RACIAL UNITY

AN IMPERATIVE FOR
SOCIAL PROGRESS

RACIAL UNITY

AN IMPERATIVE FOR SOCIAL PROGRESS

RICHARD W. THOMAS

With a Foreword by John H. Stanfield, II

PUBLISHED BY THE ASSOCIATION FOR BAHÁ'Í STUDIES

Revised edition

Bahá'í Studies Publications, Ottawa, Canada

Cover photograph: "The Bahá'í Children of Dover"
© 1991 Pepper Peterson Oldziey

Front Cover Design: Stan Phillips, Toronto
Back Cover Design: Louis Brunet, Ottawa

Printed in the United States on recycled, acid-free paper

ISBN 0-920904-25-4

To my students

*May they come to understand
how the power of racial unity
can transform the world*

———◆———

*The second edition of this book is dedicated to the memory
of my beloved Bahá'í sister Marilyn Green (1932–1992)
who for many years was the guiding spirit of racial unity
on the National Race Unity Committee of the
Bahá'ís of the United States and for countless efforts of
interracial unity and harmony*

Contents

Foreword

We are in a most profound sense already in the twenty-first century. Yet we have still to figure out what to do about the most daunting question of the century we have in many ways already left. As that great intellectual William E. B. Du Bois predicted so concisely over eight decades ago, the problem of the twentieth century would be the color line. It is still with us and promises to remain and indeed fester in dangerous ways unless we begin to look soberly into the glass darkly before us. In this thought-provoking book, Professor Richard W. Thomas offers insights into why race continues to eat away at the soul of America despite occasional episodes of race-relations reform movements in American history.

The nineteenth century was the era in which race was first fashioned as a social ideology and political weapon designed to rationalize the formation of massive modes of economic inequality such as slavery and other forced labor systems. Race became the chief cornerstone of the emotional development and status identity of European-descent colonizers and nation-state builders and of the millions of people of color they oppressed. Twentieth-century citizens witnessed the use of such dangerous myths in the stabilization and decline of European-descent and Asian-descent empires and the development of racially segmented Western nation-states.

Twentieth-century American history can only be read when this racial context is considered. No matter where we look, race has continued to matter as the twentieth-century United States has evolved gradually from being a rural to an industrial to a post-industrial nation-state. It has mattered as a central rationale for how and why twentieth-century Americans have decided to participate in wars around the world and even in terms of how Americans have defined peace. Race has figured centrally in the formation of twentieth-century American cities, employment markets, educational attainment, politics, popular culture, and organized religion. The critical involvement of Americans in the creation and entrenchment of the Cold War as a mentality as well as a way of defining and distributing international power had racial components both domestically and abroad. The emerging post-Cold War period in the world system is unleashing ancient ethnic and racial antagonisms held in uneasy check by ideological regimes while Americans stand by rather helplessly caught in the vise grip of surging urban racial violence and racialist social movements on the domestic scene.

So, as we begin to define at least the first decades of the twenty-first century, we do so with the albatross of race hanging tightly around our necks. Some of us are gasping for breath as we try to disentangle our necks from the embracing feathered beast. But, most of the world, most

Americans, remain oblivious even passive when it comes to efforts to escape from the crucible of race. They see the race riots on television and even in their neighborhoods. They continue to reside in racially homogeneous communities and work at jobs with only a few, if any, people of color, especially in authority positions. Most Americans still do not think something is wrong with statistics that reveal most whites and non-whites do not cross the color line when it comes to residence, friendship, marriage, and family development. The fact that most Americans do not question the relevance of viewing themselves and others in racial terms and basing critical life decisions on racial criteria is more than obvious. Race is such a primary factor in American perceptions of the self and the other that racelessness as a perception and as an identity is almost unheard of or is viewed as a deviant status (e.g., "nigger lover" or "Uncle Tom").

What is so tragic about the persistent though historically unique ways in which racial segmentation has remained central in the development of Americans as human beings and in the evolution of America as a nation-state is that there have been a number of missed windows for effective anti-racism which subsequently closed. The opening and shutting of such windows of opportunities to transform Americans into raceless human beings and America into a raceless nation-state have occurred with enough frequency to remind us that race continues to exist as an integral part of American lives because we want it there. Race as a way of thinking, defining status hierarchies, exploiting labor, and maintaining political and cultural control has become too profitable for most white Americans, including those who hold otherwise progressive views. It has even become profitable for not a few Americans of color who use their subordinate status as an excuse for their lowly status, as an excuse for being powerless, or as a means to exploit their own communities and people.

There are two issues that make this timely book essential reading. First, Professor Thomas reminds us of the historical windows—the chances Americans had to change the course of race relations from negatives to positives and failed to do so. It is clear that through the decades and centuries, the profitability of race has been so great that Americans in leadership positions—Presidents on down— have been more willing to preserve racial status quo than to apply democratic principles to eradicate the plight of the racially oppressed. It has been more convenient for political establishments to use race as a form of cultural currency for winning elections and for creating and maintaining divisions among the poor and middle classes than for developing a just society in which racial inequality is delegitimated as an ideology and practice. Journalists discovered in the nineteenth century, as they have in the twentieth century, that racial violence and debates over racial inferiority and superiority are more to the public's liking and thus sell more copy than do episodes of racial harmony and racelessness.

Consequently, the historical success of antiracist movements and legislation has tended to be, in the long run, quite limited. Although the early nineteenth-century abolitionist movement put moral pressure on the American public and political processes to end slavery, it did little to influence the dismantling of racial hierarchies (especially since many famous and not so famous abolitionists may have been opposed to slavery on moral grounds but viewed blacks as an inferior race). The 1950s–1960s civil rights movement maimed Jim Crow quite badly but did not completely destroy it. The emergence of the post-1970s new right and the accompanying resurgence of rabid racism has been a tragic empirical indicator that 1950s–1960s civil rights leaders were unable to complete the reform work necessary to make racial justice a permanent cornerstone of American life.

Second and most important, Professor Thomas reminds us in no uncertain terms that the battle for racial justice in the United States and elsewhere has been most successful when movement efforts have a spiritual premise. His examination of the racial unity philosophies of the Quakers, Martin Luther King, Jr., and most extensively of the Bahá'í community illustrate this contention quite well. The deeply rooted presence of race in the emotional beings of Americans often prevents even the most religious from grasping the meaning and value of racial unity (which is why, as King pointed out, the most segregated hour in America is 11 a.m. on Sundays).

Professor Thomas's narrative and interpretations offer a unique contribution to twentieth-century American cultural history in bringing to light the perspectives of the historical Bahá'í leadership, which advocated the development of an American branch, void of racism in the midst of the entrenchment of a formally segregated—Jim Crow—nation-state. The evolution of the American Bahá'í community from one with an ambiguous-to-negative perspective on racial issues to one on the forefront of civil rights is a fascinating case study in the ways in which institutions and communities can, if the collective wills it, transform themselves into instruments of change rather than of status quo maintenance. This transformational experience is especially important when it comes to religious institutions and communities in which more often than should be the case, spiritually minded people find it to be no contradiction to harbor racial prejudices.

When our lives are truly liberated spiritually from the social and cultural traditions that encourage racial criteria to taint our definitions of self and others, there is a truly revolutionary experience. This is why once a person takes a spiritual perspective and has eaten of the consequential blessed fruits of inner peace and social harmony, there is no turning back from relishing the virtues of racial unity. What gave King his strength was the spiritual revelation that he could fight for racial justice because he was located in a spiritual plane which could not be touched by human hands or even feelings. Through his visionary eyes, he could see racial unity, since he had reached a point of spiritual maturity wherein he no longer gazed at flesh and blood, but at the universal unity of human beings.

This book is important since it is now "OK" for upwardly mobile and well-established Americans to have spiritual consciousness. Everywhere we turn there is an upsurge of spiritual concern in America. Even psychiatrists are beginning to admit that having spiritual values is an important balancer, indeed anchor, in human life.

But before it was "OK," many Americans used their spiritual values as ways to prioritize in their lives and as a means to make choices. The problem with the present and historical lives of many otherwise spiritually minded Americans is that they have yet to extend their well-being to the issue of race. Their lives are still rooted in segregated or marginally integrated families, friendship circles, communities, workplaces, civic associations, and political circles. That is the real reason why this book is important. No matter what our faith, those of us who center our lives in living for a higher power must extend that faith to dismantle our private attitudes, beliefs, and conduct which are consciously or unconsciously racial. And when we are done with ourselves, we individually and collectively should turn to others and use our faith to convert them to the faith of human unity. Perhaps strange to some, the more truly spiritual (as opposed to religious) we become, the more we find that the beauty of race-free lives, institutions, and communities makes the inevitable suffering at the hands of those who do not see, worth going through and even rejoicing about. This is why truly spiritually minded people who have "been to the mountain top" cannot help but act in unity with others to liberate the world from a most fundamental source of human misery and misunderstanding—race. The more we look through the glass clearly as our spirits are cleansed from the pollutants of a racialized nation-state and world, the more activist antiracism becomes a top priority in our lives no matter who we are and no matter the material cost.

Thus Professor Thomas has performed a brilliant intellectual task in pricking our consciousness and opening our eyes to what really matters in fighting the good fight for racial justice: becoming as spiritually centered as we profess to be and then taking a fervent stand for racial justice no matter the sacrifice, no matter the pain.

JOHN H. STANFIELD, II

Frances L. and Edwin L. Cummings Professor of Sociology and American Studies and Professor of Sociology
The College of William and Mary, Williamsburg, Virginia
April 19, 1993

Preface

I would like to thank the readers of the first edition of this book for their overwhelming support for the first edition, and I apologize to those who have been waiting patiently for far too long for the second edition. After the first edition sold out, we decided to add a chapter on black–white relations in the ancient Mediterranean world and to extend the chapter on the Bahá'í community in the United States up to the present. Both the publishers and I hope that readers agree these additions were worth the wait. We feel certain that these additions will increase awareness and appreciation of the impact of racial justice and unity on social progress, and we intend to continue expanding this book in future editions. Therefore, we invite all readers to send in their comments to assist us in developing this book to meet the needs and concerns of all readers. We see this book as a collaborative enterprise of the writer, publisher, and reader in a community of service to humankind.

Preface to First Edition

This book has been germinating for many years. As a teacher and researcher in both African–American history and race relations, I have been discussing many of these issues in my courses with my students for close to twenty years. My initial interest in race relations originated from several sources: the primary source is the Bahá'í community in the United States, which has provided me with a human laboratory where I have been able to experience first-hand the interaction among racially and culturally diverse peoples. For nearly thirty years I have not only observed a process of community building among these diverse peoples but also witnessed a transformation of their traditional prejudices, fears, and anxieties into bonds of interracial and multicultural fellowship. I have watched and been involved in the painful process of confronting racism within this community, and I have experienced along with others the joy of working through the various stages of white racism and black bitterness to interracial bonding. This process continues.

The second source of my interest in race relations grew out of my involvement in the Civil Rights Movement as a young black student. Observing blacks and whites marching together confirmed my belief in the imperative of racial unity for the social good of the United States and the world.

The third source of my interest has been the classroom where for over twenty years I have been able to teach students from many racial backgrounds—but mainly blacks and whites—about the history of racism and how best to combat it and to work together for the achievement of a multiracial society based on justice, love, and fellowship. In a way, this book has been written for them.

The title of this book, *Racial Unity: An Imperative for Social Progress*, originated from a series of lectures I gave at various universities in Canada and the United States during the late 1980s. As a result of long years of teaching about the history of racism, I felt compelled to include the history of "the other tradition" of American race relations, namely: the history of the interracial struggle for racial justice, unity, love, and fellowship. People needed to know, I reasoned, both the history of racism *and* the history of those who have struggled against racism and have envisioned a social order in which people not only accept each other as equal but also have a profound appreciation of each other as members of the one human family. Chapter 8, "Towards a Model of Racial Unity: A Case Study of Bahá'í Teachings and Community Practices," is presented here as one model of "the other tradition" in the hope that the reader will find something of value in this particular multicultural religious community. While there are other multicultural religious communities, I felt that I could best serve the interests of research in the field of race relations by focusing upon the multicultural religious community of which I have the most knowledge. Furthermore, the Bahá'í community in the United States offers scholars of race relations one of the best laboratories for future research on the process by which people from diverse religious, racial, national, and cultural backgrounds are engaged in building a racially unified spiritual community. So, in one sense, this brief and very general historical essay is a statement of my belief and dearest hope that black and white Americans can transcend their common racial history and create a truly racially just, loving society that can be a model of unity for the world to emulate.

Acknowledgements

Thanks to Kyungsik Irene Shim for assistance with this project. She was joined by Kimberly Andrew, graduate student in history, Michigan State University. Both assisted in library research on chapter two.

Acknowledgements for the First Edition

This book is the product of many devoted people. Foremost among them is Christine Zerbinis of the editorial board of the Association for Bahá'í Studies who coordinated the work of all those involved in the heroic effort of getting this book ready in time for the Model of Race Unity Conference in Atlanta. Two of my graduate students, Kyungsik Irene Shim and Shobha Ramanand, also deserve a special note of thanks, Shobha for her extensive library work in verifying references and Irene for her long hours spent assisting me in historical research. Her considerable skills proved invaluable in the final stages of checking sources. Several readers contributed their time in reading portions of the manuscript: the main ones included Professor Harry Reed, History Department, Michigan State University, and Professor Ruth Harris, Department of Afro-American Studies Center, State University of New York, Brockport.

Part I

*Why Racial Unity
is an
Imperative for Social Progress
in the Modern World*

1

Racial Unity

An Imperative for Social Progress in America and Other Multiracial Societies

> Among the moral imperatives of our time, we are challenged to work all over the world with unshakable determination to wipe out the last vestiges of racism. . . . We know full well that racism is still the hound of hell which dogs the tracks of our civilization.
>
> —Martin Luther King, Jr.

Racism has cost the world dearly. Systems of racial domination in the Americas, Asia, and Africa have left a trail of blood and anguish down through history, imposing upon the present generation a legacy of hatred and racial conflict. Centuries of racial dominance have created centuries of racial distrust among the oppressed—centuries of distrust that have festered into countless manifestations of racial disunity in multiracial societies around the world. We have only to turn our attention to the periodic racial disruptions in the United States, South Africa, and England to see what the future might continue to be like for those multiracial societies that fail to address their racial problems effectively.[1]

While multiracial nations have just begun to recognize the global impact of their domestic racism and the extent to which their individual countries can be suddenly sucked into a racial maelstrom of international magnitude, many citizens of multiracial societies fail to understand the connection between their domestic racial policies and world peace. In

---

1. John Benyon and John Solomos, "British Urban Unrest in the 1980s" 3–22 and Stuart Hall, "Urban Unrest in Britain" 45–50, in John Benyon and John Solomos, eds., *The Roots of Urban Unrest*; John Rex, "Racialism and the Urban Crisis," *Race, Science and Society* 262–300; Jonathan Kaufman, *Broken Alliance: The Turbulent Times Between Blacks and Jews in America*; Lena Williams, "Officials Voice Growing Concern Over Racial Incidents on U.S. Campuses," *The New York Times*, December 15, 1986, p. A18; "Black Rage, White Fist," *Time*, August 5, 1985: 24–33.

1976, an editorial in the *Detroit Free Press* alerted its readers to such a connection when it warned: "A lot of history is bearing down on us now. . . . And the implications of . . . racial conflict, not only throughout southern Africa, but throughout much of the world, are ominous."[2]

The global ramifications of domestic racism and conflict became clearer as concerned scholars and journalists began writing on the subject, particularly during the era of urban racial turmoil in the United States. In 1967, the year of the Detroit race riot, the worst race riot in American history, Ronald Segal published a book entitled *The Race War* in which he described the future of global race relations in the following terms: "In a world where the white rich seek to preserve an order against which the coloured poor rebel, the central fact of the past will increasingly be seen as the domination of the one by the other, just as the central fact of the future will increasingly emerge as the struggle between them." Justifying the provocative title of his book, he continued: "The phrase 'race war' is a strong one, but no stronger, I believe, than the steadily increasing hostility between white and non-white fully warrants. The two colours are physically clashing in a dozen parts of the world already, whether through riots in the slums of American cities or the engagement of guns in South Vietnam and Angola." Therefore, Segal argued, "It is the contention of this book that the occasions for clash must multiply, and the war grow ever more intense, unless the circumstances which provoke the antagonisms of race are themselves removed."[3]

It was not to be. The "antagonisms of race" remain virtually untouched throughout the potential racial hot spots of the world.[4]

Although some citizens of multiracial societies have just begun to understand that social and economic justice are preconditions for racial unity and that racial unity is an imperative for social progress, multiracial societies such as the United States and South Africa are still paying the cost for refusing to learn this lesson. What is the reason for this blind and irrational refusal to abandon racial prejudice in these societies? Why have the dominant white groups in America and South Africa clung to their

---

2. Editorial, *Detroit Free Press*, September 21, 1976.

3. Ronald Segal, *The Race War* vii, 1. This theme of race war has been echoed through the centuries by such observers of race relations as Thomas Jefferson and W. E. B. Du Bois, see discussion of Jefferson (in Chapter 4) and Du Bois (in Chapter 7).

4. Throughout the late 1970s and 1980s, blacks in the South African townships, particularly Soweto, rebelled against the system of apartheid. In Britain during the 1980s, racial conflicts erupted in several cities, including Brixton, Handsworth in Birmingham, Sheffield, and Tottenham in London. In America, the worst racial conflicts of the 1980s broke out in May, 1980, in Miami, Florida. See Benyon and Solomos, *Roots* 3–14; Harris Joshua and Tina Wallace with the assistance of Heather Booth, *To Ride the Storm: The 1980 Bristol "Riot" and the State* 56–210; "Black Rage, White Fist" 24–28; "Confronting Racial Isolation in Miami" v. 26.

ideologies of white supremacy for so long? What is it about racial superiority that makes it so appealing to some segments of these societies that, for example, South Africa cannot imagine treating all human beings fairly?

Fortunately, there are great signs of hope operating throughout the world. As bad as apartheid is in South Africa, it has generated an international movement composed of people from many nations, races, and religious backgrounds dedicated to the elimination of apartheid. This international anti-apartheid movement is transforming the face of the planet, bonding many people who previously knew or cared little about their common humanity. In America, where the resurgence of racism has understandably frightened and angered many people who grew up during the Civil Rights Movement believing in "the Beloved Community," where there is still much resistance to and misunderstanding of such policies as affirmative action, and where blacks and whites in most major metropolitan areas are more segregated than ever before, brave bands of multiracial people are struggling against racism and racial conflicts. Groups and organizations such as Mothers for Race Unity and Equality in California, the Interracial Family Alliance, Focus Hope in Detroit, and the race unity programs of the American Bahá'í community are more than just isolated "points of light." Rather, they represent a new consciousness within many multiracial societies that social progress is impossible without racial justice and unity.[5]

The United Nations has long recognized the connection between racial justice and unity and social progress within the global community. The Sub-Commission on Prevention of Discrimination and Protection of Minorities, one of the United Nations' many organs, was set up in 1947 by the Commission on Human Rights. It was given the mandate "to undertake studies, particularly in the light of the Universal Declaration of Human Rights, and to make recommendations to the Commission on Human Rights concerning the prevention of discrimination of any kind . . . and the protection of racial, national, religious and linguistic minorities." In 1949, a group of experts on racial problems, meeting in Paris under the auspices of

---

5. The most dramatic example of this international movement against apartheid was seen in the world tour of Nelson Mandela, the leader of the African National Congress. However, many ordinary people also participated in this global movement for racial justice. For example, in 1984, eleven supermarket employees in Ireland were fired when they refused to handle South African fruit. After three years of pickets at the store, a court decided that the employees had been unfairly dismissed. See Martin Gottlieb, "Mandela's Visit, New York's Pride," *The New York Times*, June 24, 1990, sect. 4, p. 1; Marcus Eliason, "Irish eyes smile upon Mandelas," *Lansing State Journal*, July 2, 1990, p. 3A; Focus Hope was started in Detroit about a year after the 1967 riot. See Richard W. Thomas, "Looking Forward: The Detroit Experience after the Riots of 1943 and 1967" in Benyon and Solomos, *The Roots* 150; Mothers for Race Unity and Equality was founded by LeNeice Jackson-Gaertner in the late 1980s, leaflet, "Mothers for Race Unity and Equality," see parts 3 and 4 for information on the Interracial Family Alliance and the Bahá'í Community.

UNESCO, pointed out that the "biological fact of race and the myth of 'race' should be distinguished." In 1951, UNESCO convened a second meeting of scientists who, among similar conclusions, stated in their Statement on the Nature of Race and Racial Differences that "available scientific knowledge provides no basis for believing that the groups of mankind differ in their innate capacity for intellectual and emotional development." UNESCO convened several other conferences on race in Moscow in 1964 and again in Paris in 1967. The latter conference focused on race and racial prejudice and adopted the Paris Statement on Race and Racial Prejudice, which states that "the human problems arising from so-called 'race' relations are social in origin rather than biological. The basic problem is racism, namely anti-social beliefs and acts which are based on the fallacy that discriminatory inter-group relations are justifiable on biological grounds."[6]

From the late 1960s to the present, the United Nations and its organs have continued to address the problem of racism throughout the global community. In 1983 the General Assembly "proclaimed the ten year period beginning on 10 December 1983 the Second Decade to Combat Racism and Racial Discrimination." Building on its earlier work during the first Decade to Combat Racism and Racial Discrimination, the General Assembly approved the Program of Action for the Second Decade, which included among its activities seminars on combating racism and racial discrimination.

International efforts to combat racial discrimination within the global community have drawn attention to the fact that racism is not just limited to such countries as the United States and South Africa. Racism started as an international social virus, and it remains so today. Its most virulent strains may be found in South Africa and America, yet the virus is present in every multiracial society in the world. Some multiracial societies such as England and Brazil might have less pathological racial histories, but they share the disease of racism and must treat it effectively or suffer long-term socially debilitating effects.[7]

At the present time, many multiracial societies are struggling to find the best solutions to their racial problems. Shaken by racial conflicts and riots over the last few decades, the United States, England, and South Africa

6. Hernán Santa Cruz, *Racial Discrimination* 11–13, 22.

7. For more recent information on the United Nations' work in the area of elimination of racism and racial discrimination, see *Seminar on International Assistance and Support to Peoples and Movements Struggling against Colonialism, Racism, Racial Descrimination and Apartheid* 1. While Brazil's racial problems have not reached the volatile stage of racial problems in the United States, England, and South Africa, the country does have "problems" related to race. For example, there has been a tendency among certain groups in Brazil to see themselves as a "racial democracy" and to avoid serious discussion of racial discrimination in the country. See Thomas E. Skidmore, "Race and Class in Brazil: Historical Perspectives" in Pierre-Michel Fontaine, ed., *Race, Class and Power in Brazil* 11–24.

have tried a variety of approaches to ensure "domestic peace" but have ignored the root causes of their racial problems. In the wake of their most recent riots, both the United States and England initiated various race-relations programs, including race-awareness conferences; multiracial, multicultural organizations; and a host of scholarly productions on the "racial problem."[8] South Africa still lags far behind these two other multiracial societies.

The United States and England could serve as models for South Africa, saving it from many more decades of racial turmoil, *if* they could put their own racial houses in order. They could do so by educating the present generation of their citizens about the urgency of establishing racial justice and unity in their respective societies. Citizens of multiracial societies must be made aware of the relationship between racial unity and social progress. They must be exposed to the great historical cost in human misery and social conflict that racism has exacted from the entire society. They must be made to understand that there cannot be any lasting peace without genuine love and fellowship among racial groups. Then, it must be demonstrated to them that such love and fellowship among the various races of their societies will not only reduce and ultimately eliminate racism and racial conflicts but also elevate the entire society to new levels of material and spiritual development.

To convince the citizenry of multiracial societies of this potential, we will need a new paradigm to improve understanding of historical and contemporary race relations as related to social progress. People must realize that there is an organic relationship between racial justice and unity on the one hand, and social progress on the other. We must understand that in today's complex, interdependent world in which peoples from diverse racial and cultural backgrounds are increasingly interacting in thousands of new settings, racial unity has become an imperative for social progress. Social and economic progress in every multiracial society today depends on the degree to which racial groups learn to live, work, and play together in love and harmony. Where racial unity, based upon social justice nurtured by love and fellowship, is lacking or absent, such multiracial societies are forced to waste precious time, energy, and resources managing crises.

---

8. See part 6 in Benyon and Solomos, *The Roots*. Since Detroit had the worst race riot of the 1960s, its post-riot developments embodied valuable lessons for other cities; see Thomas, "Looking Forward" in Benyon and Solomos, *The Roots* 150–51.

2

Race and Color in the Ancient Mediterranean World
A Case Study of Black–White Relations

Scholars disagree as to the precise stage in the history of race relations at which color acquired the importance it has assumed in the modern world. One point, however, is certain: the onus of intense color prejudice cannot be placed upon the shoulders of the ancients.

—Frank Snowden

Racism has so affected the mindset of the modern world that in many segments of contemporary multiracial societies there exists the feeling that racism and racial conflicts are just the natural consequences of interactions among racially diverse people. Worse than the danger of persistent racism and racial conflict in modern societies is the pervasive belief that racism and racial conflicts have always been a part of human societies, that racism is inherently part of human nature. Here, history can be of tremendous help. There is convincing scholarly evidence not only that racism, as we have experienced it during the modern era, is a recent phenomenon but also that such racism did not exist in the virulent forms in which the modern world has come to know and experience it. As explained by Frank Snowden, one of the world's leading scholars on race and color in the ancient Mediterranean world:

Notable, therefore, is the fact that the ancient world did not make color the focus of irrational sentiments or the basis for uncritical evaluation. The ancients did accept the institution of slavery as a fact of life; they made ethnocentric judgments of other societies; they had narcissistic canons of physical beauty; the Egyptians distinguished between themselves, "the people," and outsiders; and the Greeks called foreign cultures barbarian. Yet nothing comparable to the virulent color prejudice of modern times existed in the ancient world.[1]

Commenting on the studies of other scholars of race relations in the ancient world, Snowden notes that most scholars "who have examined the evidence . . . have come to conclusions such as these: the ancients did not fall into the error of biological racism; black skin color was not a sign of inferiority; Greeks and Romans did not establish color as an obstacle to integration in society; and ancient society was one that 'for all its faults and failures never made color the basis for judging a man'."[2]

"And, of great importance for the ancient view of blacks, classical 'anthropologists', like writers from Homer to Quintus of Smyrna, developed no special theory concerning the inferiority of blacks—an approach that differed greatly from later Western outlooks, often deeply ingrained with racism in folklore, literature, and science."[3] What then, was the nature of interaction between blacks and whites in the ancient Mediterranean world? And how can our understanding of race relations during this period help us to understand better and to improve race relations in present-day society?

Ancient Origins of Black–White Relations

There is no better historical or geographical case to examine for an understanding of the historical roots of black–white relations than the ancient Mediterranean world because of the simple fact that "the encounter of African blacks and Mediterranean whites constitutes the oldest chapter in the annals of black–white relations."[4] On the basis of iconographical and written sources of the Egyptians, Greeks, Romans, and the early Christians, Snowden has argued that there are "very striking similarities in the total picture that emerge from an examination of the basic sources . . . point[ing] to a highly favorable image of blacks and to white–black relationships differing markedly from those that have developed in more color-conscious societies."[5] These sources have tended to focus on the "dark and black-skinned Africans" who lived in various areas of the Nile Valley, south of the First Cataract.

Egyptian texts and the Old Testament often referred to this region as Kush (Cush), while the Greeks, Romans, and early Christian writers referred to the same region as Aithiopa (Aethiopia).[6] This region was also

---

1. Frank M. Snowden, *Before Color Prejudice: The Ancient View of Blacks* 63.
2. Snowden, *Before Color Prejudice* 63.
3. Snowden, *Before Color Prejudice* 87.
4. Snowden, *Before Color Prejudice* vii.
5. Snowden, *Before Color Prejudice* vii.
6. Karl-Heinz Priese, "The Kingdom of Kush: The Napatan Period" and Fritz Hintze, "The Kingdom of Kush: The Meroitic Period," in Michael Botwinick, ed., *Africa in Antiquity: The Arts of Ancient Nubia and the Sudan: The Essays* 1: 74–105.

called Nubia. The ancients also described as Ethiopian, those peoples of varying shades of blackness living in parts of northwest Africa. Many blacks who eventually settled in countries of the ancient world outside black Africa originated in large part from the Nile Valley regions. Some of these blacks also came from northwest Africa, particularly during the Roman period.[7] While many scholars have differed as to what constitutes the "proper anthropological classification of the African blacks known to the ancient world," ancient artists and writers "in realistic portraits and detailed descriptions, have provided perhaps the best picture of the physical characteristics of African blacks."[8]

According to Snowden, "as early as the latter part of the third millennium B.C.," Egyptian artists were drawing African blacks with thick lips, broad noses, and tightly coiled or woolly hair. Yet, oddly enough, there is little mention of the color of the Kushites in Egyptian inscriptions and literature and only an occasional mention of their curly hair, nothing like the "detailed physical descriptions of blacks like those of later Greek and Roman authors."[9] It seems likely the only fact that could account for this lack of interest in the detailed physical description of blacks in their midst would be that blacks were not unusual but rather common and frequent neighbors. "A partial explanation of this," Snowden points out, "may lie in the fact that from earliest times Egyptians had been acquainted with blacks, had fought alongside black mercenaries at least as early as 2000 B.C., and hence, as a result of a longstanding familiarity, saw nothing unusual in the Kushites' color or their other physical characteristics."[10] Some scholars might argue that another reason for the Egyptians' lack of "detailed physical descriptions of blacks" in their midst was due to the fact that they themselves were partially "black."[11]

The ancient Egyptians were the first people "to leave a record of their experience with African blacks. . . ."[12] The first Kushite–Egyptian

7. G. Mokhtar, ed., *Ancient Civilizations of Africa: General History of Africa* 2: 141–47.

8. Snowden, *Before Color Prejudice* 5.

9. Snowden, *Before Color Prejudice* 5.

10. Snowden, *Before Color Prejudice* 5.

11. There is still much controversy on the question of the ancient Egyptians' color and race. Diop has been one of the leading exponents of the view of the African origin of the Egyptians. The symposium "The Peopling of Ancient Egypt and the Deciphering of the Meroitic Script" of 1974 in Cairo, Egypt, reflected the influence of racism on the field of Egyptology. See, "Origins of the Ancient Egyptians," in Mokhtar, *Ancient Civilizations* 15–61; "What Color Were the Ancient Egyptians?" in Martin Bernal, *Black Athena: The Afroasiatic Roots of Classical Civilization*, vol. 1: *The Fabrication of Ancient Greece, 1785–1985* 240–45; and Bruce G. Trigger, "Nubian, Negro, Black, Nilotic?" in Botwinick, *Africa in Antiquity* 26–35. A longstanding debate on the subject still continues. See Mary Lefkowitz, "Not Out of Africa," in *New Republic* 206.6 (February 10, 1992): 29–36; Martin Bernal, "Roots," in *New Republic* 206.10 (March 9, 1992): 4–7.

12. Snowden, *Before Color Prejudice* 21.

encounters resulted from "Egypt's efforts to exploit the human and natural resources of Kush, and of Kush's response to the commercial and imperial ambitions of its northern neighbors."[13] Such encounters were reported as early as the First Dynasty (ca. 3100–2890 B.C.).[14] The first three Pharaohs of the New Kingdom (1570–1085 B.C.) waged wars against Kush and finally conquered and administered it as a province for close to five-hundred years.[15] This province was administered under a "viceroy known as 'the Royal Son of Kush'." As a result, the province was "required to pay an annual tribute and to provide manpower in support of Egypt's conquests and Asiatic wars."[16]

The five-hundred-years rule witnessed the integration of large numbers of black Kushites into Egyptian society as soldiers and some "Kushites had occupied high positions in Egyptian administration."[17] After being ruled and occupied by Egypt for five-hundred years, the Napatan Kingdom of Kush "conquered Egypt, which it ruled as the Twenty-fifth Dynasty, and laid the foundations of a state that, with its later capital at Meroë (ca. 300 B.C.–350 A.D.), survived for more than . . . any [other] single period of Egyptian unification."[18] This was the period that exposed the Mediterranean world to such great black Pharaohs as Kashta, Piye (Peye) "(formally read as Piankhy)" and Shabaka.[19]

Greek and Roman Interaction with Blacks

Anyone interested in the historical development of black–white relations should examine the interaction between blacks and whites during the Greek and Roman periods. It is during these historical periods in predominantly "white" societies that we discover a far different pattern of white–black relations due in large part to the convergence of historical, social, and cultural factors nonexistent during the modern era of black–white relations. Herein lie the critical historical lessons for contemporary observers of modern racism and racial conflict: black–white relations in the ancient Mediterranean world were so vastly different from those of the modern world because of the manner in which blacks appeared on the historical stage of the Greek and Roman worlds.

The ancient Greeks were not only "the first European people to leave a record of their contacts with the Nubians of the Napatan and later the

13. Snowden, *Before Color Prejudice* 21.

14. Snowden, *Before Color Prejudice* 21.

15. For detailed information on the Egyptian–Nubian relations, see Jean Leclant, "Egypt in Nubia during the Old, Middle, and New Kingdoms," in Botwinick, *Africa in Antiquity* 62–73.

16. Snowden, *Before Color Prejudice* 23.

17. Snowden, *Before Color Prejudice* 24.

18. Snowden, *Before Color Prejudice* 24.

19. Mokhtar, *Ancient Civilization* 161–62; Snowden, *Before Color Prejudice* 25.

Meroïtic Kingdom of Kush" (black people) and ". . . who originated the name Aithiopes (Ethiopians) for blacks," they were also "among the first Europeans to confront blacks face to face in Africa." Greek mercenaries in the army of Psamtic II (594–588 B.C.) were no doubt aware of Psamtic's southern mission to prevent the black Napatans from reconquering Egypt. Snowden speculates that probably on their return home to Greece, these Greek mercenaries "doubtlessly related to friends what they had seen and heard about the history of the Ethiopians, once rulers of Egypt." Surely this would explain "the prominence given to Negro warriors in sixth-century [Greek] vase paintings. . . ."[20]

Understanding the historical significance of this first black–white contact is key: the Greeks being among the first Europeans to "confront blacks face to face in Africa" in an historical context in which blacks were known as the once rulers of Egypt would obviously influence the nature of future white–black relations. These first whites to come face to face with blacks in Africa did not see blacks as beneath them. How could they, when much that they had heard about these "Aithiopes" (Ethiopians) related to their earlier domination of Egypt? Had they, as white slave masters, met these blacks in Africa as slaves then perhaps black–white relations in the ancient world would have been similar to those of the modern era.

The black presence in ancient Greece increased during the Egyptian occupation of Cyprus under the rule of Amasis (ca. 569–525 B.C.). Ethiopians employed by Amasis as civilians and soldiers "increased Greek awareness of blacks in the sixth century."[21] The continuous presence of blacks in Greece would shed some light on Aristotle's comments on the "racial mixture in the family of a woman from Elis, who was the mother of a child by an Ethiopian."[22] Little wonder, therefore, that by the sixth century B.C., Greek artists in Naukratis demonstrated "a firsthand acquaintance with Ethiopians."[23]

Increasing contacts with the non-Greek world expanded the Greeks' awareness of racial diversity. The Hellenes soon became aware of their own physical and cultural differences as they interacted with and obtained knowledge of people as racially and culturally different as blue-eyed and red-haired Thracians and black-faced, flat-nosed, and woolly-haired Ethiopians. While many Greeks, particularly after the Persian War, looked down upon non-Greek people—mainly because of culture, rarely because of race—other Greeks respected, admired, and even idolized certain aspects of non-Greek cultures. Some Greeks such as the Sophists believed in a form of universalism among humankind.

---

20. Snowden, *Before Color Prejudice* 26–27.
21. Snowden, *Before Color Prejudice* 27.
22. Snowden, *Before Color Prejudice* 27.
23. Snowden, *Before Color Prejudice* 27.

As the Hellenistic world became more cosmopolitan, it began distancing itself from the views of Aristotle, who justified slavery on the basis of so-called innate capacities and differences of individuals. Instead, "the cosmopolitanism of the Hellenistic world emphasized a cultural rather than a racial differentation."[24]

The ancient Greeks' observations and contrasts of racial types offer students of modern race relations valuable insights into how ancient peoples felt about race and color. It appears that the Greeks' observations "on races of other physique and other cultures often took the form of antitheses involving racial extremes . . ."[25] but without the attendant racism of the modern era. Greek Janiform art objects (made in Naukratis) contrasting Caucasian and Negroid types dating back to the seventh century B.C. offer dramatic evidence of the ancient Greeks' appreciation of racial diversity and what Snowden refers to as "antitheses involving racial extremes."[26]

Travellers to Egypt and Ethiopia further expanded the Greeks' knowledge of blacks. For example, Herodotus, "whose history includes the first detailed extant account of Ethiopia and Ethiopians, traveled as far south as Elephantine."[27] But it was not until the 480–479 B.C. campaign of the Persian ruler Xerxes in Greece that mainland Greeks for the first time saw blacks in large numbers. Xerxes' Ethiopian mercenaries undoubtedly made a lasting impression on the Greek population and likely explained "the popularity of Negroes in the art of the fifth century and of Ethiopian themes in the theater was probably a reflection of an interest stimulated both by the experience of Greek residents in Egypt and contemporary reports of Ethiopian soldiers."[28] Stone figures of blacks uncovered by a Swedish–Cypriot expedition in Cyprus during a 1927–1931 excavation[29] are further testimony of not only the increasing awareness of blacks among Greek artists but also the growing popularity of blacks as models for Greek artists.[30]

While some Greeks obtained their knowledge of blacks from the Napatan Kingdom of Kush and others obtained their information "from travelers in Egypt or from the history of Herodotus," Snowden argues that "it was, however, primarily the Meroïtic Ethiopians who at various times from about 300 B.C. to 350 A.D. evoked the attention of classical writers and attracted visitors to Nubia."[31]

24. Snowden, *Blacks in Antiquity: Ethiopians in the Greco-Roman Experience* 170.
25. Snowden, *Blacks in Antiquity* 171.
26. Snowden, *Blacks in Antiquity* 171.
27. Snowden, *Before Color Prejudice* 27; *Herodotus,* vol. 1, book 2: 28–29, 305–7.
28. Snowden, *Before Color Prejudice* 27.
29. Snowden, *Before Color Prejudice* 27, n. 26.
30. Jean Vercoutter, et al., eds., *The Image of the Black in Western Art: From the Pharaohs to the Fall of the Roman Empire.*
31. Snowden, *Before Color Prejudice* 28.

The Meroïtic Kingdom was an ancient African civilization that commanded great administration and respect from both Greeks and Romans. According to Shinnie, a scholar of Meroe: "Meroe was an African civilization, firmly based on African soil, and developed by an African population. That an urban, civilized, and literate state existed deep in the African continent and lasted nearly a thousand years in itself constitutes an achievement of outstanding importance."[32]

Meroe was very familiar to the classical world. Herodotus became the first of the classical writers to mention Meroe by name. However, earlier writers "from Homer onwards had known in general terms of the Ethiopians, the 'burnt faces'. . . ."[33]

Diodorus Siculus, Strabo, Pliny, Seneca, and Juvenal all mentioned Meroe.[34] Therefore, notwithstanding its geographical remoteness from the main centers of civilization of the classical world, "it [Meroe] was known to that world and . . . there was coming and going between the Mediterranean and the Upper Nile."[35]

More contact between blacks of the Meroïtic period of Nubia (Kush) and the Mediterranean whites occurred during the periods of the Ptolemies, particularly when Philadelphus (283–246 B.C.) took over part of the country of the "black Ethiopians" in which he "conducted elephant-hunting expeditions, and organized a great procession in Alexandria that paraded elephants and Ethiopians carrying tusks of ivory, ebony logs, and vessels of gold and silver."[36] The Ptolemies also wanted to get at the gold mines in Nubia and the eastern deserts, and they needed elephants for military purposes. The blacks resisted Ptolemic commercial policies and military campaigns by besieging Ptolemaic positions and joining Egyptian rebellions against the Ptolemies.

According to Snowden, "It is not unlikely that respect for the courage and reputation of Ethiopian warriors gave rise to a Ptolemaic policy of recruiting southern mercenaries. Because of their experience and skill in handling elephants, Ethiopians were probably employed by the Ptolemies as elephant trainers and mahouts."[37] By the end of the third century B.C., these Ethiopian blacks and the Ptolemies must have developed "amicable relations" as evidenced by the "building programs of Meroïtic rulers at Philae, a border area under Ptolemaic control."[38]

---

32. *Meroe: A Civilization of the Sudan* 169; *cf.* Mokhtar, *Ancient Civilization* 172–84; Hintze, "Kingdom of Kush" 89–105.

33. Shinnie, *Meroe* 13.

34. Shinnie, *Meroe* 16–22.

35. Shinnie, *Meroe* 22–23.

36. Snowden, *Before Color Prejudice* 28.

37. Snowden, *Before Color Prejudice* 29.

38. Snowden, *Before Color Prejudice* 29.

The Ptolemaic era, therefore, was another historical watershed in ancient black–white relations in that it stimulated an increase in the knowledge of Ethiopia and Ethiopians. This expansion of knowledge about blacks seemed to have started with the reign of Philadelphus (283–246 B.C.). For example, Pliny's list of visitors to Meroe included Timosthenes, a commander of the navy of Philadelphus and someone named Dalian reported "to have been the first Greek to penetrate Ethiopia beyond Meroë."[39]

The Romans had frequent contact with Meroïtic blacks during their occupation of Egypt dating from the Augustan era to the sixth century A.D. In fact, during this period the Romans saw these blacks as a military threat to their southern boundary. Yet notwithstanding various military conflicts, Romans and the Meroïtic blacks enjoyed extended periods of peaceful interaction. "The peaceful Ethiopian–Roman relations of the first centuries after Christ, interrupted only by an occasional military engagement, such as that in the second century A.D. between a Roman cavalry unit and the Ethiopians," Snowden explains, "undoubtedly owed not a little to Augustus' foresight and to the diplomatic negotiations of Ethiopian and Roman ambassadors, some of whose names appear in inscriptions dating from 13 B.C. and later."[40]

However, the same relationship did not exist between the Romans and another group of blacks, the Blemmyes, "described variously" by ancient and modern scholars as "a black-skinned Ethiopian race, burnt-colored and woolly-haired" related to the present Beja tribes from the region of the Red Sea Hills.[41] Between the middle of the third century to the late sixth century A.D., the Blemmyes caused the Romans and others much trouble by attacking settlements near the Roman frontier, taking part in rebellions, and attacking Christian communities. The Blemmyes created so much havoc for Romans that by the end of the third century, the Roman Emperor Diocletian abandoned lower Nubia and withdrew the Roman frontier to the First Cataract, placed another people, the Nobatae, "as buffers between the Blemmyes and the new Roman boundary; [and] promised an annual tribute to both the Blemmyes and Nobatae, which they were still receiving more than two hundred years later."[42] In addition, the Romans settled Roman, Blemmye, and Nobatae priests at certain temples and altars "with the hope that the experience of common worship would result in friendship with Rome's southern neighbors. . . ."[43]

---

39. Snowden, *Before Color Prejudice* 29.
40. Snowden, *Before Color Prejudice* 30–31.
41. Trigger, "Nubian, Negro, Black, Nilotic?" 22–23; Snowden, *Before Color Prejudice* 31.
42. Snowden, *Before Color Prejudice* 31.
43. Snowden, *Before Color Prejudice* 31.

The Image of Blacks in the White Mediterranean Mindset

Most of the blacks known to the Greeks and Romans came from the Nile Valley. However, the Roman contact with blacks from northwest Africa began with the Punic Wars and continued intermittently during the period of the Roman occupation of Africa. The image of blacks and elephants on third-century B.C. coinage suggests that Romans "encountered blacks of the pronounced Negroid type as mahouts in the Carthaginian army."[44] Some scholars argue that these black mahouts formed the first impression of blacks in Italy. Blacks from northwest Africa served in Roman military units "continuing a Mediterranean practice of employing black troops dating back to pharaonic times," and a black was among the auxiliaries of Septimius Severus in Britain.[45]

It is often difficult for those of us who live in the modern world of race relations to understand the historically unique pattern of race relations that existed in the ancient world. Thus far we have examined the contacts between blacks and whites within the broad framework of changing civilizations; the interaction of black and white soldiers sometimes within the same armies, sometimes as opposing armies, and a few times as ambassadors. The modern mindset, still heavy with the burden of racial impressions rooted in the legacy of slavery, racial segregation, race riots, and racial stereotyping, cannot but ask the questions: "Did the presence of black aliens in their midst and other factors such as color symbolism or aesthetic preferences trigger emotional or negative reactions in whites? How did blacks actually fare in their day-to-day contacts with whites outside Nubia?"[46]

Obviously blacks from Nubia and elsewhere in Africa were conspicuous by their color when they travelled throughout the predominantly white Mediterranean world. Yet they also were common sights in many areas. For centuries blacks not only found careers in the Egyptian army but also achieved high rank and "positions of security and prestige."[47]

Apparently racial integration did not constitute the difficult problem it would later become in the modern world. Perhaps one reason for this lack of difficulty was the way in which black–white interaction was portrayed in classical mythology, which both reflected and influenced the ancient view of white–black relations. For example, ". . . the presence of black gods or heroes and their interracial amours presented no embarrassment and evoked no apologies from [classical] poets or artists."[48]

One of the most powerful images of blacks to emerge in classical mythology was the image of Ethiopians as very pious and just, so much so

44. Snowden, *Before Color Prejudice* 31.
45. Snowden, *Before Color Prejudice* 33.
46. Snowden, *Before Color Prejudice* 88.
47. Snowden, *Before Color Prejudice* 89.
48. Snowden, *Before Color Prejudice* 94.

that, as Homer tells us, Zeus and the other gods were fond of visiting and feasting with them:

> Only yesterday Zeus went off to the Ocean River
> to feast with the Ethiopians, loyal, lordly men,
> and all the gods went with him. But in twelve days
> the Father returns to Olympus.[49]

As *The Iliad* draws to a close, the goddess Iris tells the winds that she cannot remain because she is going to attend a sacred feast to be put on by the Ethiopians:

> No time for sitting now. No, I must return
> to the Ocean's running stream, the Aethiopians' land.
> They are making a splendid sacrifice to the gods—
> I must not miss my share of the sacred feast.[50]

In Homer's *Odyssey,* Poseidon goes off to visit the land of the "sunburnt races" to feast:

> . . . all but Poseidon, raging cold and rough
> against the brave king till he came ashore
> at last on his own land.
>
> But now that god
> had gone far off among the sunburnt races,
> most remote of men, at earth's two verges,
> in sunset lands and lands of the rising sun,
> to be regaled by smoke of thighbones burning,
> haunches of rams and bulls, a hundred fold.
> He lingered delighted at the banquet side.[51]

This image of pious and just Ethiopians emerged throughout the work of classical writers. Herodotus was the first among the Greek writers to mention the piety and justice of the Ethiopians. According to Herodotus, Sabacos, one of the Ethiopian rulers of Egypt, "never put to death Egyptian wrong-doers but instead required them, according to the severity of their offence, to contribute to civic improvement by raising the embarkments of their cities."[52]

Diodorus echoed Herodotus' accounts of the "piety and uprightness" of Sabacos but added that "the piety and uprightness [of] Sabaco(s) far

---

49. Homer, *The Iliad* 91–92.
50. Homer, *The Iliad* 566.
51. Homer, *The Odyssey* 14.
52. Snowden, *Blacks in Antiquity* 145; cf. *Herodotus,* Book 2: 137–38; 441.

surpassed his predecessors."[53] In another account of the piety of the Ethiopians, Diodorus reports that Actisanes, an Ethiopian King of Egypt "carried his good fortune as a man should" and treated his subjects with kindness. Clearly impressed by the justice of the Ethiopian king, Diodorus compared and contrasted the justice of this king with the "harshness, injustice, and arrogance of the Egyptian Amasis."[54]

Diodorus' interpretations of the Homeric references to the Olympian visits among the Ethiopians, as pointed out by Snowden, contain great significance "for the question of the classical image of Ethiopian piety and justice. . . ."[55]

> And they say that they [Ethiopians] were the first to be taught to honour the gods and to hold sacrifices and festivals and processions and festivals and the other rites by which men honour the deity; and that in consequence their piety has been published abroad among all men, and it is generally held that the sacrifices practised among the Ethiopians are those which are the most pleasing to heaven. As witness to this they call upon the poet who is perhaps the oldest and certainly the most venerated among the Greeks; for in the *Iliad* he represents both Zeus and the rest of the gods with him as absent on a visit to Ethiopia to share in the sacrifices and the banquet which were given annually by the Ethiopians for all the gods together. . . . And they state that by reason of their piety towards the deity, they manifestly enjoy the favour of the gods, inasmuch as they have never experienced the rule of an invader from abroad; for from all time they have enjoyed a state of freedom and of peace one with another, and although many and powerful rulers have made war upon them, not one of these has succeeded in his undertaking.[56]

This image of "just Ethiopians, beloved of the gods,"[57] is still present during the Empire. Seneca, Strabo, Statius, and Lucian made references to piety and justice among the Ethiopians. Referring to the inhabitants of heaven, Statius comments how they "burst forth from their secret portals whenever they wish the pleasure of visiting the homes and shores and lesser banquets of the red Ethiopians."[58]

Pausanias believed that the most just Ethiopians lived in the city of Meroe and the often-called Ethiopian plain. Aelian pointed out that Ethiopia is where the gods bathe. Continuing the image of just and pious Ethiopians in the Homeric tradition and other early writings, Heliodorus portrays the Ethiopian king Hydaspes as "a model of wisdom and

53. Snowden, *Blacks in Antiquity* 145.
54. Snowden, *Blacks in Antiquity* 145.
55. Snowden, *Blacks in Antiquity* 145.
56. Diodorus. 3.2.2–3.1, quoted in Snowden, *Blacks in Antiquity* 146.
57. Snowden, *Blacks in Antiquity* 147.
58. Quoted in Snowden, *Blacks in Antiquity* 147.

righteousness, resembling in some respects the Ethiopian kings described by Herodotus and Diodorus."[59]

Snowden refers to Lactantius Placidus, a sixth-century A.D. (?) grammarian, to provide "an appropriate summary of the classical tradition of divine love for the Ethiopians and of the ancient records on Ethiopian justice. . . ."[60]:

> Certainly they [the Ethiopians] are loved by the gods because of justice. This even Homer indicates in the first book by the fact that Jupiter frequently leaves heaven and feasts with them because of their justice and the equity of their customs. For the Ethiopians are said to be the justest men and for that reason the gods leave their abode frequently to visit them.[61]

Much more could be said concerning the image of Ethiopians as symbols of justice, but the above examples should be sufficient to demonstrate how and why such an image affected the racial perceptions of generations of Mediterranean whites.

Racial Attitudes among the Early Christians

The early Christians' racial attitudes reflected in large part the racial attitudes of the larger Greco–Roman world. Once again the excellent scholarly work of Snowden sheds light on this topic:

> The early Christian view of the Ethiopian was in the same tradition as the Greco–Roman outlook, adumbrated at first by the environmental approach of the Greeks to racial differences and developed in later ideas of the unity of mankind.[62]

According to Snowden, the early Christians not only "adapted to their credo a frame of reference which had been employed frequently by Greeks and Romans to express their opinions on the equality of men" but in addition these early Christians also "used the Ethiopian as a prime motif in the language of conversion and as a means to emphasize their conviction that Christianity was to include all mankind."[63]

So unlike the long, tortuous, racial history of the modern era in which tens of millions of later Christians were contaminated by the virus of anti-black racism, a legacy of African enslavement, the early Christians were not put off by those Ethiopians, "the blackest and most remote of men."

---

59. Snowden, *Blacks in Antiquity* 148.
60. Snowden, *Blacks in Antiquity* 148.
61. Lactantius quoted in Snowden, *Blacks in Antiquity* 148.
62. Snowden, *Blacks in Antiquity* 196.
63. Snowden, *Blacks in Antiquity* 196.

Instead, ". . . the Ethiopian was in many ways a convient symbol for certain patterns of Christian thought." Whereas in the modern era Christian thought and tradition would buckle under the repeated blows of the racial oppression of black humanity and then erect an elaborate system of racial theoretical justification both to belittle and deny the historical enormity of the impact of such oppression on the lives of generations of blacks (and other non-whites), the blackness of the Ethiopian within the early Christian community gave rise "neither to a theory of racial superiority nor to an inferior treatment."[64]

Early Christian writers such as Origen, Gregory of Nyssa, Jerome, and St. Augustine, accepted racial diversity and unity as the measure of faith in the early Christian communities. In St. Augustine's commentary on a verse of one of the Psalms, he mentioned "that under the name 'Ethiopians' all nations were signified."[65] In an interpretation of another verse of the Psalms, St. Augustine commented that "the Catholic Church has been foretold not to be in any particular quarter of the world, as certain schisms are, but in the whole universe, by bearing fruit and growing even unto the very Ethiopians, indeed the remotest and blackest of men."[66]

At a time when the vast majority of Christian churches in the United States and elsewhere have been racially segregated by tradition and choice, the early church could teach modern-day Christians a lesson on race relations. "That membership in the early Church was actually to include Ethiopians was a cardinal principle from the very beginning," Snowden comments, "for one of the acts of the apostles, Philip's baptism of an Ethiopian eunuch, foreshadowed what was to be the practice of the early Church."[67]

The first six centuries of Christianity witnessed blacks' being "summoned to salvation and . . . welcomed in the Christian brotherhood on the same terms as other converts."[68] Philip's baptism of the Ethiopian eunuch inspired the north Italian poet Arator to revive aspects of the marriage of Moses to an Ethiopian woman. Both for Arator and readers of the Acts, blacks "continued to be a dramatic symbol of Christianity's catholic [universal] mission. . . ."[69]

It should be pointed out that this positive, unific use of black Ethiopians to demonstrate the universality of the early Christian church occurred "in spite of the association of blackness with ill omens, demons, the devil, and sin. . . ." Instead, we see an image of blacks that emphasized "the

64. Snowden, *Blacks in Antiquity* 196.
65. Quoted in Snowden, *Blacks in Antiquity* 204.
66. Quoted in Snowden, *Blacks in Antiquity* 204.
67. Snowden, *Blacks in Antiquity* 206.
68. Snowden, *Before Color Prejudice* 106.
69. Snowden, *Before Color Prejudice* 107.

ecumenical character of Christianity and adumbrated the symbolism of the black wise man in the Adoration of the Magi."[70]

The modern world would turn these positive images of blacks into icons of anti-black racism to rationalize slavery and the role of much of European Christendom in the dehumanization of people of color. The white West would gradually move away from the early church's image of black as the symbol of "the ecumenical character of Christianity." Instead, in the wake of African slavery, a new color symbolism would emerge in Christian thought, as explained by one scholar:

> The entire history of Western painting bears witness to the deliberate whitening or bleaching effort that changed Christ from a Semitic to an Aryan person. The dark hair that Christ was thought to have had came to be rendered as very light-colored, and his big dark eyes as blue. It was necessary that this man, the incarnation of God, be as far removed as possible from everything that could suggest darkness or blackness, even indirectly. His hair and his beard were given the color of sunshine, the brightness of the light above, while his eyes retained the color of the sky from which he descended and to which he returned.
>
> The progressive Aryanization of Christ is in strict accordance with the logic of the color symbolism. It did not start, however, until Christianity came into close contact with the other races—with the African race, in particular. Christian artists began to avoid the darker tints in depicting Christ in order to remove as much as possible of their evil suggestion.[71]

Notwithstanding the historical process that transformed early Christian views of humankind as one community in Christ into the modern view and practice of a racially segregated community in Christ, the ancient Mediterranean world has given to the modern world a great gift of interracial understanding. It has taught the modern world that blacks and whites in particular have a much older history of interracial harmony than of interracial conflict. But much more important, it has taught the modern world that white racism and white notions of racial superiority are social and spiritual diseases of the recent past and not, as many would have us believe, a natural consequence of interactions of different racial types.

---

70. Snowden, *Before Color Prejudice* 107.
71. Roger Bastide, "Color, Racism, and Christianity" 315–16.

3

European Global Conquest and Expansion and the Emergence of the Ideology of White Racial Superiority in America

The race to which we belong is the most arrogant and rapacious, the most exclusive and indomitable in history. It is the conquering and unconquerable race, through which alone man has taken possession of the physical and moral world. All other races have been its enemies or its victims.

—J. J. Ingalls
Speech to the United States Senate, 1890

The modern world is still paying the social costs of historic racism. We are only just beginning to understand the extent to which the system of racial domination imposed upon millions of non-Europeans by European nations over the past few centuries still governs the conscious and unconscious relationships between whites and nonwhites throughout the world. Racism has wounded generations of nonwhites far more deeply than whites will ever know. Many whites, however, still partake of the privileges of color bequeathed to them by the legacy of historic racism, unable or unwilling to divest themselves of the advantages of being "white" in a world that still touts white cultural values and allocates rewards for accepting such values. As a result, racial fear and hatred still dominate interracial interactions in most multiracial societies.

Everywhere we look today, in the United States, England, and South Africa, we observe the long hand of racism reaching across the centuries into the present. The black underclass in American cities, trapped in poverty, crime, and violence, is not composed of disconnected entities floating in time and space. Blacks are the human flotsam and jetsam of a historical process of dehumanization that started with the first slave ship which landed in the British colonies. The angry black students in Soweto, South Africa, who refuse to go to school under an apartheid educational system, are linked to other blacks around the world by the same history of white racial dominance. Native–American adults and youth seeking escape through drugs and alcohol, as well as the Hispanic and Indo–Chinese struggling to carve a niche for themselves in a world in which whites largely determine the size and shape of the niches, all share a common history of racial victimization that still exerts tremendous influence throughout the global community.

The Role of African Slavery in the Development of Global Racism

The above statements should be not interpreted as a wholesale indictment of the white race. Rather, they should be viewed as an indictment of an historical system of racial dominance that developed in parallel to the European world economy from the sixteenth century onwards. Almost imperceptibly at first, Europeans developed racist attitudes towards Indians, Africans, and other nonwhites as they went about their business exploring the "New World," conquering the indigenous peoples and then taking their lands, and buying and selling Africans to till those lands. The European banking houses, ship captains, planters, soldiers, and sailors, and a host of other "whites" who participated in this Grand Adventure were not necessarily evil people. Like people of all ages and nations, they found themselves thrust into an historical process that many neither fully understood nor controlled. For example, the unquestioned evils of the African slave trade that drove Western civilization down the long path of racial turmoil, the contemporary by-products of which periodically rise up to greet us on the front pages of our morning newspaper in the form of racial conflicts, began in part as a response to a shortage of labor. As Immanuel Wallerstein has argued:

> But why Africans as the new slaves? Because of exhaustion of the supply of laborers indigenous to the region of the plantations, because Europe needed a source of labor from a reasonably well-populated region that was accessible and relatively near the region of usage. But it had to be from a region that was outside its world-economy so that Europe could feel unconcerned about the economic consequences for the breeding region of wide-scale removal of manpower as slaves. Western Africa filled the bill best. [1]

Before the fateful choice was made to use West Africans as the main labor force for the New World plantation systems, Europeans in their greed

---

1. Immanuel Wallerstein, *The Modern World-System: Capitalist Agriculture and the Origins of the European World-Economy in the Sixteenth Century* 66.

for more land and profits had committed genocide and near genocide of the Indian populations. Indian populations on most Caribbean islands "disappeared entirely." In New Spain (Mexico), the Indian population numbered about 11 million in 1519. By 1650, the population had declined to about 1.5 million. Indian populations in Brazil and Peru experienced a similar decline. Some scholars have argued that the two key factors responsible for the decline in indigenous populations were the disease and damage "to Indian cultivation caused by the domestic animals that the Europeans bred." But, the most likely explanation for the decline seems to be have been the "sheer exhaustion of manpower, especially in the mines."[2] In short, the Indian populations were practically killed off by varying means, brought on by the imposition of a European-based world economy reinforced by racial selection.

The early brutal exploitation of Indian and African labor by Europeans set the stage for similar exploitation of nonwhite labor throughout the European world-system. By the late nineteenth century, European nations had carved up Africa and subjugated millions of nonwhites in various parts of Asia.

The European exploration of the New World in the fifteenth century led to centuries of brutal conquest, colonization, and protracted wars of extermination. At the same time that the indigenous peoples were being systemically forced from their lands by the use of subterfuge and guns, millions of Africans were being forcibly removed from their homelands by international slave cartels to supply the labor needs of plantations in the New World. Millions of Africans died on their way to the slave ships; others died crossing the ocean; still others died or were maimed and murdered while laboring on plantations established to satisfy the needs of European planters, merchants, and banking houses.

The New World alone could not satiate the appetite of a Europe that had lost its soul in pursuit of material gain. All the lands populated by non-Europeans found themselves the target of European mercantile capitalism. Wherever a European ship could sail and find a sponsor to make a profit, the people and the land and resources upon or beneath it became fair game for the global market, dominated by a people who would soon consider such domination their divine right simply by virtue of race and culture.

The Emergence of the Ideology of White Superiority

As Europeans increasingly took over the lands and the resources of non-Europeans in Asia, Africa, the Americas, New Zealand, Australia, and various other regions of the world dominated by Europeans on behalf of "White Christian Civilization," they increasingly saw themselves as the stewards of world civilization, placed on earth to elevate and guide the

---

2. Wallerstein, *The Modern World-System* 67.

nonwhite masses. This collective feeling of racial superiority developed gradually over the centuries as the European peoples established contact with non-European peoples for the purposes of conquest and exploitation.[3] The English played a leading role both in the conquest of peoples of color and the development of the ideology of racial superiority.

According to historian Winthrop Jordan, the English had a peculiar disposition toward racist feelings about blacks:

> In England perhaps more than in southern Europe, the concept of blackness was loaded with intense meaning. Long before they found that some men were black, Englishmen found in the idea of blackness a way of expressing some of their most ingrained values. No other color except white conveyed so much emotional impact.[4]

According to *The Oxford English Dictionary*, before the sixteenth century, the meaning of the word *black* in English culture had the following connotations: "Deeply stained with dirt; soiled, dirty, foul. . . . Having dark or deadly purposes, malignant; pertaining to or involving death, deadly; baneful, disastrous, sinister. . . . Foul, iniquitous, atrocious, horrible, wicked. . . . Indicating disgrace, censure, liability to punishment, etc."[5] Jordan continued to explain the deepseated cultural symbolism of blackness within the collective psyche of the English. "Black was an emotionally partisan color, the handmaid and symbol of baseness and evil, a sign of danger and repulsion." But, if blackness symbolized everything negative in the English collective mind, what about whiteness? "Embedded in the concept of blackness," Jordan explains, "was its direct opposite—whiteness. No other colors so clearly implied opposition. . . ."[6] What preceded the establishment of African slavery in the United States and the subsequent development of ideological racism as a rationale and defense for the practice was an historical and cultural predisposition among the English populace that saw blackness as embodying everything negative. It is necessary, then, to probe further into the English cultural history to understand what happened to them when they became "white" Americans. Jordan explains further:

> White and black connoted purity and filthiness, virginity and sin, virtue and baseness, beauty and ugliness, beneficence and evil, God and the devil. Whiteness, moreover, carried a special significance for Elizabethan Englishmen:

---

3. E. Franklin Frazier, *Race and Culture Contacts in the Modern World* passim.

4. Winthrop D. Jordan, *White Man's Burden: Historic Origins of Racism in the United States* 5–6.

5. Quoted in Jordan, *White Man's Burden* 6.

6. Jordan, *White Man's Burden* 6.

it was, particularly when complemented by red, the color of perfect human beauty, especially *female* beauty. This ideal was already centuries old in Elizabeth's time, and their fair Queen was its very embodiment: her cheeks were "roses in a bed of lilies."[7] (Italics in original.)

An adoring nation knew precisely what a beautiful queen looked like. This "adoring nation" visualized their queen in the following manner:

> Her cheeke, her chinne, her neck, her nose,
> This was a lillye, that was a rose;
> Her bosome, sleeke as Paris plaster,
> Held upp twoo bowles of Alabaster.[8]

The English were no less ethnocentric than other peoples who also saw themselves as the standard of all beauty. Most certainly at this point in their cultural history they were acting quite normally. The ideal for them was just that: "Her cheeke, her chinne, . . . This was a lillye, that was a rose. . . ." The beauty standards of the English had evolved over the centuries before they made contact with black Africans. The English voyagers were about a century behind Portugal's Prince Henry the Navigator in making contact with Africans. When they did make contact around 1550, the African's color arrested their attention probably more than anything else. In some ways, one could say the English suffered an intense cultural shock due mainly to the trauma of being thrown into sudden contact with people so very different from them in terms of color. Here again, Jordan explains this process:

> The powerful impact which the Negro's color made upon Englishmen must have been partly owing to suddenness of contact. Though the Bible as well as the arts and literature of antiquity and the Middle Ages offered some slight introduction to the "Ethiope," England's immediate acquaintance with "black"-skinned peoples came with relative rapidity.[9]

The English had known people much darker than themselves, but few as black as the West Africans. To them, northern Africans, whom they referred to as Moors, were really black. In Shakespeare's time, the Moors were considered dark, and the terms *Negro* and *black* carried the same connotations. When the English made contact with the really "black" peoples of West Africa, they began refining their first perceptions. They called these blacks, "blacke Moores." "The impact of the Negro's color was the more powerful upon Englishmen, moreover, because England's

---

7. Quoted in Jordan, *White Man's Burden* 6.
8. Jordan, *White Man's Burden* 6.
9. Jordan, *White Man's Burden* 5.

principal contact with Africans came in West Africa and the Congo," Jordan argues, "which meant that one of the lightest-skinned of the earth's peoples suddenly came face to face with one of the darkest."[10]

Where, then, did this English cultural predisposition towards "blackness" place black people? Where did blacks rate in the English standards of beauty? If one had to be lily-white with red cheeks to be beautiful, certainly then, the West Africans were lowest on the English scale of beauty. "By contrast, the Negro was ugly, by reason of his color and also his 'horrid Curles' and 'disfigured' lips and nose,"[11] Jordan states. A century after their first sustained contact with West Africans, the English were still struggling with the social and psychological ramifications of blackness. Their discovery of the black African made their "whiteness" all the more dear. Such contrast in color in such a short period of time proved too much. Whiteness had to be right and correct and divine. Yet, many English writers of the period understood that Africans also had their own standards of beauty based on blackness. Indeed, in 1621, one English writer probably shocked his readers by reporting that some Africans painted the devil white in contempt for the color.[12]

In Great Britain, probably more so than in any other European country, the duality of black and white permeated the literature. There were indeed few European cultures whose literature abounded with such black and white symbolism as England's. William Shakespeare used this symbolism in such plays as *The Merchant of Venice*, *Titus Andronicus*, and *Othello*. William Blake also made use of such symbolism in his poem, "The Little Black Boy."[13]

Reading about black Africans and interacting with them a safe distance from home provided one kind of unique experience. However, when planters began bringing blacks into Britain, it created problems. As blacks started arriving in Britain in large enough numbers to be noticed, it was not long before voices were being raised against them, led by Queen Elizabeth I herself. In 1596, the queen sent a letter to the Lord Mayor of London and to the mayors of other cities, complaining that there were of late too many blacks in the country. By 1601, the queen felt the problem was so severe, particularly because of the poverty of many people during this period, that she issued a royal proclamation ordering all "blackamoors" out of the kingdom. The royal proclamation proved ineffective because

> By the end of sixteenth century London's black minority had become sufficiently large to cause the government concern. Yet it was Elizabeth's

---

10. Jordan, *White Man's Burden* 5.
11. Jordan, *White Man's Burden* 6.
12. Jordan, *White Man's Burden* 9–10.
13. Lemuel A. Johnson, *The Devil, the Gargoyle, and the Buffoon: The Negro as Metaphor in Western Literature* 38, 54.

encouragement of the trade with Africa, from which she stood to gain financially, that brought about black immigration. Black servants were in the employ of royal favourites at Court and of others less well-placed. Not all Africans were enslaved domestics. Some had gained their freedom and actively participated in their local churches. Some were sufficiently independent to pay their own taxes while a small minority even possessed property. Within twenty years of Elizabeth's attempt to purge the country of its Africans, the black minority had firmly integrated itself into socially acceptable positions. Employment of Negroes as servants in early Stuart England—and once again after the Restoration in 1660—reinstated the Africans in the ranks from which Elizabeth had tried to dislodge them.[14]

By this time, the historical combination of English involvement in the African slave trade and their cultural predisposition towards blackness had evolved into a set of racist values appropriate for formulating a fairly formidable ideology of racism. Many of these values were brought by those English who later settled America. There was not only a continual transatlantic interchange of commodities and people but also an interchange of dominant values, theories, and practices concerning blacks. In fact, the system of African slavery under the English created one of the most sophisticated forms of white racial dominance and ideological racism. As one scholar explains this development:

> It was in the British plantation colonies in the Western hemisphere that race relations emerged in their clearest form: the whites, as masters, were the superior race; the blacks, as slaves, were the inferior race. A basically similar model of race relations also emerged in the Eastern hemisphere once the British had consolidated their hold over the Indian sub-continent.[15]

The United States and Britain were well on their way to becoming racist societies when they became dependent on African slave labor. This dependency would not have necessitated an ideology based upon racism had these societies been able to reconcile their religious, moral, and political traditions with African slavery and the conquest of the native peoples.

Economic need for plentiful cheap labor drove lawmakers in the Colony of Virginia to write slavery into law in 1660. Soon other colonies followed this example.[16] The American Revolutionary War and the post-war period presented some problems as to how the new nation would resolve the fundamental moral and political contradiction of holding slaves while preaching and fighting for freedom. As it would also successfully do in future

14. James Walvin, *The Black Presence: A documentary history of the Negro in England, 1555–1860* 13.

15. Dilip Hiro, *Black British, White British* 298.

16. Jordan, *White Man's Burden* 39–50.

situations, America fashioned a special brand of political and moral compromise that helped it to rationalize both the conquest of the native peoples and the enslavement of blacks. Since America was not about to abandon slave labor or its policy of dispossessing the native peoples of their land, the only real and practical choice was to minimize the nature of its sins: blacks and the native peoples (Indians) were not to be considered on the same level of humanity as whites; blacks were heathen and amoral, next to the apes in the scale of evolution. Gradually an ideology emerged in the United States and Britain which explained that white racial dominance was a blessing.

As slavery continued to become more profitable to the United States and Britain, the moral contradictions became more apparent and blatant. Both countries began formulating a racist ideology to cover those moral contradictions that collided with certain Christian and Enlightenment beliefs in the universality of the human race. By the eighteenth century, there emerged a wide array of antiblack theories and views of which racist apologists could have their choice. There was the work of Dr. Charles White, a famous English physician and surgeon, who developed so-called scientific arguments for the multiple origins of the human race. He believed that blacks occupied a different "station" on the human scale than whites, indeed, that blacks comprised an intermediate species between the whites and the apes.[17] Another scholar, Lord Kames, also contributed his share to the development of the ideology of racism. This Scottish jurist argued that blacks were not even of the same species as whites.[18] Voltaire believed that both Indians and blacks comprised separate species. Thomas Jefferson joined in the parade of dignitaries who believed that nonwhites were essentially inferior to whites.[19] The ideological rationale for slavery and white racial dominance over nonwhite peoples developed even more under the attacks of the antislavery forces in the United States and Britain. (These were the social forces that contributed to the movement for racial unity, which we will discuss later.)

In the 1760s, a "paper war" broke out in Britain between the slave lobby and the antislavery forces. The former maintained (as did their American counterparts) that blacks were an inferior species. The latter, sometimes to the detriment of blacks, maintained the counterbelief that blacks were "innocent child[ren] of nature."[20] Unfortunately, the proslavery forces in both countries had more influential people supporting them. David Hume, the Scottish philosopher and historian, contributed greatly to the development of ideological racism when he remarked:

---

17. Thomas F. Gossett, *Race: The History of an Idea in America 47*–48.
18. See Gossett, *Race: The History of an Idea in America* 45.
19. See Gossett, *Race: The History of an Idea in America* 42–44.
20. Walvin, *Black Presence* 21.

I am apt to suspect the Negroes to be naturally inferior to the Whites. There never was a civilised nation of any other complexion than white, or even any individual eminent either in action or speculation. No ingenious manufacturer among them, no arts, no sciences. There are Negro slaves dispersed all over Europe, of which none ever discovered any symptom of ingenuity.[21]

Similar views were expressed across the Atlantic by Jefferson and other influential white Americans. Jefferson, however, played a major role in fostering ideological racism in America during the formative years of white America's thinking on race and the place of blacks within the American Grand Experience.

21. Quoted in Walvin, *Black Presence* 21.

4

Thomas Jefferson's View of a Multiracial America

I advance it, therefore, as a suspicion only, that the blacks, whether originally a distinct race, or made distinct by time and circumstances, are inferior to the whites in the endowment both of body and mind.
—Thomas Jefferson

Thomas Jefferson was not only a slave owner like his contemporary George Washington and others among the "founding fathers," but, unlike many of the others, Jefferson was also a man of letters whose writings influenced generations of Americans and Europeans. As two scholars of Jefferson have pointed out: "No leader in the period of the American Enlightenment was as articulate, as wise, as conscious of the implications and consequences of free society as he."[1] That being the case, Jefferson wielded enormous influence on the thinking of his age in the areas of science and politics, but especially in race relations. What he thought and wrote about race was key to the thinking of future American generations. "In the years after the Revolution the speculations of Thomas Jefferson were of great importance because so many people read and reacted to them," another scholar wrote. "His remarks about Negroes in the only book he ever wrote were more widely read, in all probability, than any others until the mid-nineteenth century."[2] Unfortunately, Thomas Jefferson, one of America's greatest leaders and thinkers, was also one of the first Americans to formulate an ideology of racism, particularly antiblack racism. In short, Thomas Jefferson was the first among America's ideological racists.

The scholar of American racism finds in Thomas Jefferson's life and

---

1. Adrienne Koch and William Peden, eds., *The Life and Selected Writings of Thomas Jefferson* xv.
2. Jordan, *White Man's Burden* 165.

writings many racial phobias and beliefs that still plague contemporary white America. Jefferson worried about slavery much as many contemporary white Americans worry about racism and the plight of the black community: solely in regard to its impact on the whites. Like many contemporary white Americans, Jefferson harbored racist beliefs about blacks. He feared black uprisings and entertained all kinds of notions about black sexuality. He firmly believed in the superiority of whites over blacks. According to Jefferson, blacks and whites could never co-exist on equal terms in America. These views were incorporated in his *Notes on the State of Virginia,* written between 1781 and 1782. No one can say that Jefferson was not concerned about the evils and social and historical consequences of slavery upon American society. He was among the first to recognize the costs of slavery on the moral and psychological development of white children, even as he neglected to articulate fully slavery's deadening effects upon the body, mind, and souls of generations of black slaves and their descendants. Of the effects on whites, he wrote:

> There must doubtless be an unhappy influence on the manners of our people produced by the existence of slavery among us. The whole commerce between master and slave is a perpetual exercise of the most boisterous passions, the most unremitting despotism on the one part, and degrading submissions on the other. Our children see this, and learn to imitate it. . . . From his cradle to his grave [man] is learning to do what he sees others do. If a parent could find no motive either in his philanthropy or his self-love, for restraining the intemperance of passion towards his slave, it should always be a sufficient one that his child is present. . . . The parent storms, the child looks on, catches the lineaments of wrath, puts on the same airs in the circle of smaller slaves, gives a loose to the worst of passions, and thus nursed, educated, and daily exercised in tyranny, cannot but be stamped by it with odious peculiarities. The man must be a prodigy who can retain his manners and morals undepraved by such circumstances.[3]

Jefferson could see the pathology of racial dominance inherent in slavery and how it affected white children. He reveals the process by which white Americans reared under slavery developed their sense of racial superiority. He was obviously very concerned for the moral and psychological health of white children. The effects of their racism on black children, within that "circle of smaller slaves," is mentioned only parenthetically, clearly a shadow issue in Jefferson's mind. Slavery destroys not only the morals of a people but also their industry, as Jefferson remarked:

> With the morals of the people, their industry also is destroyed. For in a warm climate, no man will labor for himself who can make another labor for him.

---

3. Quoted in Koch and Peden, *Life and Selected Writings* 278.

This is so true, that of the proprietors of slaves a very small proportion indeed are ever seen to labor. And can the liberties of a nation be thought secure when we have removed their only firm basis, a conviction in the minds of the people that these liberties are of the gift of God? That they are not to be violated but with His wrath?[4]

The costs of slavery, then, weighed heavily on white slaveholders. The greatest cost, perhaps, was their disinclination to work. "No man will labor for himself who can make another labor for him." Slavery, then, not only distorted the hearts and souls of whites who held slaves but also destroyed the sanctity of labor itself, or at least the hard, difficult, backbreaking labor that the slaves were forced to do on behalf of whites. As bothersome as these costs of slavery were to Jefferson, he worried more about a great possible cost to America exacted by God for the crime of slavery. That cost might possibly come in the shape of black rebellions, which Jefferson and most planters who owned slaves constantly feared:

> Indeed I tremble for my country when I reflect that God is just; that his justice cannot sleep forever; that considering numbers, nature and natural means only, a revolution of the wheel of fortune, an exchange of situation is among possible events; that it may become probably by supernatural interference! The Almighty has no attribute which can take side with us in such a contest.[5]

Jefferson lived long enough to see his worst fears of God's wrath realized, but (happily for him and his fellow white Americans), in another region—Haiti. Haiti had been under French rule until black slaves under the leadership of a black military genius (Toussaint l'Ouverture) defeated Napoleon's troops in a two-year bloody war that ended in 1793 with the black slaves gaining their freedom.[6] To Jefferson, this revolt of black slaves was only the first chapter: ". . . if something is not done," he warned, ". . . we shall be the murderers of our own children."[7] Here again, Jefferson was calculating the great cost whites would have to pay if they did not free black slaves. Jefferson spent much of his life agonizing over the issue of slavery. But that agony did not prevent him from contributing his considerable share to racist thought in the United States.

Thomas Jefferson's views on blacks were among the most racist of his time. Some would say that he reflected his time, that he was shaped by the slave-holding culture of which he was but a part. While such an explanation is certainly true to some extent, it fails to account for the tremendous

---

4. Quoted in Koch and Peden, *Life and Selected Writings* 278–79.

5. Quoted in Koch and Peden, *Life and Selected Writings* 279.

6. C. L. R. James, *The Black Jacobins: Toussaint L'Ouverture and the San Domingo Revolution* ix–xi.

7. Quoted in Jordan, *White Man's Burden* 169.

intellectual efforts Jefferson devoted to demeaning blacks as human beings. It is in this context that we must regard him as the premier ideological racist of his day. Jefferson believed not only that blacks were inferior but also that they could never join white Americans as equals in the Great Republic:

> It will probably be asked, Why not retain and incorporate the blacks into the State and thus save the expense of supplying by importation of white settlers, the vacancies they will leave? Deep-rooted prejudices entertained by the whites; ten thousand recollections, by the blacks, of the injuries they have sustained; new provocations; the real distinctions which nature has made; and many other circumstances, will divide us into parties, and produce convulsions, which will probably never end but in the extermination of the one or the other race. To these objections, which are political, may be added others, which are physical and moral. The first difference which strikes us is that of color. . . . And is this difference of no importance? Is it not the foundation of a greater or less [sic] share of beauty in the two races?[8]

Jefferson made a strong case for not incorporating blacks into the body politic. The prejudices of whites and the recollections of blacks would be, it seemed to him, too volatile, too irreconcilable. On this point, we can perhaps sympathize with Jefferson. He had few if any examples of multiracial societies in which former black slaves and their former white masters had come together on an equal basis to build a nation. At this juncture of modern history with all its potential for great human glory and tragedy, even the greatest visionaries found difficulty incorporating a peoplehood of black, red, and white. Few such visions transcended the pervasive ethnocentric views of the English-turned-Americans who still struggled with the perjorative meaning of blackness lodged in their innermost being. Not only did Jefferson have difficulty envisioning blacks and whites sharing a common country on an equal basis, he also had difficulty imagining that blacks could ever be as beautiful as whites:

> Are not the fine mixtures of red and white, the expressions of every passion by greater or less suffusions of color in the one, preferable to that eternal monotony, which reigns in the countenances, that immovable veil of black which covers the emotions of the other races? Add to these, flowing hair, a more elegant symmetry of form, their own judgment in favor of the whites, declared by their preference of them, as uniformly as is the preference of the Oran-utan [sic] for the black woman over those of his own species.[9]

Continuing, Jefferson points to more differences between blacks and whites, which differences, he contends, separate blacks and whites. Blacks

---

8. Quoted in Koch and Peden, *Life and Selected Writings* 256.
9. Quoted in Koch and Peden, *Life and Selected Writings* 256.

"seem to require less sleep. A black after hard labor through the day, will be induced by the slightest amusements to sit up till midnight, or later, though knowing he must be out with first dawn of the morning." It did not not seem to occur to Jefferson that black slaves had to have a life of their own whenever they could get it. He could only see from a white planter's point of view, namely, that slaves should work hard all day then sleep as much as they could so they would be able to work harder for the master. At one point when he credited blacks with being "at least as brave, and more adventuresome" than whites, he quickly added, "But this may perhaps proceed from a want of forethought, which prevents their seeing a danger till it be present." Of black love and affection, Jefferson had this to say: "They are more ardent after their female; but love seems with them to be more an eager desire, than a tender delicate mixture of sentiment and sensation." And of black grief, "Their griefs are transient. Those numberless afflictions, which render it doubtful whether heaven has given life to us in mercy or in wrath, are less felt, and sooner forgotten with them." In addition, the general state of blacks, Jefferson believed, was little more than an existence that "appears to participate more of sensation than reflection. To this must be ascribed their disposition to sleep when abstracted from their diversions, and unemployed in labor."[10]

One can readily see how Jefferson became the premier ideological racist of his day. He seemed unwilling to recognize the slightest indication of black humanity. Blacks could not be brave and more adventuresome without being seen by Jefferson as lacking forethought. The love of the black man for the black woman was too ardent for Jefferson's taste "more an eager desire, than a tender delicate mixture of sentiment and sensation." Of all of Jefferson's views of blacks, his views of black male sexuality revealed the deep-rooted fears and anxieties of generations of white males.[11] As a

---

10. Quoted in Koch and Peden, *Life and Selected* 257. Jefferson's fears and anxieties concerning black male sexuality became such an obsession that he once proposed a bill to the Virginia legislature to require a white woman who had borne a child by a black man to leave the state or be placed beyond the protection of the law. See John Chester Miller, *The Wolf by the Ears: Thomas Jefferson and Slavery* 64.

11. Miller, *The Wolf by the Ears* 62. White male fear of black male–white female sexual relations has played a major role in the psychohistorical development of racial attitudes in the larger white society, going back to the earliest contacts between the English and the Africans. See Winthrop D. Jordan, *White Man's Burden* 32–40. This phobia on the part of southern white males assumed pathological proportions during the post-emancipation period when white males felt that they were losing control of black males. They responded by inventing a mental image of the black, former slave as "beast rapist," "insatiable satyr," preying on the fair damsels of the South. See Joel Williamson, *A Rage for Order: Black/White Relations in the American South Since Emancipation* 186–91. For some insights into how this sexual–racial phobia manifests itself in present-day American society, see Bob Blauner, *Black Lives, White Lives: Three Decades of Race Relations in America* 247–51.

slaveowner who more than once commented on the tragic effects of slavery on whites, Jefferson did not seem overly concerned by the burden of slavery upon his black slaves. He tended to trivialize their grief as "transient," which he thought "sooner forgotten with them." Adding much insult to injury, he then reduced their general existence to little more than that of "sensation" rather than of "reflection."

Jefferson also made a central contribution to racist thought in America with his comments on black mental inferiority. It is in this area that Jefferson, the founding father of white America, laid the foundation for the racism that still works to divide white America from black America. Jordan places the blame squarely on Jefferson's shoulders: "Of far more serious import for the Negro's future were Jefferson's remarks on mental capacity. More than any other single person he framed the terms of the debate still carried on today."[12] Jefferson also provided generations of white Americans with an intellectual defense of white racism. Indeed, this following quotation gave Jefferson the historical distinction of being a founder of the most popular and oldest school of racist thought in America:

> Comparing them by their faculties of memory, reason, and imagination, it appears to me that in memory they are equal to the whites; in reason much inferior, as I think one could scarcely be found capable of tracing and comprehending the investigations of Euclid; and that in imagination they are dull, tasteless, and anomalous. It would be unfair to follow them to Africa for this investigation. We will consider them here, on the same stage with the whites, and where the facts are not apocryphal on which a judgment is to be formed. It will be right to make great allowances for the difference of condition, of education, of conversation, of the sphere in which they move. Many millions of them have been brought to, and born in America. Most of them, indeed, have been confined to tillage, to their own homes, and their own society; yet many have been so situated, that they might have availed themselves of the conversation of their masters; many have been brought up to the handicraft arts, and from that circumstance have always been associated with the whites. Some have been liberally educated, and all have lived in countries where the arts and sciences are cultivated to a considerable degree, and all have had before their eyes samples of the best works from abroad. The Indians, with no advantages of this kind, will often carve figures on their pages not destitute of design and merit. They will crayon out an animal, a plant, or a country, so as to prove the existence of a germ in their minds which only wants cultivation. They astonish you with strokes of the most sublime oratory; such as prove their reason and sentiment strong, their imagination glowing and elevated. But never yet could I find that a black had uttered a thought above the level of plain narration; never saw even an elementary trait of painting or sculpture. In music they are more generally gifted than the whites with accurate ears for tune and time. . . .

12. Jordan, *White Man's Burden* 171.

Whether they will be equal to the composition of a more extensive run of melody, or of complicated harmony, is yet to be proved.[13]

Jefferson's analysis of blacks' mental abilities as compared to whites and Indians revealed the emergence of an historical pattern of white ideological racism that would persist for many generations. Anti-environmentalism formed the crux of this historical pattern of racist thought. Basically, it argued that no amount of opportunity or exposure could alter the mental capacity of blacks. They were, by nature, inferior. Even the Indians, who lacked the so-called advantages of blacks, could do better. By focusing on the carefully contrived deficits of blacks within equally contrived situations in which they should have been able to demonstrate great ability but failed to do so, Jefferson was able to give the impression that he was measuring both blacks and Indians with the same yardstick. But Jefferson was committed to rationalizing his racist interpretation of blacks by any means at his disposal for the simple reason that to fail to do so would place the total burden of racial guilt upon white society. Here again, he was among the first American ideological racists to use this method of victim-blaming to deflect blame away from a system of white racial oppression.

Comparing black efforts to great Indian achievements despite lack of advantages supposedly available to blacks was another device employed by Jefferson to blame blacks for their condition. Although both blacks and Indians suffered at the hands of white Americans, Jefferson chose to place Indians on a more equal basis with whites than he did blacks. In fact, he once even stated that in intelligence and morality Indians were the equals to whites. Unlike his intense negative feelings toward blacks' physical attributes, he found the color of Indians close to that of Mediterranean Europeans. In contrast to his views of black–white intermixture, Jefferson, much like many other contemporary whites, accepted racial mixing between whites and Indians while rejecting similar mixing between blacks and whites. He was proud of the fact that both of his daughters had married descendants of Pocahontas and that the blood of Indian royalty therefore flowed in the veins of his grandchildren. In Jefferson's view, racial unity was possible but only between whites and Indians. Addressing the Indians on this subject, he stated, "Your blood will mix with ours and will spread with ours over this great land," until white and Indian become one people and one nation. The Indian, therefore, in contrast to the black, was in Jefferson's view a Noble Savage.[14]

To return to Jefferson's use—or more accurately put, misuse—of the contrast of blacks and Indians in relation to white America, this device of comparing blacks with other ethnic groups so as to deflect attention and

---

13. Quoted in Koch and Peden, *Life and Selected Writings* 257–58.
14. Quoted in Miller, *Wolf by the Ears* 65.

blame from the historical costs and consequences of white racial oppression upon black people has been used repeatedly by white Americans. As we have seen and as other scholars of Jefferson's racial views have noticed, Jefferson "seemed incapable of complimenting Negroes without immediately adding qualifications."[15] This racist tendency would also be transmitted across countless white generations to the present day: Blacks were good at music with some qualification but probably not good at more complicated musical forms. Although blacks were overly burdened with misery, which Jefferson commented is "often the parent of the most affecting touches in poetry," he snatched from blacks even the mind and spirit to produce good poetry from their misery: "Among the blacks is misery enough, God knows, but no poetry. Love is the peculiar oestrum of the poet. Their love is ardent, but it kindles the senses only, not the imagination."[16] As for the famous black–American poet Phillis Wheatley, born in Africa and brought to America as a small child and reared by a wealthy white Boston family, and who published her first poem in 1770,[17] she was simply not good enough to alter Jefferson's views of black inferiority. "Religion, indeed, has produced a Phyllis Whately [sic]," he conceded, "but it could not produce a poet. The compositions published under her name are below the dignity of criticism."[18]

Phillis Wheatley's work had impressed some of Jefferson's contemporaries, such as George Washington and Voltaire, and five editions of her book of poetry were published before 1800. In addition, she translated segments of Ovid, which should have impressed Jefferson even more, given his classical orientation. She received much acclaim in England from a host of nobles, including Lord Dartmouth, and when she returned to Boston, the *Gazette* sounded a rousing welcome for her in its pages, calling her "the extraordinary Poetical Genius."[19] But Jefferson was still too encumbered with his racist views to allow even these achievements to persuade him to appreciate this first great black poet in the United States.

However, Jefferson was trying in his own unique way to understand his views concerning blacks. Benjamin Banneker, a free black from Maryland, known for his achievements as a mathematician, astronomer, and a clockmaker, forced Jefferson to modify some of his racist beliefs concerning blacks, though Jefferson continued to cling to most such beliefs even after acknowledging Banneker's great achievements. In 1791, Banneker sent Jefferson a manuscript of an almanac he had put together. No doubt aware

15. Jordan, *White Man's Burden* 172.

16. Koch and Peden, *Life and Selected Writings* 258–59.

17. John Hope Franklin and Alfred A. Moss, Jr., *From Slavery to Freedom: A History of Negro Americans* 87; cf. Franklin and Moss, *From Slavery* 408–510.

18. Quoted in Koch and Peden, *Life and Selected Writings* 259.

19. Quoted in Miller, *Wolf by the Ears* 76.

of Jefferson's and some of his contemporaries' antiblack biases, Banneker informed Jefferson in no uncertain terms that he hoped Jefferson would see the manuscript as the long sought-after evidence of what blacks could achieve. He went on to comment that he had heard Jefferson was friendly towards blacks. Therefore, he believed that Jefferson, as the author of the Declaration of Independence, would be open to proof of achievement regardless of race. Banneker then proceeded to chastise Jefferson for violating his principles by holding slaves in a state of "tyrannical thralldom and inhuman captivity," and of being insensitive to the "cruel oppression" of thousands of blacks. Banneker also reminded Jefferson of how different the present state of affairs was from the days of 1776 when people were committed to eliminating every trace of oppression.[20] Jefferson accepted both the manuscript and the scolding from Banneker. In his reply, Jefferson demonstrated his respect for Banneker's feelings and some indications that the manuscript provided the long-awaited proof that blacks were quite capable of remarkable achievements:

> Sir,—I thank you sincerely for your letter of the 19th instant, and for the Almanac it contained. Nobody wishes more than I do to see such proofs as you exhibit, that nature has given to our black brethren, talents equal to those of the other colors of men, and that the appearance of a want of them is owing merely to the degraded condition of their existence, both in Africa and America. I can add with truth, that nobody wishes more ardently to see a good system commenced for raising the condition both of their body and mind to what it ought to be, as fast as the imbecility of their present existence, and other circumstances which cannot be neglected, will admit. I have taken the liberty of sending your Almanac to Monsieur de Condorcet, Secretary of the Academy of Sciences at Paris, and member of the Philanthropic Society, because I considered it as a document to which your color had a right for their justification against the doubts which have been entertained of them. I am, with great esteem, Sir, your most obedient humble servant.[21]

In his cover letter to Banneker's almanac sent to the Marquis de Condorcet, Jefferson expressed his delight and approval that it was possible for a black to become a very respectable mathematician who could produce "very elegant solutions of Geometrical problems." However, Jefferson could not avoid his tendency to place qualifications once again on Banneker's achievements. According to Jefferson, Banneker's great achievements did not, as Banneker desired, furnish proof that blacks if given a chance were capable of achieving as much as whites. Banneker was considered to be only an exception. While agreeing in part that Banneker's achievements were

---

20. Quoted in Miller, *Wolf by the Ears* 76.
21. Quoted in Koch and Peden, *Life and Selected Writings* 508–9.

impressive, Jefferson was too influenced by his own racism to see blacks as ever being equal to whites, no matter how much individual blacks achieved. "I shall be delighted to see these instances of moral eminence so multiplied as to prove that the want of talents observed in them, is merely the effect of their degraded conditions, and not proceeding from any difference in the structure of the parts on which the intellect depends."[22]

It is important to note that Jefferson was reflecting a cultural tendency that would come to characterize certain kinds of prejudiced patterns of thinking among white Americans. In cases where racism is so deep that to uproot it would cause prejudiced people great emotional upheaval by forcing them to change their view of the world radically, these people engage in countless qualifications—what the late Gordon Allport described as "re-fencing." Allport's explanation is very helpful in understanding Jefferson's tendency to place qualifications on black achievements:

> For our purposes it is important to understand what happens when categories conflict with evidence. It is a striking fact that in most instances categories are stubborn and resist change. After all, we have fashioned our generalizations as we have because they have worked fairly well. Why change them to accommodate every new bit of evidence? . . . To do so would only disturb our satisfactory set of habits.
>
> We selectively admit new evidence to a category if it confirms us in our previous belief. . . . But if we find evidence that is contradictory to our preconception, we are likely to grow resistant.
>
> There is a common mental device that permits people to hold to prejudgments even in the face of much contradictory evidence. It is the device of admitting exceptions. . . . By excluding a few favored cases, the negative rubric is kept intact for all other cases. In short, contrary evidence is not admitted and allowed to modify the generalization. . . .
>
> Let us call this the "re-fencing" device. When a fact cannot fit into a mental field, the exception is acknowledged, but the field is hastily fenced in again and not allowed to remain dangerously open.[23]

In the case of Banneker and other "exceptional" blacks, Jefferson, and those of his contemporaries who shared his racist views of blacks, would find the use of re-fencing critical to the maintenance and perpetuation of ideological racism. Future generations of whites would employ this device almost unconsciously in their attempts to avoid confronting their antiblack prejudices. Some whites, however, placed no such qualifications upon black achievement. While Banneker was most certainly an exceptional black, in their eyes he was also an example of what the black race as a whole was capable of achieving if given a chance. James McHenry, who later became

---

22. Quoted in Miller, *Wolf by the Ears* 76.
23. Gordon W. Allport, *The Nature of Prejudice* 23.

Secretary of War in the cabinet of John Adams and who assisted Banneker in obtaining important contacts within the national government, took the opposite position from Hume and Jefferson, who might on occasion accept the accomplishments of "rare" blacks but remained convinced that the majority of blacks were still inferior to the majority of whites. McHenry did not engage in such re-fencing. To him, Banneker represented "fresh proof that the powers of the mind are disconnected with the color of the skin, or, in other words, a striking contradiction to Mr. [David] Hume's doctrine, that the Negroes are naturally inferior to the whites, and unsusceptible of attainments in arts and sciences."[24] McHenry was not alone in his rejection of the anti-black views of Hume, Jefferson, and others. When Banneker arrived in the District of Columbia to take up his duties, the Georgetown *Weekly Ledger* contradicted Jefferson's qualified acceptance of Banneker as proof of what blacks could achieve by describing him as "an Ethiopian whose abilities as surveyor and astronomer already prove that Mr. Jefferson's concluding that that race of men were void of mental endowment was without foundation."[25]

In all fairness to Jefferson, he did assist Banneker in obtaining a job as a surveyor in the District of Columbia where the new federal city was to be located. But Jefferson paid a dear price for even corresponding with Banneker. When his first letter to Banneker appeared in print, Jefferson found himself in serious political trouble. Although he still harbored anti-black prejudices that he would take to his grave, Jefferson had violated sacred southern mores by writing to a black man and calling blacks, "his black brethren." As his party's candidate for president in 1796, Jefferson was taken to task by an avowed racist, William Smith, a South Carolina Federalist. "What shall we think of a *secretary of state* thus *fraternizing* with negroes, writing them complimentary epistles, styling them *his black brethren,* congratulating them on the evidences of their *genius,* and assuring them of his good wishes for their speedy emancipation" (italics in original).[26] Jefferson lost the presidency to John Adams by a margin of three votes in the electoral college. He had paid a high price for even his qualified acceptance of individual black achievements and limited future possibilities. "Thus it was again borne in upon Jefferson," according to a scholar of Jefferson's views on slavery, "that the course of political wisdom was to ignore the blacks and the problems they created. . . . Expediency dictated that slavery be treated as though somehow, sometime, and by means as yet undisclosed, it would go away of its own accord."[27]

---

24. Quoted in Franklin and Moss, *From Slavery* 112–13.
25. Quoted in Franklin and Moss, *From Slavery* 113.
26. Quoted in Miller, *Wolf by the Ears* 78.
27. Miller, *Wolf by the Ears* 78.

Over time, this self-serving attitude on the part of Jefferson and other members of the slave-holding class created greater and greater costs. The moral compromise over slavery eroded the very spirit of white planters who, as Jefferson had pointed out, would not labor so long as they had someone to labor for them. Slavery also necessitated the brutalization of blacks and created the need to demean them systematically in both their own eyes and the eyes of white society. With blacks as slaves and important statesmen as slave owners and articulate ideologues of white supremacy, few Americans could envision a multiracial society based on justice, equality, and racial unity. Only the Quakers came close to this vision of a racially unified America.[28] Jefferson and the majority of white Americans could only see the forceful expansion of white civilization over the land and bodies of red peoples, with black people somewhere tucked away from sight or better yet, emancipated from slavery and shipped away to their African or Haitian homelands.

Whatever grand legacy Jefferson left to future generations of Americans and the world, the vision of a multiracial society where peoples from all racial backgrounds could live in justice and peace was not part of this legacy. Jefferson, as did so many of his contemporaries, believed first and foremost in the establishment of a white nation, with whites in charge, fulfilling their spiritual destiny. As much as Jefferson enjoyed looking into the future of America, he could not envision an America where blacks and whites lived on terms of equality. "Nothing is more certainly written in the book of fate," he wrote in his autobiography, "than that the two races, equally free, cannot live in the same government. Nature, habit, opinion have drawn indelible lines of distinction between them."[29] Driven by his twin fears of racial war and miscegenation between blacks and whites, Jefferson and many of his contemporaries could only see a white America achieved through the gradual emancipation and relocation of blacks far "beyond the reach of mixture." To this end, Jefferson supported the efforts of the American Colonization Society, organized in 1816 to remove free blacks from American soil to any place where they would not come into contact with whites. The plan failed because of numerous reasons, including the cost of transporting blacks as their numbers increased, the refusal of many free blacks to abandon a place that they considered their home, and other organizational problems.[30]

---

28. Jordan, *White Man's Burden* 139–41.

29. Quoted in Miller, *Wolf by the Ears* 278.

30. Miller, *Wolf by the Ears* 264–72; Several major white American leaders were unable to conceive of a multiracial society where whites were not in total control of blacks. They could not envision racial unity between blacks and whites. Even Abraham Lincoln, the "Great Emancipator," labored to get rid of blacks so as to achieve a white-only America. See, Charles H. Wesley, "Lincoln's Plan for Colonizing the Emancipated Negroes," *The Journal of Negro History* 4.1 (January, 1919): 7–21; most free blacks rejected white leaders' attempts

Jefferson, desperate to get rid of blacks so that white America could proceed with its business of spreading white civilization over the Western hemisphere, even proposed separating black children from their parents, training and supporting the children as wards of the State until they were ready to live on their own, and then shipping them to Africa or any other convenient place away from contact with whites. The remaining older blacks would then simply die off naturally, and America's racial problem would be solved. Such a desperate proposal by Jefferson moved one historian to comment: "That Thomas Jefferson, by nature a kindhearted, benevolent, well-intentioned man, should have recommended such a Draconian method for attaining the 'beatitude' of an all-white society reveals how urgent he deemed it to be to separate physically the two races." Unable or unwilling to envision racial unity among blacks and whites, Jefferson was determined to "dispose of an unassimilable and potentially dangerous race which, in his opinion, endangered the peace, well-being, and racial purity of the American people."[31]

Notwithstanding his other great accomplishments, Jefferson contributed to the development of the evils of racism in America. He could have made a contribution to the vision of racial unity—like Benjamin Rush and scores of Quakers—but he could see only a white America. A year before he died in 1826, Jefferson was visited by Lafayette, who had not been to America since 1784. The latter was shocked by many of the changes that had occurred, but, the most startling change was the increase in racial prejudice. He sadly but accurately concluded that the American Revolution had benefitted only whites.[32]

At this stage of American race relations—the stage of shaping the image of blacks in the American white mind—it is crucial to understand the psychohistorical aspects of Jefferson's views of blacks. In many ways Jefferson reflected the evolving white views of the black presence. Confronted by the enormity of the contradiction of enslaving a people while advocating freedom and building a nation (for whites mainly and perhaps Indians if they conformed), Jefferson and generations of whites after him would simply and systematically rationalize their oppression of black slaves. They would consciously and unconsciously nurture the seed of white-skin privilege, of the unquestioned rights of whites to conquer and

---

to colonize them because blacks felt that they had contributed to the development of America. In this sense, one could argue that these blacks played a key role in shaping the vision of America as a multiracial society. For black Americans' views on African colonization and their role in the future of America, see: Bella Gross, "The First National Negro Convention," *The Journal of Negro History* 31.4 (October, 1946): 435–43; Louis R. Mehlinger, "The Attitude of the Free Negro toward African Colonization," *The Journal of Negro History* 1.3 (July, 1916): 276–301.

31. Miller, *Wolf by the Ears* 271.
32. Miller, *Wolf by the Ears* 273–74.

rule nonwhite peoples not only in America but also throughout the world. The human cost of this lack of interracial vision led to the continuation of slavery with its attendant evils of racial hatred and fear and to a sectional conflict that triggered a bloody civil war, costing thousands of lives. Worse still, the racial ramifications of that war and its subsequent historical developments of segregation, race riots, racial fear, and hatred still poison the core of America's national life and culture.

Part II

*Barriers to Racial Unity
and Multiracial Progress*

5

White Manifest Destiny and the Victimization of Native and African Peoples

Humanity has often wept over the fate of the aborigines of this country, and philanthropy has been long busily employed in devising means to avert it, but its progress has never for a moment been arrested, and one by one have many powerful tribes disappeared from the earth. To follow to the tomb the last of his race and tread on the graves of extinct nations excite melancholy reflections. But true philanthropy reconciles the mind to these vicissitudes as it does to the extinction of one generation to make room for another.

—President Andrew Jackson
Second Annual Message to Congress, 1830

Lost Opportunities for Building a Multiracial Society Based on Harmony and Justice

The greatest historical cost of the European conquest and development of the United States was the systematic victimization and dehumanization of the Native and African peoples. We will never know what kind of multiracial society the United States would have been had those Europeans who chose the historical track of conquest and slavery over peoples of color instead chosen the track leading to racial unity, love, and fellowship. We can only wonder at what great material and spiritual achievements would have been possible had the other track been chosen. Centuries of bloodshed and hatred would have been avoided. The tremendous energy channelled into the conquest of the Native peoples and the enslavement of Africans could have gone into developing methods of greater and greater cooperation among all racial groups, cooperation that in turn would have released and channeled the combined cultural and spiritual talents of

African, Indian, and European peoples to build one of the greatest human civilizations in the history of the human species.

Had this historical convergence of different races and peoples been energized by some great spiritual force sweeping the world, there would have been a tremendous synergistic revolution in human material and spiritual relationships. The entire world would have been spared much racial strife, but this convergence of peoples occurred during the time of European expansion and conquest, when human greed was fast overtaking the quest for spiritual growth and development. Several centuries would have to pass before people came to understand the connection between racial unity and social progress and to have sufficient spiritual guidance to make a choice. At the time of the great European discoveries and conquests, minds were turned to gold, silver, land, and great adventures, at the expense of non-European peoples. Social progress came to mean white manifest destiny.

It is so easy and always tempting to look back over history and engage in endless speculation about what could have happened if only we had done such and such, much like the proverbial Monday-morning quarterback who relives the Great Game that took place over the past weekend. However, if we, as human beings living in a world where conflict and violence have become common, do not look back over the Great Games of human experience and learn from them, we, as George Santayana put it, "who cannot remember the past are condemned to repeat it." The history of racial contacts between Europeans on one side and Native and African peoples on the other side embodies profound lessons for the entire human race. Understanding these lessons is all the more important in the wake of the five-hundredth anniversary of Columbus's first voyage to the so-called New World. As governments and historical societies throughout the Western world celebrated this event, many questions surfaced concerning the historical lessons learned since the time Columbus first landed in the Americas.

Depending on one's historical and futuristic perspectives on the "meaning" of human history in the broadest sense of the term, the last 500 years can be interpreted in many ways. Most certainly, one must acknowledge the traditional interpretations that focus on the European exploration of the Western Hemisphere, exploration that led to the rise and development of African slavery within the world system of capitalism, along with the emergence of semi-democratic State systems. For our purposes, however, the most significant aspect of this period is that it witnessed the historical convergence of peoples from very distinct racial and cultural backgrounds, albeit within very tragic and far-reaching historical circumstances: the European extermination of several indigenous peoples and cultures and the enslavement of Africans.

This process of systematic victimization was no historical aberration of European exploration and settlement of the Western Hemisphere. Rather, it evolved as a direct consequence of the emergence of the European world economic system. While this world economic system provided the historical and structural context in which European and non-European peoples in the Western Hemisphere first established contact, the nature and direction of these first formative multiracial contacts were in many ways predetermined by a set of culturally based perceptions and values Europeans brought with them to the New World. Foremost among these perceptions and values was the notion that they, as Europeans, were a chosen people with a destiny that included the expansion of their "European Christian Civilization" over the face of the earth. Non-Europeans had no voice in the matter. One such theory—called by some historians "the European theory of the right of discovery"—grew out of an ancient claim by Christians that they had the right to dispossess non-Christians of their land anywhere in the world. This theory was reinforced by an even more ethnocentric theory transformed into tradition called *vacuum domicilium,* which "held that land not 'occupied' or 'settled' was available to any 'civilized' person—that is, Christian—who, of course, had the exclusive right to determine whether or not a land was 'settled'."[1]

These two views sanctioned the right of European Christians to dispossess the Native peoples in the New World of their land. Another European view that further eroded the possibility of building a just and harmonious multiracial society in the New World was the "idea that someone else should do the hard manual work of the world," namely Indians or Africans. This view, according to one scholar of race relations in the New World, "appealed strongly to sixteenth-century Spaniards, who inherited a taste for martial glory and religious conquest and a distaste for physical labour from their medieval forefathers who had struggled for centuries to free Spain from the Moslems."[2] While the Spaniards were prepared to fight to the death to plant their flag, serve their king, and advance Christianity, "they were not prepared, however, to settle down as farmers to till the soil or as miners to extract gold and silver from the bowels of the earth. That was work for Indians."[3] When adequate Indian labor was not available, the Spaniards were dumbfounded and complained to the king. It was inconceivable that they themselves should do such work. At one point in the colonial history of Spanish America, the town officials of Buenos Aires were forced by circumstances to inform the king "affairs were so bad there that Spaniards actually had to dig in the earth and plant crops if they were to eat." In still another case, Spaniards

---

1. Forrest G. Wood, *The Arrogance of Faith: Christianity and Race in America from the Colonial Era to the Twentieth Century* 217.

2. Lewis Hanke, *Aristotle and the American Indian: A Study in Race Prejudice in the Modern World* 13.

3. Hanke, *Aristotle* 14. Africans later were enslaved to do this work.

reported how they had seen their fellow Spaniards die of hunger and others working in the fields with "their own hands"—something these observers had never before witnessed.[4]

This negative view of labor came to dominate the thinking of Spaniards and other Europeans throughout the New World and in most areas of the world in which Europeans colonized non-Europeans.[5] "Throughout the whole of the colonial period and in all lands colonized by Spain," Lewis Hanke has written, "this same attitude prevailed."[6] These views of labor and work became linked to race and culture soon after the Europeans began their conquest of the New World. This historical linkage determined in large part the future of race relations in the Americas. In short, it was part of the first set of barriers placed in the path of genuine racial unity and cooperation between European and Native peoples. The philosophical rationale of the linkage was provided by the Aristotelian doctrine of natural slavery.

The Aristotelian doctrine of natural slavery, which argued some human beings were set apart by nature to serve others, appealed to many Europeans seeking ways to exploit the vast mineral and human resources of the New World.[7] John Major, a Scottish professor in Paris, helped pave the way for the application of this doctrine to the Indians of the New World. He was not only the first to apply the doctrine of natural slavery to Indians but also the first to support the idea that force against the Indians should be used in preparation to teaching them Christianity. His views were published in 1510.[8] One can readily see how such racial views would contaminate the relationships between peoples from different cultures and destroy or delay any attempt to build a multiracial society based on justice.

Without being an incorrigible optimist, one could still argue that even with all the racial and cultural "baggage" European colonizers brought with them, options for creating a multiracial society based upon justice and cooperation were still possible at various historical points of the encounters with Native peoples, Africans, and Europeans. However, given the perceptions, values, and power of the Europeans in this historical drama, such an idea was not attractive. As any other people might have been under similar circumstances, European colonizers of the New World were beside themselves with cultural arrogance. Their so-called discovery of the New World was intoxicating. Some Europeans found it difficult not to think that they were indeed "God's gift to the world." Not even the universal

---

4. Hanke, *Aristotle* 14.

5. For an analysis of some aspects of this historical relationship between European use of the labor of non-European people, see "White Capital and Colored Labor" in E. Franklin Frazier, *Race and Culture Contacts in the Modern World* 127–56.

6. Hanke, *Aristotle* 14.

7. Hanke, *Aristotle* 14.

8. Hanke, *Aristotle* 14.

ideas of the Enlightenment and the American Revolution could stem the tide of racial pride among certain European groups. By the time Joseph Arthur de Gobineau published his famous book on the inequality of the human races in 1854, he was merely "summarizing and amplifying more than half a century of ideas on race rather than inaugurating a new era."[9] The seeds of those racial ideas were sown centuries earlier.

The English brought with them a special brand of racial ethnocentrism that in contact with Native and African peoples grew into a systematic form of racial dominance supported by an equally systematic theological and "scientific" rationalization. The English arrived and began their conquest of the New World with the notion that they had a divine racial right to rule over both the land and the people. As historian Reginald Horsman explained it:

> Although the concept of a distinct, superior Anglo-Saxon race, with innate endowments enabling it to achieve a perfection of governmental institutions and world dominance, was a product of the first half of the nineteenth century, the roots of these ideas stretch back at least to the sixteenth and seventeenth centuries. Those Englishmen who settled in America at the beginning of the seventeenth century brought as part of their historical and religious heritage a clearly delineated religious myth of a pure English Anglo-Saxon church, and in the seventeenth and eighteenth centuries they shared with their fellow Englishmen an elaborately developed secular myth of the free nature of Anglo-Saxon political institutions.[10]

These racial ideas took root in America as the English went about proclaiming their divine right to rule over both Native and African peoples. The Puritans, as we shall see, arrived with a view of the Indians that did not encourage building a multiracial society. Their vision of the new world included only people like themselves. For a while, the noble ideas of the Enlightenment kindled the hearts of many Europeans and had the moral potential of providing a philosophical foundation for building a multiracial society in America. The Enlightenment view of the human race saw all people as members of one human species capable of infinite progress. This view held sway among many European and American thinkers before 1815. It was expressed best by the philosophy of environmentalism, which argued that environment, not "innate racial differences, accounted for the marked gaps in achievement between different peoples and different nations."[11] This view of humankind was so influential that it not only fired the imagination of the generation of the American Revolution but also held the hearts and minds of American intellectuals well into the early years of the

---

9. Reginald Horsman, *Race and Manifest Destiny: The Origins of American Racial Anglo-Saxonism* 2.

10. Horsman, *Race and Manifest Destiny* 9.

11. Horsman, *Race and Manifest Destiny* 98.

nineteenth century.[12] This period was one of those crucial crossroads in American history where much hung in the balance, where compromise and the wrong moral choice threw America's greatest historical possibilities far off course. The ideas of the Enlightenment fell victim to the crushing and overpowering demands of the English push for racial dominance over Indians and Africans. It was a struggle, Horsman explains, "between a theoretical view of mankind and race provided by Enlightenment thought and a practical view stimulated by overt contacts between white Americans and blacks or Indians on the North American continent."[13]

We can only look back and regret what America lost as a result of building a society based upon white racial manifest destiny instead of upon multiracial justice, cooperation, and harmony. As we shall see, the former approach took America down the path of racial victimization and dehumanization of Indians and Africans and in the process poisoned the spiritual core of America. In addition to the great historical, cultural, psychological, economic, and spiritual costs of centuries of racial oppression of these peoples, white racial manifest destiny in America delayed the achievement of world unity and peace by supporting similar racist ideas throughout the world.[14]

The First Barrier to Racial Unity: The American Indian and White Racial Manifest Destiny

Considering that in 1992 millions of people throughout the Western world celebrated the five-hundredth anniversary of Columbus's first contact with the "New World," we should understand not only what he and other Europeans thought of the Native peoples of the Americas but also how Europeans' different cultural views of land, peoples, and religion led to the eventual subjugation of the Native American peoples. Here again, we revisit history not to belabor the role of European racial domination in the United States but to emphasize the cost of domination and to note the lost possibilities of achieving racial unity and social progress. While historians might differ on the historical junctures where racial unity based upon justice and equality was possible but was not achieved due to the expanding system of European racial dominance, they tend to agree that many of the first contacts between Europeans and Native peoples were friendly and

---

12. Horsman, *Race and Manifest Destiny* 98.

13. Horsman, *Race and Manifest Destiny* 98.

14. As we have already seen, Jefferson's writings on blacks were read throughout Europe, a fact that no doubt contributed to Europeans' negative views of African-Americans. This trend continued as white American writers on race became the leaders in the field of racist religious and quasi-scientific tracts, books, and articles throughout the nineteenth and early twentieth centuries. See Gossett, *The History of an Idea in America* 54–122, 370–408; Wood, *Arrogance* passim.

could have developed into lasting bonds of racial unity. However, they also agree that since these relationships took place at a time when European nations were in a state of economic, political, intellectual, and religious change, it was also inevitable that the expansionist tendencies and military technological superiority of the Europeans would tip the scale towards a European racial dominance based solely on the belief that God had given them a divine right to rule over the nonwhite races of the world. When we study Columbus's first report of the first Native peoples he encountered, we cannot help but notice the characteristics he emphasized, such as the absence of iron and steel weapons:

> The people of this island and of all the other islands which I have found and of which I have information, all go naked, men and women, as their mothers bore them, although some of the women cover a single place with a leaf of a plant or with a net of cotton which they make for the purpose. They have no iron or steel or weapons, nor are they fitted to use them. This is not because they are not well built and of handsome stature, but because they are very marvelously timorous. . . . It is true that, after they have been reassured and have lost this fear, they are so guileless and so generous with all that they possess, that no one would believe it who has not seen it. They refuse nothing that they possess, if it be asked of them; on the contrary, they invite any one to share it and display as much love as if they would give their hearts. They are content with whatever trifle of whatever kind that may be given to them, whether it be of value or valueless. . . .[15]

This idyllic view of Native peoples could not but have been attractive to certain Europeans bent on trade and conquest, events that did in fact take place not long thereafter. Columbus's report of the Native people continued in this vein:

> They do not hold any creed nor are they idolaters; but they all believe that power and good are in the heavens and were very firmly convinced that I, with these ships and men, came from the heavens, and in this belief they everywhere received me after they had mastered their fear. This belief is not the result of ignorance, for they are, on the contrary, of a very acute intelligence and they are men who navigate all those seas, so that it is amazing how good an account they give of everything. It is because they have never seen people clothed or ships of such a kind. . . .
> In all these islands, I saw no great diversity in the appearance of the people or in their manners and language. On the contrary, they all understand one another, which is a very curious thing. . . .
> In all these islands, it seems to me that all men are content with one woman,

---

15. Quoted in Robert F. Berkhofer, Jr., *The White Man's Indian: Images of the American Indian from Columbus to the Present* 6.

and to their chief or king they give as many as twenty. It appears to me that the women work more than do the men. I have not been able to learn if they hold private property; it seemed to me to be that all took a share in whatever any one had, especially of eatable things.[16]

Columbus, like most Europeans of his day, would have been interested in private property among the Native peoples, who it would be discovered had a far different view of land and the use to which it should be put than did their European visitors. Differing views of land would become the cause of some of the first conflicts between Europeans and Native peoples. Aside from these fairly positive impressions of Indians that gained popularity among educated Europeans, Columbus also created some of the first negative images of these Native peoples. While he had "found no human monstrosities, as many expected, but on the contrary the whole population is very well formed. . . ." he did claim to have come across Native peoples who

are regarded in all the islands as very fierce and who eat human flesh. They have many canoes with which they range through all the islands of India and pillage and take whatever they can. . . . They are ferocious among these other people who are cowardly to an excessive degree, but I make no more account of them than of the rest.[17]

Notwithstanding the view of the loving, good-natured Natives willing to give everything they owned to outsiders, the view of Native people as cannibalistic, depraved, and hostile, gained as much if not at times more popularity among Europeans. More than the "good Indian" image, this "bad Indian" image provided a rationale for the later expansionist designs of those Europeans who saw the New World as a place that had to be rescued from the devil and saw Native peoples as barriers to be moved by God to make way for the development of a white Christian civilization. For example, Cotton Mather considered his Puritans to be "a people of God settled in those, which were once the *Devil's* Territories. . ." and believed that "the Devil was exceedingly disturbed, when he perceived such a People here accomplishing the Promise of old made unto our Blessed Jesus, *That He should have the Utmost parts of the Earth for his Possession* (italics in original)."[18] The logical conclusion was clear: the Native peoples occupied unsacred land, "the *Devil's* Territories" that had to be claimed by the Puritans, who considered themselves to be the "Chosen People."

The Chosen-People complex of the early Puritans provided one of the

---

16. Quoted in Berkhofer, *White Man's Indian* 6.
17. Quoted in Berkhofer, *White Man's Indian* 7.
18. Quoted in Wood, *Arrogance* 228.

first theological rationalizations for the victimization and dehumanization of the Native peoples of New England. Puritans believed that New England was an extension of their mandate that had begun in England before their migration of 1630–1642. Every barrier they overcame represented God's favor and confirmation of their spiritual destiny, even if at times God, according to their interpretation, had to destroy Native people to clear the way for his Chosen Ones. For example, the epidemic that had virtually destroyed all the Native peoples in the region just prior to the arrival of the Puritans was perceived by the Puritans as a great blessing. So firmly did early Puritans believe that this 1617 epidemic emanated from God on their behalf, that for years after the event Puritan leaders prayed thanks to God for his assistance.[19]

The same rationale prevailed in the Puritan mindset after they almost destroyed the entire Pequot tribe in 1637 and during subsequent wars against the Indian tribes in the region.[20] The Puritans' worldview made it impossible for them to coexist in a biracial society on equal terms. Many Puritans simply could not divest themselves of the rigid notion that they had a divine right to dominate the land. Puritan religious leaders and lay persons could only see their history in one way: namely, the struggle to realize their racial–religious manifest destiny. Not even the best of the "good Indians" could deter them from pursuing this vision of themselves. "Good Indians," such as Squanto, who helped the Pilgrims of the Plymouth Plantation to survive, were not seen as evidence of the potential for biracial coexistence but as God's intervention on behalf of his Chosen People, the Pilgrims. While they expected God to use the Native people as just one more instrument to help them realize their destiny, they also "expected the horrors of Indian warfare both because of [their belief in] the unregenerate state of the Indians who were trapped in the 'snare of the Divell' and because God must from time to time send a scourge to chastise His chosen people in their pride and in their departure from His word."[21] Such thinking could not but lead Puritans to see Native peoples as being both instruments of good and bad fortune in the unfolding destiny of a superior people. "Thus," as Berkhofer comments, "the images of the good and bad Indian served the same didactic purposes for the Puritan imagination."[22]

Even if the Puritans and other European religious denominations had been less rigid in their worldviews, encouraging instead a creative interracial coexistence between themselves and Native peoples, their other worldviews concerning the land occupied by the Natives would have remained as

19. Wood, *Arrogance* 210.
20. Wood, *Arrogance* 210.
21. Berkhofer, *White Man's Indian* 83.
22. Berkhofer, *White Man's Indian* 83.

barriers to interracial cooperation. European Christians operated on the belief that they had a "right to discovery." Therefore, since native peoples were not Christians or were not divesting themselves of their Native cultures to the satisfaction of European Christians to qualify as "real Christians," then the real Christians, or Chosen People, had a right to the land. Puritans could also take possession of Native peoples' land under the European legal theory of *vacuum domicilium* by claiming that "land not 'occupied' or 'settled' went by forfeit to those who attached themselves to it in a 'civilized' manner."[23] Puritan leaders like John Winthrop applied this theory to the Native peoples even before the Puritans arrived in the New World, as Winthrop himself wrote before he landed on the shores of New England:

> As for the Natives in New England, they inclose noe Land, neither have any setled habytation, nor any tame Cattle to improve the Land by, and soe have noe other but a Naturall Right to those Countries, soe as if we leave them sufficient for their use, we may lawfully take the rest, there being more than enough for them and us.[24]

Here again, we see the philosophical building block of the early Puritan sense of religious manifest destiny. They arrived with the arrogant assumption that they had the right to take the land of Native people whose way of life did not conform to European standards because they had "inclose[d] noe land, neither have any settled habytation, nor any tame Cattle to improve the land. . . ." The land question constituted one of the most difficult barriers to Indian–white cooperation. Few historians would deny the major role European racial and cultural arrogance played in this conflict, a conflict that still plagues Indian–white relations today.[25]

Racial unity and cooperation between Native peoples and Europeans might have had a better chance of succeeding if their two worldviews had been more compatible, but the weight of history proved too great. Their converging histories, based upon two vastly different worldviews, were almost certainly destined to clash. However, in terms of the potential of racial unity and social progress for both European and Native peoples, at the point of their initial contacts the Native worldview was far more compatible to that end. The restless, expansionist nature of the European, coupled with an ethnocentric religious vision of Europeans as the Chosen People, simply was incompatible with any joint biracial venture in universal social progress. Far too many Europeans arrived in the New World with either a chip on their shoulders or a Bible and gun in their hands. Most did

---

23. Gary B. Nash, *Red, White, and Black: The Peoples of Early America* 79.
24. Quoted in Nash, *Red, White, and Black* 79–80.
25. The latest and most published Indian–white conflict over land in North America took place in Oka, Québec, Canada, July–September, 1990.

not come to join hands with the "good Indians" in building a biracial society based upon justice and social progress for all peoples, but like the Puritans to carve a white Christian civilization out of the "Devil's Territories." In many ways, the Native people offered a much more humane way of building a multiracial society. Had Columbus and his contemporaries and those who followed them been less concerned about wealth and power, they might have been able to build upon the great spiritual power of many of the Natives they first encountered. By focusing upon wealth and power and by prostituting Christianity to obtain these ends, they lost great opportunities to build a multiracial society in the New World based upon genuine respect, justice, equality, and social harmony. Many of the Native people could have taught the Europeans a new way of viewing the land. Rather than regarding the land as just a resource "to be exploited for man's gain . . . [and] a commodity to be privately held" and fenced in, Europeans might have learned to see the land as a natural world that is sacred, and "inhabited by a great variety of 'beings', each possessing spiritual power and all linked together to form a sacred whole."[26] To the Indian, the European notion of land being privately owned was senseless. While Native peoples did recognize territorial boundaries among tribal groups, land was held in common within these boundaries. Contrary to the European view of land as a form of commodity, Native peoples tended to view land as a part of Nature given to humans by the Creator to be used and respected. This view of land as entrusted to humans by the Creator lent a special meaning to the relationship among the people who shared the trust. As the Moravian missionary John Heckewelder discovered during his stay with the Delaware Indians in the eighteenth century, the Native view of God was that of a Creator who

> made the Earth and all that it contains for the common good of mankind; when he stocked the country that he gave them with plenty of game, it was not for the benefit of a few, but of all: Every thing was given in common to the sons of men. Whatever liveth on the land, whatsoever groweth out of the earth, and all that is in the rivers and waters . . . was given jointly to all and every one is entitled to his share. From this principle hospitality flows as from its source.[27]

Commenting on this approach, Nash says, "Thus, land was a gift of the Creator, to be used with care, and was not for the exclusive possession of particular human beings."[28] One can only imagine what kind of race relations would have evolved if Europeans had been able to accept and practice this view of the land and its relationship to people. Given that many

---

26. Nash, *Red, White, and Black* 25.
27. Quoted in Nash, *Red, White, and Black* 26.
28. Nash, *Red, White, and Black* 26.

European wars had been triggered by conflicts over land, the adoption of this Native–American approach to the Earth might have been of great benefit to the economic, social, and political stability of Europe. Most certainly, the Native view of land was less ethnocentric than those of the Puritans and later generations of white American officials who formulated land policies that victimized and dehumanized generations of Native peoples.

Early America could also have benefitted from other aspects of Native peoples' cosmology, which no doubt would have contributed to a smoother transition to a multiracial society and universal social progress. For example, the typical European interpersonal values tended to be acquisitive, competitive, and centered around the role of the individual. These values fostered the insatiable expansionism that characterized European contacts with non-European people around the world. "Wider choices and greater opportunities for the individual to improve his status—by industriousness, valor, or even personal sacrifice leading to martyrdom—were regarded as desirable," Nash points out, "Personal ambition, in fact, played a large role in the migration of Europeans across the Atlantic in the sixteenth and seventeenth centuries."[29] The values of many Native peoples were just the opposite of the Europeans who colonized the New World. According to one scholar, "In contrast to the exalted position of man in Judeo–Christian tradition, [the Native American] cosmology conferred upon the Indian a rather humble stature." Therefore, ". . . individualism was more likely to lead to ostracism than admiration in Indian communities."[30] Once again we can only speculate how very different race relations might have been if the more universalistic values of many Native peoples had been allowed to govern at least some of the relations among the races in early American history. That this did not occur was due mainly to the persistence of European expansion and domination in the New World.

By the end of the eighteenth century, the chances for achieving a multiracial society based on equality and justice for all peoples—black, white, and red—were rapidly diminishing. Historical circumstances and the relentless greed for land and power among many European settlers in America precluded any possibility for racial justice and cooperation. The period between 1815 and 1855 witnessed a steady transformation in the collective self-image of white Americans. Examining themselves against the multiracial backdrop of their developing nation, many could only see one historical scenario: the continual expansion of white Christian civilization across America, expansion that by its nature would include the removal or extermination of the Native peoples and the continual enslavement of blacks or their removal, preferably to another country, if freed. During this

---

29. Nash, *Red, White, and Black* 26.
30. Calvin Martin quoted in Nash, *Red, White, and Black* 26.

period most white Americans overcame decades of moral qualms concerning the rights of Native and African peoples. They buried the high ideals of the Enlightenment and the American Revolution beneath layers of racist rationalizations and the practical power politics of the emerging white nation. Nation-building to these white Americans could only include white people. To gain credibility for both what they had already done to Native and African peoples in the past and were planning to do to them in the future, white Americans adopted an American Anglo-Saxon ideology that had the dual effect of anesthetizing them to whatever lingering moral qualms they might have had towards the victimization and dehumanization of Indians and Africans and of articulating a racial mission loudly enough to drown out any audible voices still preaching justice, equality, and the belief in the unity of the human race.

This racial ideology propounding the right of white Anglo-Saxon Americans to dominate peoples of another color in the whites' expansion across the continent has been explained by one scholar of racial manifest destiny: "Internally it was made quite clear that the American republic was a white Anglo-Saxon republic; other white races would be absorbed within the existing racial mass while nonwhite races would be rigorously excluded from any equal participation as citizens."[31] This racial ideology had a devastating impact on both Native and African peoples.

As white Americans engaged in the business of building a white nation during the period between 1815 and 1850, they found themselves in a struggle between those who still believed in the Enlightenment view of the Native "as an innately equal, improvable being" and those who believed "the Indians to be inferior, who did not wish them to be accepted as equals within American society, and who expected them ultimately to disappear." Unfortunately for the Indians, the latter view was held by those whites who were steadily gaining in political power and whose main concern was how best to remove Indians from the path of white expansion.[32] The eighteenth-century view of the Indian as a "noble savage" was slowly fading from the public to be replaced by the image of the Indian as a tragic figure doomed to extinction by the forward motion of expansion.

As more and more white settlers moved into the Mississippi Valley and into the cotton lands in the southern states, Indian lands became barriers to so-called white progress. Even those Indians who had accepted the ways of white civilization by giving up certain vital aspects of their own culture (to adopt the Jeffersonian model of Indian transformation and assimilation) by becoming small-scale farmers and property owners, could not escape the grinding wheel of white racial manifest destiny. While before 1815 and for

31. Horsman, *Race and Manifest Destiny* 189.
32. Horsman, *Race and Manifest Destiny* 190.

sometime after, many whites had attacked the Indian for being unwilling or unable to accept the culture of the whites because of their "savage nature" and could point to many demoralized, scattered Indian tribes as proof of the inability of the Indians to adapt to white civilization, there were thousands of Indians in the southern states who had demonstrated their ability to adopt the ways of whites and even prosper. One would have thought that such a demonstration of Indian assimilation should have been sufficient for most whites who claimed that their anti-Indian attitudes were based upon the inability of Indians to assimilate into white society, but that was not the case. Too many whites wanted Indian land, and too many whites were willing to do whatever they had to do to get that land. Assimilated Indians, like freed blacks, constituted barriers to the process of white nation-building. No matter how much they became like white Americans, they were not white.[33]

Between 1815 and 1830, the policy of Indian Removal best reflected the ideology of white racial manifest destiny as applied to the Native peoples. Not only did it represent the height of racist thinking in white–Indian relations, it also demonstrated how far many white Americans were willing to go to victimize and dehumanize Indians solely out of avarice. It was one of the lowest points in the moral and spiritual history of white America. It involved not only moral and spiritual compromise among the white public (who grew increasingly insensitive to the rights of Indians) but also a twisting of the very fabric of historical truth as the general public willingly accepted and perpetuated the racial beliefs and myths rationalizing the victimization and dehumanization of the Native peoples. It was during this period in American history, when white America was forging its racial self-image and expanding and consolidating its dominance over nonwhite peoples, that even more possibilities for building a multiracial society were lost.[34]

Indian Removal as a policy of racial manifest destiny had the strongest supporters in Tennessee, Georgia, Alabama, and Mississippi. These states led the fight in pressuring the federal government to remove the Indians from their states for no other reason than they wanted the Indians' land. It did not matter that the Indians wanted to stay. The Cherokees were the very Indians who had demonstrated the "greatest success in assimilation [and] would be the most hurt by removal westward." One of their greatest leaders, Sequoyah, who devised an alphabet for his people, exemplified the degree to which the Cherokees had assimilated and mastered the culture of whites. The Cherokees even devised a written constitution as they put forth every effort to prove that they could adapt to white culture. But to little

---

33. For an example of how assimilated Indians were treated, see Horsman, *Race and Manifest Destiny* 195–207; Wilcomb E. Washburn, ed., *The Indian and the White Man* 376.

34. Horsman, *Race and Manifest Destiny* 190.

avail. It mattered even less to those whites who coveted their land that these were the very Indians who "had followed Jefferson's injunctions to assume white ways."[35] All that mattered was that whites in these states and their representatives wanted Indians to be removed so as to make way for whites. A long battle ensued as white political leaders at the state and national levels debated the Indian Removal policy. By the late 1820s, the relentless pressure by the governments of southern states on the federal government for Indian Removal caused the federal government to capitulate and renege on previous guarantees and promises. Gradually, many friends of the southern Indians gave up from despair and frustration. As many of these "friends" abandoned the cause of the southern Indian, they began justifying their abandonment with the rhetoric of white manifest destiny: Indians were destined to become extinct before the advancement of white civilization.[36]

With the election of Andrew Jackson as president of the United States in 1828, the fate of the southern Indians was sealed. Few white leaders were as virulent in their hatred and disregard for the rights of Indians as was Jackson during his days as a soldier. While fighting against the Creeks in 1813–14, "Jackson denounced his Indian enemies as 'savage bloodhounds' and 'blood thirsty barbarians'" and "urged his troops to exterminate them."[37] In early 1814, at the battle of Horse Shoe Bend, Jackson manifested a hatred for Indians that would stain American history for decades. His troops surrounded about 800 Indians and killed almost all of them, including the women and children. After the battle, Jackson sent the cloth that had been worn by the slain Indian warriors to the ladies of Tennessee. Not satisfied with the carnage they had inflicted on the Indians, Jackson's soldiers proceeded to desecrate the dead bodies of the Indians by cutting "long strips of skin" from them (which they used for bridle reins) and by cutting off the tips of each "dead Indian's nose to count the number of enemy bodies."[38]

The savage manner in which the Creek Indians had been treated by Jackson and his men revealed a deep current of racial disregard for the Indian people as members of the human race. The killing of Indian women and children and the deliberate desecration of the Indian dead could not but have eroded any lingering sense of a common and shared humanity between Indians and whites in the minds of Jackson and his men and by extension, in the minds of most of the general public who saw Jackson as a great hero. In the actions of Jackson and his men, one cannot help but see a bizarre celebration of the dehumanization of Indian people both living and dead that has found itself a secure place in the annals of American popular history

35. Washburn, *Indian* 376: Horseman, *Race and Manifest Destiny* 195.
36. Horsman, *Race and Manifest Destiny* 200.
37. Ronald T. Takaki, *Iron Cages: Race and Culture in Nineteenth-Century America* 95.
38. Takaki, *Iron Cages* 96.

and culture, e.g., cowboys and Indians. But even more to the point: these celebrations of offering the cloth of slain Indian warriors to white women and fashioning bridle reins from strips of skin from dead Indian bodies signaled a highwater mark in the pathology of white racial hatred of nonwhites.

When Jackson was elected to the presidency in 1828, people still remembered him as the "heroic fighter." In their minds he represented their interests as whites advancing against the "red savages" standing in their way. Jackson personified the supreme architect of white racial manifest destiny at the expense of the Native peoples. After the protracted struggle between southern Indians and their white supporters and the Jackson anti-Indian forces in 1828, the federal government ordered the army to round up 15,000 Cherokees. After first being placed in detention camps, they were then "marched west beyond the Mississippi in the dead of winter, more than 4,000 Cherokees died on the 'Trail of Tears'."[39] Summing up the impact of Jackson's role in the victimization and dehumanization of southern Indians, one historian writes:

> During the age of Jackson, some seventy thousand Indians were removed from their homes in the South and driven west of the Mississippi River. Due to violence, disease, starvation, dangerous travel conditions, and harsh winter weather, almost one-third of the southern Indians died. By 1844, the South was, as far as Indians were concerned, a "white man's country."[40]

Jackson was not the founder of the movement of racial manifest destiny that undermined and later discarded the more racially egalitarian ideas of the Enlightenment and erected ideological barriers to the development of a multiracial society based upon justice and cooperation. However, he willingly inherited it and willingly carried it out and passed it on to posterity. For decades to come, advocates of white racial manifest destiny would continue to break treaties with Indian peoples as well as to take their land for the sole benefit of whites.[41] As late as the 1890s, a future president of the United States, Theodore Roosevelt, could still boast of the right of white people to take land from Indians and rationalized doing so: "It is nonsense to talk about our having driven most of these Indians out of their lands. They did not own the land at all *in the white sense,* [italics added] they merely occupied it as the white buffalo hunter did. . . ."[42]

---

39. Takaki, *Iron Cages* 100.
40. Takaki, *Iron Cages* 96.
41. George Sinkler, *The Racial Attitudes of American Presidents: From Abraham Lincoln to Theodore Roosevelt* passim.
42. Quoted in Sinkler, *Racial Attitudes* 334.

The Second Barrier to Racial Unity: The Enslavement of Africans and the Development of White Racist Attitudes

The same white American mindset that perceived Native peoples as barriers to the progress of white Christian civilization, that saw whites as the most important people on the continent with a racial destiny to be carried out with guns and Bibles, and that by the 1850s felt little remorse for the systematic victimization and dehumanization of the Native peoples then under way, also perceived black people less as barriers to their progress and more as a form of raw material to be fashioned and used as instruments in the building of a white-only nation. Jefferson had paved the way for this view of nation building in his *Notes on the State of Virginia.* While Jefferson did consider sharing the nation-building process with Indians,[43] by the time of Jackson, the Jeffersonian view of Indian–white cooperation in the nation-building process was fast fading from the public mind. As the process of white nation building marginalized the Native people through conquest and removal, that same process was at work shaping black slave labor into an instrument of white economic development. The land that whites forced the Indian to abandon was all too often cultivated by black slave labor under the lash of white planters who saw both Indians and Africans as different sides of the same racial coin: their humanity could be violated without qualms for the benefit of the expanding white Christian civilization. Thus, advocates of white racial manifest destiny either could not or would not conceive of social progress emanating from racial unity; rather, they could only conceive of white social progress emanating from white racial dominance over red and black peoples.

As the dual process of removal of Indian people and the institutionalization of African slavery began, the few brave whites who visualized a country where people from all racial backgrounds could live together found themselves confronted by the behemoth of racial manifest destiny. Fewer and fewer whites were troubled by the moral contradictions of white nation building on the stolen land of Indians and the bowed backs of African slave labor. Fewer and fewer historical windows of opportunity remained open through which white America could pass towards building a multiracial society based upon justice and cooperation. The institutionalization of African slavery as an essential component of white nation building soon materialized as the second formidable barrier to racial unity. Once African slavery was in place legally (and in the "moral comfort zone" of most of white Americans), the last historical windows for achieving unity vanished, not to appear again until the short experimental period of racial democracy during Reconstruction.[44]

---

43. See discussion of Jefferson in Chapter 3.

44. John Hope Franklin and Alfred A. Moss, *From Slavery to Freedom: A History of Negro Americans* 216–23.

The enslavement of the African, later rationalized by tortured logic and moral gyrations, worked a strange uneasiness into the collective psyche of white America. What might have been simply another chapter in the long history of human oppression turned out to be a protracted struggle, particularly for southern whites, to define themselves in an environment heavily peopled by blacks. The social, political, cultural, and psychological ramifications of black enslavement radiated throughout white southern society and penetrated deep into the region's white collective psyche and later poisoned the soul of the nation for centuries. From the institutionalization of slavery in the mid-seventeenth century to about the 1830s, slavemasters experimented with several images of blacks to rationalize their enslavement of people whom they knew to be as human as themselves. The black sex-hungry-savage image performed one key function for white masters needing to subject the slave to harsh treatment, but some slavemasters liked the image of the happy slave who was loyal, dependent, and affectionate—in short, a Sambo. As one slavemaster put it, "At present, we have in South Carolina, two hundred and fifty thousand civilized and peaceable slaves, happy and contented. . . ."[45] This image helped slavemasters to convince themselves that perhaps slavery was justified if only because it had transformed savage Africans into civilized, happy slaves.

These rationalizations, however, did not quiet the consciences of slavemasters. There were moral contradictions warring within the larger society that could not be easily dismissed or buried. During the period before 1830, many slavemasters admitted that slavery was plainly amoral. The American Revolutionary period held up a mirror to the slavemasters and forced them for the first time to see how blatantly hypocritical they were being in fighting for their own rights while holding others in bondage. Many, gazing in the mirror of their society, confessed that they could not justify slavery, which they knew to be "repugnant to humanity" and "destructive of liberty."[46] So troubled by this moral war waging in their collective soul were they, that not even the invention of the cotton gin and the subsequent expansion of cotton production, which infused a new life and greatly increased the profitability of black enslavement, could silence the voice of conscience among some slavemasters. They could not live with the moral contradictions stemming from the enslavement of black people. Slavemasters found themselves describing slavery in such terms as "an evil," a "curse," which was "felt and acknowledged by every enlightened man"[47] in the South. So persistent was this moral torment among some planters that even after the proslavery apologists had developed sophisticated

---

45. Quoted in Takaki, *Iron Cages* 119.
46. Takaki, *Iron Cages* 119.
47. Takaki, *Iron Cages* 120.

arguments defending the enslavement of blacks, these slavemasters still felt the moral contradiction connected with human bondage.[48]

Despite these moral qualms, most whites clung to and rationalized slavery because of its economic benefits. For example, black slave labor was the very foundation of Thomas Jefferson's life and of his many contributions to the process of white nation building, as a scholar of his life has pointed out so well:

> Thomas Jefferson was intimately associated with slavery from the cradle to the grave. His first memory was of being carried on a pillow by a slave; and a slave carpenter made the coffin in which he was buried at Monticello. The labor of black slaves made possible Jefferson's cultivation of the arts; the building of Monticello and the Virginia State Capitol, his principal architectural monuments; the acquisition of the books which made his library one of the largest private libraries in the United States (and which eventually formed the nucleus of the Library of Congress); the accumulation of choice wines and the fine food prepared by a French chef, both of which made dinner at the President's House a notable event in the lives of congressmen; and the leisure which he devoted to science, philosophy, and politics. Even Jefferson's salaries as Secretary of State, Vice-President and President were indirectly paid in large part by slaves: their labor provided the tobacco, cotton, and sugar, the export of which stimulated Northern shipping, manufacture, banking, and insurance and enabled the United States to make remittances for imported manufactured goods and to attract the foreign investment capital vital to the agricultural, industrial, and commercial development of the Republic. Next to land, slaves constituted the largest property interest in the country, far larger than manufacturing and shipping combined. Truly, one of the main pillars of world of Thomas Jefferson was black slavery.[49]

Black slave labor not only was a major pillar of Jefferson's life but also contributed substantially to the economic development of the country. This might explain in part Jefferson's obsessive need to degrade (and by extension to dehumanize) blacks in his writings. However, he was not alone in his attempt to resolve his moral contradictions by resorting to racial rationalizations. The black presence during the early stages of white nation building posed other problems besides the moral contradictions over enslaving people chiefly for one's own economic welfare. In the process of confronting, conquering, and enslaving peoples of color, the English found it necessary to redefine themselves in a manner that would clarify (to themselves) their special role in the multiracial society they were largely responsible for creating. In fact, the process of white nation building within the context of racial manifest destiny involved dramatic shifts in whites' racial self-perception. Jordan explains this shift:

---

48. Takaki, *Iron Cages* 120.
49. Miller, *The Wolf by the Ears* 1.

Most suggestive of all, there seems to have been something of a shift during the seventeenth century in the terminology which Englishmen in the colonies applied to themselves. From the initially most common term *Christian*, at mid-century there was a marked shift toward the terms *English* and *free*. After about 1680, taking the colonies as a whole, a new term of self-identification appeared—*white*.[50]

As whites became more conscious of their "whiteness," they became less concerned about the traditional distinctions of religion and nationality and more concerned about what they had in common. As more Africans (joined by non-English whites) arrived in the colonies and became assimilated into the English colonial culture, the English found themselves in a multiracial society their actions had created but that their collective minds could not begin to understand in terms of short- and long-term psychosociological effects. As both the black and the white races increased, the English, being in the dominant position in the colonies and still carrying the cultural baggage of traditional English attitudes, could not help but notice that the most profound differences were not among whites of varying religious, ethnic, and national backgrounds but between blacks and whites. "As time went on," Jordan argues, "English colonists turned increasingly to what they saw as the striking physiognomic difference"[51] between the Africans and European peoples populating the colonies. In 1692, this emerging racial consciousness of whites was reflected in a revised Maryland law prohibiting miscegenation.[52] In the revised form, the term *Christian* was dropped, but the terms *white* and *English* were retained,[53] indicating where English colonists within an emerging multiracial society wanted the emphasis to be placed. The gradual substitution of the term *white* for *Christian* in the cultural and racial transformation of the English colonies suggests that most whites were beginning to see themselves in strictly racial terms instead of in terms of potential Christian brotherhood and sisterhood. Retaining the term *Christian* might have kept some options open to build a multiracial society based upon an appreciation of racial diversity and justice, but by this time the institution of slavery was erecting a high wall that few visionaries and advocates would be able or willing to scale to live in a just society. Being white had too many advantages that most whites in early English colonies would not forgo for visions of multiracial harmony.

The enslavement of Africans parallel to the development of a white nation supposedly based upon the high ideals of the Enlightenment and the American Revolution required racial rationalizations both to quiet the

---

50. Jordan, *White Man's Burden* 52.
51. Jordan, *White Man's Burden* 52.
52. Jordan, *White Man's Burden* 52.
53. Jordan, *White Man's Burden* 52.

consciences of many whites who could not live with the moral contradictions and to educate generations of whites who were expected to carry out the mission of racial manifest destiny. A convincing system of racial rationalization was particularly crucial for the latter group because they had to be free of all moral qualms related to the conquest and removal of Indians and the enslavement of blacks if they were to be able to carry out their "divine" racial mission. By the mid-1660s, the English colonists were becoming accustomed to thinking of Africans more as chattel than as human beings. Already preconditioned by Elizabethan cultural images and perceptions of blackness that were further distorted by their sudden and traumatic contact with West Coast Africans and lower primates, English colonists were predisposed to enslave black people and be at peace with themselves while doing so.

But other factors also contributed to the enslavement of Africans. According to Gary B. Nash, an historian of race relations in America, "Certainly a latent and still forming prejudice against people with black skin was partially responsible for the subjugation of Africans. But the chronic labor shortage in the colonies and the almost total failure to mold the Indians into an agricultural labor force were probably more important factors."[54] The key point is: once the enslavement of Africans was institutionalized in early America, it "cast the Negro in such a lowly role that the initial bias against him could only be confirmed and vastly strengthened. It was hardly possible for one people to enslave another without developing strong feelings against them."[55] Mass enslavement of Africans was triggered by the initial "unfavorable impressions of Africans and economic conditions which encouraged their exploitation. . . ,"[56] but much more was required to produce a racist culture and people who could oppress people with black skin without moral qualms. That "something" was the systematic institutionalization of not only African slavery but also the rationalization of white racial dominance over black people—slave or free. However, slavery was the foundation that "harden[ed] negative racial feelings into a deep and almost unshakable prejudice which continued to grow for centuries to come."[57] The enslavement of Africans, therefore, created the need among the vast majority of white Americans to understand their "whiteness" in relation to "the black presence" in their midst and to do so in a way that would preserve their image of themselves as moral and God-fearing people. They had to rationalize the enslavement of black human beings in order to minimize an obvious social evil. The best way to

54. Gary B. Nash, "Red, White and Black: The Origins of Racism in Colonial America" in Gary B. Nash and Richard Weiss, eds., *The Great Fear: Race in the Mind of America* 16.

55. Nash, "Red, White and Black" 16.

56. Nash, "Red, White and Black" 16.

57. Nash, "Red, White and Black" 16.

do this was by degrading the victims of their racial oppression as being unworthy of humane treatment, as not being as fully human as whites, or as being "beasts" or "children."

One of the first and most persistent rationalizations white Americans adopted to justify slavery and various other forms of racial social controls over the centuries was the idea of the insatiable sexual appetite of black people that required blacks be held in check. "Arising from the fear of the black slave bent upon sexual revenge," Nash explains, "was the common perception of the Negro as a hypersexual creature, another view which has transited the centuries so enduringly as to suggest that it fills a need in the white psyche."[58] Because white males dominated most aspects of early American society and culture, most white rationalizations of racial dominance of blacks on the sexual level embodied long-held sexual anxieties and fears of white males. From before Jefferson to the present, white males have used a variety of sexual myths to rationalize their domination of black people. During the Colonial Period, white males created a network of laws controlling sexual relations primarily between black men and white women, while at the same time exercising their right of sexual dominance over black women.[59] According to Nash, during the Colonial Period the image of blacks as hypersexual creatures intensified through white males' frequent sexual relations with black females. At the same time, since white men had almost complete control of blacks, they often required black women to have sexual relations. But they found such sexual behavior troublesome since it reflected those same sexual urges they had attributed to their "hypersexual" black slaves. White men who found themselves caught up in such socially contradictory behavior could extricate themselves by projecting their sexual urges and behavior onto black women. As Nash explains:

> Little evidence can be found to show that the black woman *was* physiologically a more sexually responsive person. Instead, the white man *made* her into a symbol of sexuality because he could thus act out with her all of the repressed libidinal desires which were proscribed by his own moral code, and because by

---

58. Nash, "Red, White and Black" 20.

59. According to one scholar of "law and the American legal process during the Colonial Period," the colonial legal system is best understood by "recognizing that it was a system controlled by a white male-dominated culture, a society generally antagonistic toward blacks, a society wherein white males wanted to maintain their domination over *both* white and black females, and finally a society in which white males fervently desired to preclude any sexual relationships between black males and white females." These white male-created antimiscegenation laws were not declared unconstitutional by the United States Supreme Court until 1967. See A. Leon Higginbotham, Jr., *In the Matter of Color: Race and the American Legal Process, The Colonial Period* 38, 41–42.

assigning to her a promiscuous nature he could assuage his own guilt that festered inevitably as a result of his illicit and exploitative activities.[60]

These white-male sexual projections fed into a complex system of racial myths about blacks that rationalized white racial manifest destiny. This racial–sexual rationalization of black slavery intensified during and after black slave revolts and insurrections. White Southerners "always stressed the physical threat black revolt posed for white women."[61] The Nat Turner Insurrection of 1831 in Virginia, which left fifty-seven whites dead and eventually led to the death of all the black insurrectionists, fueled white males' fears of black men throwing off the chains that had kept their sexual bestiality in check. When the Civil War ended slavery, the sexual fears and anxieties of many southern whites persisted. Without slavery, how could blacks be controlled? By the 1890s, the image of black men in the southern white mindset assumed the character of "the insatiable satyr, specially built both physically and mentally for the libidinal women they served." Such post-Emancipation sexual images of black men and women would be used by generations of whites to rationalize decades of further racial oppression of black people. Blacks became the scapegoats for those southern whites struggling to adjust to a changing social, political, and economic order.[62]

The enslavement of blacks not only enabled whites to turn blacks into instruments of their economic and political development but also forced them constantly to revise their image of blacks to fit their collective psychological needs. For example, during the Jacksonian era, blacks were not seen as barriers to white expansion as were the Indians. Millions of slaves were not to be removed from white society but were instead tied more firmly to white society. In short, black slaves were seen as essential to the social and economic progress of white society. The image of the black "child/savage" emerged to facilitate the rationalization of an enslavement that had burdened the consciences of many slaveholders during the Revolutionary Era. As historian Ronald T. Takaki has argued, this image of blacks had a "unique regional function" that served the needs of southern whites who needed a Sambo who was "childlike, docile, irresponsible, given to lying and stealing, lazy, affectionate, and happy."[63]

White slaveowners cherished the Sambo image because it suggested that the racist social order was correct and moral: everybody was happy, both master and slave. Planters could defend their slave society against attacks by pointing to the happy slaves being cared for by loving, caring masters who

---

60. Nash, "Red, White and Black" 20.
61. Dorothy Ann Gay, quoted in Joel Williamson, *A Rage for Order: Black–White Relations in the American South Since Emancipation* 28.
62. Williamson, *Rage for Order* 188, 198.
63. Takaki, *Iron Cages* 116.

overlooked their slaves' childish behavior. But as Takaki explains, ". . . the slavemasters' need for a Sambo was more complex than the desire to defend the peculiar institution and to mitigate guilt: The image helped to assure them that the slave was contented and controlled. Surely a happy slave would not violently protest his bondage; surely he would not slit his master's throat at night."[64]

In contrast to the savage, insurrectionist image of blacks such as Nat Turner, the Sambo image was conducive to the white planters' image of the racially unified social order where racial peace and cooperation could lead to social progress—as long as everybody stayed neatly in their places and did not threaten the racial social order. For decades these white views of blacks vacillated between the Sambo and the Rebel or beast–rapist according to the psychosociological needs of certain segments of the white community. By the late nineteenth century, the black image in the white collective mind ranged from seeing blacks as children to fearing them as insurrectionists or beast–rapists out to destroy white society. These two polar views characterized the South between the 1890s and about 1915. The beast–rapist view of black men tended to dominate the period. This view grew out of a new period of race relations in the South among insecure whites who no longer had the institution of slavery to set them apart from blacks. With slavery gone, their social universe lost its order. Everything was in flux, but one way of maintaining the order was by creating new forms of racial oppression to provide whites with some semblance of past racial glory. Lynching blacks became one way of maintaining racial dominance and was one of the most barbaric and sadistic forms of inhumanity in the history of Western civilization.[65] Those whites who engaged, encouraged, and observed this social ritual that included hanging, burning, amputating sexual organs and other body parts for souvenirs, represented the sociopathological depths to which racists could sink in their hatred of blacks. This pathological racial hatred even reached to the office of some southern governors, such as Cole Blease, the "pro-lynching governor of South Carolina, . . . received the finger of a lynched black in the mail and planted it in the gubernatorial garden."[66]

Lynching was primarily aimed at black males, who for centuries had been at the core of the white-male dominated, white culture's fears, anxieties, and fantasies concerning black people in general. Lynching and

---

64. Takaki, *Iron Cages* 121.

65. Williamson, *Rage* 71–125; lynching blacks involved more than just hanging, which was rarely sufficient to satisfy the pathological antiblack hatred of many southern whites. Torture and dismemberment of black victims provided an outlet for these whites to vent their frustrations. As Williamson puts it so well, these whites "needed devils" (182); for a chronology of lynching, see Ralph Ginzburg, *100 Years of Lynchings: A Shocking Documentary of Race Violence in America* passim.

66. Williamson, *Rage* 125.

other physical forms of white racial dominance were intended to break the spirit of black males and to make them subservient. Thus, much of the history of black–white relations in the United States involved formal and informal means of controlling black males. In a white-male dominated society, dedicated for much of its history to the expansion and maintenance of white economic, political, and cultural hegemony, the control of nonwhite males, especially black males, was seen by most whites as the best way to promote social peace in a multiracial society.[67]

The enslavement of blacks had a catalytic effect on many areas of white American life and culture as related to race. It contributed to the creation of a white culture fraught with moral and political contradictions that created a wellspring of psychosociological tensions, periodically expressed through wide swings of racial projections, physical violence, institutional constraints, pro-black rights advocacy, and genuine love and fellowship. Had science and religion been able to escape the influence of racism, they might have been able to turn the tide during the formative period of much of American racist thought after 1830. Unfortunately, the swings toward racism received strong support from religion and science.

Religion and science were used by racists throughout the formative period of American race relations to support the enslavement of blacks and were used periodically for many decades after slavery to rationalize both racial segregation and the long-term effects of racism on black behavior and attitudes.[68] The American churches failed abysmally in protecting the

---

67. Since American society has been controlled largely by white males, who had long exhibited irrational fears and anxieties about black males, most of the formal and informal means of white racial dominance have been designed to control black males. Castration of black males was one of the most drastic forms of racial dominance use by white males. According to Jordan, this practice goes back to the American Colonial Period and was motivated by white males' fears of black males' sexual aggression. "The white man's fears of Negro sexual aggression were equally apparent in the use of castration as a punishment in the colonies. This weapon of desperation was not employed by angry mobs in the manner which became familiar after Emancipation. Castration was dignified by specific legislative sanction as a lawful punishment in Antigua, the Carolinas, Bermuda, Virginia, Pennsylvania, and New Jersey. . . . Yet castration was not simply another of the many brands of hideous cruelty which graced the colonial criminal codes: it was reserved for Negroes and occasionally Indians. In some colonies, laws authorizing castration were worded so as to apply to all blacks whether free or slave. As a legal punishment castration was a peculiarly American experiment, for there was no basis for it in English law" (Jordan, *White Man's Burden* 81). Confining black males to the most marginal forms of employment protected white males from having to compete on a fair basis with black males. See Philip S. Foner, *Organized Labor and the Black Worker, 1619–1973* passim; for decades, black baseball players were not allowed to compete with white baseball players for slots in the major leagues. See Jules Tygiel, *Baseball's Great Experiment: Jackie Robinson and his Legacy* passim.

68. J. Oliver Buswell, III, *Slavery, Segregation and Scripture* 111. Some social scientists tended to blame the black victims of white racism for the very pathologies created by that racism. See Daniel P. Moynihan, *The Negro Family: The Case for National Action.*

human rights of Indians and blacks. While many individual white Christians struggled on behalf of blacks, both slave and free, and a few Christian denominations such as the Quakers and the Mennonites opposed slavery when other denominations had long since twisted the Bible to support the enslavement of black people, American churches in general failed to confront the ideology and beliefs of white racial manifest destiny.

As soon as the proslavery forces were able to convince the general public that slavery was good for blacks as a means of civilizing them, the rush was on to reinterpret key biblical passages to conform with and rationalize the enslavement of blacks. Just before the Civil War, the slavery issue split the white American Christian community into regional denominations, e.g., Southern Baptists, Northern Baptists, and the like.[69] So pervasive was the influence of racism within the white Christian community that it prompted one religious historian to comment that denominational unity among certain northern white Protestants was possible only because a "growing number of northern Protestants were willing to sacrifice Negro rights."[70] Another historian argued that if there is any consistent theme in the religious experience of Americans, "it has been that where a racial factor is present, the values of 'forgiveness, reconciliation, and love' have been largely impotent—even in church—to resolve conflict and stave off strife."[71] Goen commented further that racism, more than any other factor, "has undermined the credibility of Christian charity throughout American history."[72] By its refusal to use its moral forces to combat racial oppression against Indians and blacks, the white American Christian community lost its soul and the opportunity to be in the spiritual vanguard of the progressive forces supporting racial unity and justice as a means of universal social progress.

Much like religion, science, too, fell under the spell of the racism that sprang from the enslavement of blacks. Scientists on both sides of the Atlantic found themselves searching for answers to the conundrum of black skin and features in contrast to those of whites. Science was soon enlisted in the debate over slavery and white supremacy, and the power of the ideas of white supremacy and black inferiority found "scientific" support in the work of many renowned and respected scientists who pioneered in the fields of ethnography, anthropology, geography, and egyptology, and who published their theories and research in some of the most respected scientific journals and books in the United States. Beginning in the early nineteenth century, a group of American scientists began raising questions about traditional views of human equality and the unity of the human race.

---

69. Wood, *Arrogance* 43–73, 83–111, passim.
70. D. H. Reimers, *White Protestantism and the Negro,* quoted in Wood, *Arrogance* 338.
71. C. C. Goen, *Broken Churches, Broken Nation,* quoted in Wood, *Arrogance* 338.
72. C. C. Goen, *Broken Churches, Broken Nation,* quoted in Wood, *Arrogance* 338.

They were known as "the American School," and they strongly pursued the idea that the different races of humankind were actually distinct species. The irony of this development was that many whites who believed in white racial manifest destiny, white racial supremacy, and black inferiority, could not embrace the very "scientific view" that supported their racism because it struck at the heart of their religious belief in the Creation based on one Adam and one Eve. Race scientists of the American School, however, were not deterred by the beliefs of the racists within the religious community, and they continued to pursue their interests in separate species that contributed to the racist thought of the nineteenth century.[73]

Enslavement of blacks, therefore, created racial myths about blacks that still prevail today in the thinking of many whites. As these racial views began serving functional psychological and social needs for whites, they found them too difficult to relinquish. The more whites came to believe that they had a special racial mission, the less they could envision building a multiracial society based upon racial justice and equality. From the Colonial Period to the late nineteenth century, most attempts to foster racial justice and unity failed due to the persistence of the majority of whites' attempting to build a social order for whites only. So persistent was the racism of whites that by the time of the emancipation of slaves in 1863, the majority of white Americans had internalized the most rampant racial beliefs about blacks. Emancipation could have provided the United States with another chance at building a new multiracial society based upon racial justice and unity, but far too many whites viewed the emancipation of blacks as a threat to the welfare of whites. They could only see social progress in white terms. To these whites, social progress could only mean white racial dominance over peoples of color. After a short period of racial democracy during Reconstruction, white America continued to erect barriers to racial unity. By the twentieth century, the legacy of racism had taken the nation far down the path of racial hatred, conflict, and disunity.[74]

73. William Stanton, *The Leopard's Spots: Scientific Attitudes toward Race in America, 1815–59* passim.

74. Forrest G. Wood, *Black Scare: The Racist Response to Emancipation and Reconstruction* 17–39; C. Vann Woodward, *The Strange Career of Jim Crow* passim.

6

The Legacy of White Racism in the Twentieth Century

What white Americans have never fully understood—but what the Negro can never forget—is that white society is deeply implicated in the ghetto. White institutions created it, white institutions maintain it, and white society condones it.
—*Report of the National Advisory Commission on Civil Disorders,* 1968

The Persistence of White Racism

By the twentieth century, more than two centuries of white racial dominance over Native peoples and African–Americans had created in the minds of generations of whites the image that America was essentially a white nation moving towards its great racial destiny. The last of the great central plains Indians had been subdued and placed on reservations, and the ex-slaves and the first generation of their descendants had lived to see their greatest dreams—emancipation from slavery—realized, destroyed, replaced by newer forms of slavery and racial dominance.[1] Native peoples and the African–Americans had little to look forward to in the midst of the newer and more sophisticated forms of white racial dominance that white America was extending to other lands populated by nonwhite peoples.[2]

---

1. Takaki, *Iron Cages: Race and Culture in Nineteenth-Century America* 186–87. For the historical impact of Indian reservations on Native peoples' lives and culture, see Vine Deloria, Jr., *God is Red* 17, 27–32, 218–22, 251–58; Edgar S. Cahn, ed., *Our Brother's Keeper: The Indian in White America*; Rayford W. Logan, *The Betrayal of the Negro: From Rutherford B. Hayes to Woodrow Wilson* passim; Leon F. Litwack, *Been in the Storm So Long: The Aftermath of Slavery* 337–449.

2. Beginning in the early 1890s, white American leaders began extending their racial dominance to Hawaii in complete disregard for the wishes of the majority there. They imposed a similar policy of racial dominance and expansionism on the people in the Philippines. Theodore Roosevelt was a firm believer in "the white man's burden" and justified the United States' taking over the Philippines because he once said it benefitted the

The end of the nineteenth century had witnessed the infamous European scramble for Africa that would lead to decades of further racial oppression. In fact, peoples of color around the world, in India, Africa, China, and the "New World," shared a common oppression at the hands of whites.[3]

The United States could have changed the course of the racial history of the modern world, but it missed more and more opportunities to do so. These missed opportunities represented fading lights to a watchful world badly in need of Grand Models of racial unity and fellowship. Instead of building on its heritage of democracy by extending it to all peoples, by the twentieth century white America was preoccupied with building a nation dedicated first and foremost to the social and economic well-being of whites. Not withstanding the anti-immigrant bias of white native Americans, the most widespread and deeply felt bias was directed toward black Americans. The legacy of racism once again took America down the racial path of least resistance, and the country embarked upon a new century of racial injustice.[4]

From the end of the Civil War to the turn of the century, the focus of American race relations shifted more and more to black–white issues in the South. The emancipation of the slaves and their subsequent shortlived political participation in regional politics placed them at the center of national attention. As a result, black–white issues came to dominate American race relations. By the turn of the century, Native peoples had been pushed to the margins of society to such an extent that they constituted far less a threat to white Americans than did black Americans. With the pacification of the Native peoples, only blacks were left as a perennial problem for whites, and the South (where the majority of blacks lived) was expected to offer a solution. This solution turned out to be another form of white racial dominance that would victimize and dehumanize black people far into the twentieth century.

Southern Racial Segregation

This path of least resistance and compromise—what historian C. Vann Woodward has called the "Capitulation to Racism" in reference to the racial changes in the Reconstruction and Post-Reconstruction South—opened the era of racial segregation that tainted the history of American democracy for most of the twentieth century.[5] The South became a seed-bed for this newly emerging form of racial domination, and the North happily acquiesced as southern states began passing countless laws and ordinances

people. See Rubin Francis Weston, *Racism in U.S. Imperialism: The Influence of Racial Assumptions on American Foreign Policy, 1893–1946* 37–47.

3. Frazier, *Race and Culture Contacts in the Modern World* passim; Segal, *The Race War* vii–1.

4. Logan, *Betrayal* 359–92; Gossett, *Race: The History of an Idea in America* 253–409.

5. Woodward, *The Strange Career of Jim Crow* 44–96.

segregating blacks from whites. "The mushroom growth of discriminatory and segregation laws during the first two decades of this century," Woodward states, "piled up a huge bulk of legislation."[6] But the trend toward racial segregation had started several decades earlier. Beginning with the 1890s, the South was rapidly influencing the nature and direction of race relations in the nation as a whole, in effect demonstrating to the North that since the majority of blacks had always lived in the South among white southerners, southerners knew what was best for blacks. No wonder southern states such as Mississippi, South Carolina, Louisiana, North Carolina could amend their constitutions so as to disenfranchise most blacks yet allow even the most unqualified whites to vote. As it had on previous occasions, the highest court in the land, the United States Supreme Court, supported the very laws that contributed the most to the racial oppression of blacks. Rayford W. Logan, one of the first scholars to study the impact of racial segregation during the Post-Reconstruction period, wrote: "Practically all the relevant decisions of the United States Supreme Court during Reconstruction and to the end of the century nullified or curtailed those rights of Negroes which the Reconstruction 'Radicals' thought they had written into laws and into the Constitution."[7] During the 1870s and 1880s, the Supreme Court supported discrimination by individuals on public carriers and in public places and approved racial segregation by state action. The most infamous of the Court's decisions, *Plessy* v. *Ferguson* in 1896, saw the Court for the first time invoke "the doctrine of police powers to deny in effect the equal protection which the framers of the Fourteenth Amendment thought they had established. It was this decision by which the Supreme Court accepted the doctrine of 'separate but equal accommodations'."[8] With the sanction of the highest tribunal in the land, the South had a free hand to oppress blacks. White violence against blacks during this era of Supreme Court compliance with racial oppression was so widespread that it prompted one scholar of constitutional history and racism to comment: "This was an era in which the Supreme Court supported federal police power to regulate lotteries and oleomargarine, yet constricted the use of federal police power in incidences of racial violence."[9]

People around the world celebrated the turn of the century with expositions and congresses. Many saw a future "wherein man's aspirations for his fellows would be realized through the wonders of technology. The threshold of the century also seemed to mark a quickening in man's social

---

6. Woodward, *Strange Career* 82.

7. Logan, *Betrayal* 105.

8. Logan, *Betrayal* 105, 119; for the essential aspects of *Plessy* v. *Ferguson,* see Derrick A. Bell, Jr., *Race, Racism and American Law* 204.

9. Mary Frances Berry, *Black Resistance/White Law: A History of Constitutional Racism in America* 126.

awareness."[10] In the United States, white Progressives joined in the founding of the National Association for the Advancement of Colored People (NAACP) and the National Urban League (NUL), the two major organizations that would lead the way in interracial cooperation for racial justice and the uplifting of black urban dwellers.[11] But they were mere flickers of light in a long dark tunnel of racism. Southern states, the federal government, and several presidents supported the racial status quo.[12] Maintaining their role in the vanguard of white racism, southern states continued to pass an array of laws—some almost comical in form had they not been so cruel—to segregate blacks and whites in every area of life. "In 1903, Arkansas directed that in the state penitentiary and in county jails, stockades, convict camps, and all other places where prisoners were confined" blacks and whites be segregated. Ten years later, most southern states had similar laws. The same policy of racial segregation was applied to the "white and Negro insane, feeble-minded, blind and deaf, paupers, tubercular patients, and juvenile delinquents. . . ." In 1906, Montgomery, Alabama, ordered blacks and whites to use separate streetcars. In 1915, South Carolina passed a law that prohibited textile factories from allowing their black and their white employees "to work together in the same room, or to use the same entrances, or pay windows" to receive their paychecks, or to use the same exits, "toilets, drinking-water buckets, pails, cups, dippers, or glasses at any time."[13] In 1905, it became illegal for blacks and whites to use the same park facilities at the same time. Donors of land for playgrounds were obligated to specify for which race's use. Blacks and whites in Atlanta, Georgia, were not permitted to visit the municipal zoo at the same time until 1940. In 1929, it was illegal for blacks and whites to use the same fishing, boating, and bathing facilities. In 1935, Arkansas went even further by segregating blacks and whites "at all race tracks and gaming establishments." Starting in 1910, several southern cities outlawed blacks and whites from living in the same areas, such as blocks and districts. These laws were declared unconstitutional in 1917. In 1915, Oklahoma ordered telephone companies "to maintain separate booths for white and Negro patrons."[14] Florida and North Carolina even had a policy of segregating textbooks used by black students in addition to strict regulations for fumigating textbooks. In 1922, Mississippi outlawed blacks and whites from riding together in a cab unless there were more than seven passengers in the

10. Berry, *Black Resistance* 123.

11. Berry, *Black Resistance* 123; Nancy J. Weiss, *The National Urban League: 1910–1940*; Charles Flint Kellogg, *NAACP: A History of the NAACP*, vol. 1, 1909–20, 23–104.

12. Logan, *Betrayal* 23–104, 347–48; Sinkler, *Racial Attitudes* 289–372.

13. John Hope Franklin, "History of Racial Segregation in the United States," *The Annals of the American Academy of Political and Social Science* 304 (March 1956): 7–8.

14. Franklin, "History" 8.

cab, and the vehicle "was traveling from one city to another." And New Orleans had an "ordinance separating Negro and white prostitutes."[15]

Notwithstanding the regional concentration of these legal forms of white racial control, their influence spread throughout the nation. Since the vast majority of blacks lived in the South, the larger white public looked to the white South for their information about blacks. And much of what the white South said and wrote about the black South became "facts" in the minds of generations of white Americans outside the region. Northern and southern whites who supported racial segregation in the South had to defend it, and the best way to defend racial segregation was to follow the examples of the proslavery apologists and racial theorists who placed the blame of slavery on the backs of black slaves. Between 1900 and 1930, the defenders of racial segregation in the South produced a range of antiblack literature. I. A. Newby, a scholar who studied antiblack thought among white Americans during this period, points out, "These were the years in which anti-Negro thought reached its zenith, the years which produced the greatest proliferation of anti-Negro literature, and the years in which that literature enjoyed its broadest appeal."[16] Much like their nineteenth-century counterparts, twentieth-century racists clothed their racial theories and beliefs in scientific rationales. "The science of race which developed in this country in the early twentieth century," Newby argues, "was all inclusive, especially as it applied to the Negro. It commenced by affirming that his inferiority began with the racial differentiation of mankind, and it concluded with scientific justification for Southern race policies and prejudices."[17]

Racial segregation in the South received its greatest support from the churches. Armed with many of the proslavery religious arguments, twentieth-century religious racists continued to pervert Christianity and the Bible to support white racial dominance. Unlike the community of scientists and scholars, most white churches clung to their racist beliefs long after such beliefs lost favor in other areas of American society. As Newby once again explains:

> . . . organized religious bodies still endorsed or failed to condemn racist policies. Long after scientists and scholars had dropped their belief in racial inequality, anti-Negro ideas endured among many American church groups. Especially true of fundamental churches in the South, this fact indicated the peculiar way in which American churches reflect popular opinion.[18]

---

15. Franklin, "History" 8.
16. I. A. Newby, *Jim Crow's Defense: Anti-Negro Thought in America, 1900–1930* xi.
17. Newby, *Jim Crow's Defense* 21.
18. Newby, *Jim Crow's Defense* 85.

Racism and Racial Conflict in the Industrial North

Although the South led the way in expanding and perfecting institutional mechanisms of white racial dominance of blacks, the North played a complementary role by not only adopting a "hands-off policy" but also by supporting southern racial practices in word and deed.[19] The North, however, soon found itself facing its own variety of racism and racial conflicts when World War I triggered a need for southern black labor to replace thousands of European immigrants returning to their homelands to fight in the war. Almost overnight northern industrial centers found themselves inundated with tens of thousands of southern black "peasants" eager to work in the high-wage factories. In the space of a few years, northern cities with only a few blacks before the war had thousands of blacks in their postwar populations. The migration of southern blacks into northern cities radically changed the nature of race relations in the United States. No longer was the South the center of the nation's racial problems.[20] The war and the northern demand for cheap, abundant black labor changed all that. Now, the North had to share in carrying the burden of the country's most persistent social problem.

Northern cities soon developed serious racial problems. In their haste to meet the demand for war production, many industrialists imported southern black workers to break the strikes of white workers. This soured relations between blacks and whites for decades and led to several serious race riots in the North, the worst being the Chicago race riot of 1919.[21] As more southern blacks left the South to work and live in the North, they began to clash with whites over housing. Largely because of racially restrictive convenants that were not declared constitutionally unenforceable until 1948,[22] blacks were increasingly forced to live in the worst areas of the cities.

By the 1920s, black ghettoes, infested with crime and violence, had become the norm in many northern black areas. Much as they had done in the South, many northern white city officials erected barriers to control the population movement of northern blacks. These officials were supported by white citizens who organized countless white neighborhood associations to prevent blacks from moving into white neighborhoods. Throughout the

---

19. Logan, *Betrayal* 165–241.

20. Charles Johnson, "Substitution of Negro for European Immigrant Labor" in *National Conference of Social Work Proceedings* (May–June, 1926) 319–20; Harold M. Baron, "The Demand for Black Labor: Historical Notes on the Political Economy of Racism" in *Radical America* 19–21; Emmett J. Scott, *Negro Migration during the War* 26; Florette Henri, *Black Migration: Movement North, 1900–1920* 49–80.

21. William M. Tuttle, Jr., *Race Riot: Chicago in the Red Summer of 1919* 108–56.

22. Clement E. Vose, *Caucasians Only: The Supreme Court, The NAACP, and the Restrictive Covenant Cases* 1–12, 177–210.

1930s and 1940s, many northern whites resorted to violence to keep blacks from purchasing homes in white neighborhoods.[23]

These whites were encouraged to practice such racism against blacks seeking decent housing by an agency of the federal government, the Federal Housing Administration (FHA), which encouraged and supported racially restrictive covenants. The result of such government-supported, institutionalized racism was increased racial conflict between blacks whose housing needs were not being met and those whites who believed that their property values would decrease if blacks moved into their neighborhoods. In Detroit, during the summer of 1942, racial conflicts over housing exploded into a race riot. By the next summer, another race riot, linked to a combination of racial conflicts over jobs and housing, shocked the nation. It was the worst race riot in American history.[24]

Racial tension and conflict in northern cities were almost always associated with institutionalized racism. Racial discrimination in housing and employment clashed with the increased expectations of those southern blacks who had migrated North not only to get better paying jobs in northern factories but also to escape the racially repressive atmosphere of the South. Once in the North, many refused to accept even the more moderate forms of white racism. The generation that grew to maturity in the North became known as the "The New Negro."[25] Much more radical and self-assured than their parents could afford to be in the South, this new generation of blacks demanded equal treatment from whites. When such treatment was not given, they formed powerful protest groups and fought for their rights. During the 1930s, this generation of northern blacks was able to use their increased population base to exercise their political muscle in city, state, and, particularly, national presidential elections. When World War II broke out, this generation of blacks refused to defer their agenda for the sake of the war. Led by such leaders as A. Philip Randoph of the Brotherhood of Sleeping Car Porters, they threatened a march on Washington, D.C., if President Roosevelt did not take action against discrimination in war industries. He responded with an executive order against racial discrimination in war-production industries, but white racism persisted.[26]

---

23. See chapter "Life and Death in the Inner City," Henri, *Black Migration* 93–131; for examples of whites using bombs to force blacks out of white neighborhoods, see Tuttle, *Race Riot* 157–83; Karl E. Taeuber and Alma F. Taeuber, *Negroes in Cities: Residential Segregation and Neighborhood Change* 43–55.

24. Taeuber and Taeuber, *Negroes in Cities* 20; Vose, *Caucasians Only* 124–25, 225–27; Dominic J. Capeci, Jr., *Race Relations in Wartime Detroit: The Sojourner Truth Housing Controversy of 1942*; Robert Shogan and Tom Craig, *The Detroit Race Riot: A Study in Violence.*

25. Alain Locke, *The New Negro* passim.

26. Florence Murray, ed., "National Defense Chronology for the Year, 1941," *The Negro Handbook* 76–77; Louis Ruchames, *Race, Jobs, & Politics: The Story of FEPC* 20–21.

In some ways World War II resembled World War I in its impact on American race relations. Both wars triggered black migration to northern cities and increased racial tensions and conflicts because of the unwillingness of whites to alter the racial status quo. However, the political empowerment of blacks in northern cities during the 1930s and early 1940s provided them with leverage to challenge and alter some aspects of institutional racism. In addition, northern blacks entered into several very effective interracial coalitions with progressive whites in labor and politics, coalitions that greatly augmented their struggle against racism. For example, the movement of industrial unionism led by the Congress of Industrial Organizations (CIO) supported racial equality on the job and supported black workers in their fight against racial discrimination in housing.[27]

World War II also aroused white fears and anxieties concerning the increase and expansion of the black population. The racial status quo was under attack everywhere, particularly since the war was seen by many in part as a struggle against the racist theories of Hitler's Germany. Roosevelt's executive order against racial discrimination, the first of its kind in history, constituted in the minds of many whites a challenge to their racial privileges. This was the period when the labor market was characterized by what some labor market scholars now called a dual labor market, which segregated black and white workers on the basis on color instead of skills.[28] Generations of whites had in many cases gained benefits over blacks on the basis of their color instead of their skills. No matter what skill level black workers had, the vast majority were forced to work in the most dangerous and dirtiest jobs— those jobs rejected by whites. For years many labor organizations, such as the railroad brotherhoods and the American Federation of Labor (AFL), supported such white racial privileges. As efforts mounted against such racist practices and traditions in the labor market, white workers in various industries throughout the country responded with "hate strikes," so-called because their only objective was to preserve the racial privileges of those white workers who refused to work alongside black workers.[29]

Perhaps the worst case of government-sponsored racism during the war involved the relocation and internment of thousands of West Coast Japanese–Americans to concentration camps in other states. Due to the anti-Japanese hysteria that resulted from the Japanese bombing of Pearl Harbor, the United States government forced entire Japanese–American communities to leave their friends and property. Forced by a deadline to

27. *CIO News*, June 28–August 21, 1943.

28. David M. Gordon, *Theories of Poverty and Underemployment: Orthodox, Radical, and Dual Labor Market Perspectives* 43–52; for an example of how a dual labor market affects black workers, see Harold M. Baron and Bennett Hymer, "The Negro Worker in the Chicago Labor Market," in Julius Jacobson, ed., *The Negro and the American Labor Movement* 232–85.

29. Philip S. Foner, *Organized Labor and the Black Worker, 1619–1973* 265–66, 280.

leave by an appointed date, many Japanese–Americans had no choice but to sell their homes and businesses at a great loss. Many of these people had been born in the United States. But a long history of anti-Asian racism on the West Coast and the bombing of Pearl Harbor combined in a groundswell of fear and hatred that forced their removal and internment. No other American ethnic group whose native country was at war with the United States ever suffered such humiliation and shame. It was inconceivable to most white Americans to consider such treatment for German–Americans. Notwithstanding this humiliation and shame, Japanese–Americans served with distinction in the United States Armed Services.[30]

The increased racism and racial conflicts generated by the war forced some white leaders to reflect more seriously on the long-term effects of racial discrimination. Until World War II and the full revelations of the genocide against European Jews and other so-called non-Aryan peoples, far too many observers and scholars of race relations did not realize the extent to which the racism created by Europeans centuries ago could grow into such a monster. As long as the victims of American and European racism belonged to the non-white races, most whites either showed little concern or considered it a problem that society could take its time solving. The prevailing view was that racism would fade away in due course as whites became more enlightened and as nonwhites became more civilized. However, Germany changed that thinking for many American whites who, had they been in Germany during the Third Reich, might not have been Aryan enough for its racial theorists.

The racial theories of the Third Reich emanated in part from centuries of European racist thought that had victimized and dehumanized nonwhites around the world. European Jews were among the first large-scale "white" victims of practices based on those theories. The Nazis, therefore, did not invent any startlingly new racial theories to justify their special brand of European racism. As George L. Mosse, in his groundbreaking book on the history of European racism has explained: "The Nazis did not invent racism; they merely activated it. . . . The Nazi implementation of racial policy was essentially the climax of a long development . . . from its source in the eighteenth century. The stream flows on into the future."[31]

Unfortunately, the racial lessons of the Jewish holocaust as related to the racial discrimination against blacks in the United States were lost on many white Americans during the post-war period, and the connections between blacks and Jews as victims of the same stream of European racism are often ignored in current discussion of the holocaust. "Historically, Jews and

---

30. Bill Hosokawa, *Nisei: The Quiet Americans* 224–378, 393–422.
31. George L. Mosse, *Toward the Final Solution: A History of European Racism* 231.

blacks have always played the outsider, the villain who threatens the tribe. Who knows," Mosse points out, "but that 6 million Jews might not have been joined by as many blacks had these lived in the midst of the peoples of Europe."[32] Writing in 1978, Mosse reminds the reader that

> the holocaust has passed. . . . But racism itself has survived. As many people as ever before think in racial categories. There is nothing provisional about the lasting world of stereotypes. That is the legacy of racism everywhere. And if, under the shock of the holocaust, the postwar world proclaimed a temporary moratorium on anti-Semitism, the black on the whole remained locked into a racial posture which never varied much from the eighteenth century to our time. . . . nations which had fought against National Socialism [in Nazi Germany] continued to accept black racial inferiority for many years after the end of the war, and did not seem to realize that all racism, whether aimed at blacks or Jews, was cut of the same cloth.[33]

After World War II, race riots and hate strikes in major northern industrial cities followed on the heels of new waves of southern black migrants eager to find work and new homes. The war years brought even larger numbers of southern blacks to northern cities where, unfortunately, even when they could find jobs, they could not find decent housing. Throughout the war and the early years of the postwar period, blacks could only find housing in traditionally black areas. As the ghettoes swelled to capacity, spawning crime and violence, black leaders, led by the NAACP, began chipping away at the various legal mechanisms used to keep the expanding black population locked in ghettoes. The vast majority of whites were determined to keep blacks from leaving the ghettoes. They had powerful white-dominated institutions, government agencies, and professional organizations to assist them. Even after the 1948 Supreme Court decision declared racially restrictive convenants unenforceable, local white real estate boards, still acting under the powerful influence of the National Association of Real Estate Boards, penalized white real estate salespersons for selling property in white areas to blacks.[34] The nature of this resistance to legal changes in the racial status quo proved revealing, as one scholar of the period explained:

> The Supreme Court's decision in the 1948 cases did not change the minds of most [white] real-estate salesmen. That decision made their position of greater importance for they could enforce segregation whereas the Court would not.[35]

---

32. Mosse, *Toward the Final Solution* xi.
33. Mosse, *Toward the Final Solution* 235–36.
34. Vose, *Caucasians Only* 223–25.
35. Vose, *Caucasians Only* 223.

The manner in which the white real-estate establishment went about circumventing the spirit of the law of the highest tribunal in the land demonstrated the extent to which many whites would go to maintain their racial privileges. One method they used was the following:

> The method now being employed here in St. Louis . . . is to have the Real Estate Exchange zone the city and forbid any member of the exchange under pain of expulsion to sell property in the white zone to a Negro. If the real estate men refused to participate in the sale, the breaches will at least be minimized to those who deal with each other directly or through a . . . non-member of the exchange who could be easily identified and boycotted more or less by all the people to whom the knowledge comes.[36]

Such methods kept thousands of blacks from exercising their rights to buy decent homes in which to rear families and contribute to the larger society. For decades, these and other methods, such as redlining[37] by banks, forced blacks who could afford to purchase homes to live in increasingly crowded ghettoes. The whites who designed and supported these racist methods contributed to the web of urban institutionalized racism that created and maintained black ghettoes. Several decades later, after the black urban rebellions of the 1960s, the Kerner Commission Report correctly placed the blame squarely on institutionalized racism for the creation of the black ghettoes: "What white Americans have never fully understood—but what the Negro can never forget—is that white society is deeply implicated in the ghetto. White institutions created it, white institutions maintain it, and white society condones it."[38]

During the 1940s and 1950s, race relations between blacks and whites underwent dramatic and complex changes due largely to the convergence of economic, political, social, and technological changes within the larger society. New highway construction opened the suburbs to young, white, middle-class families anxious to leave the crowded city with its expanding black populations. Innercity factories and related businesses soon joined the exodus. Technological changes and the need to compete forced many industries that had once depended heavily upon several generations of unskilled southern black workers to rely more on technology instead of black brawn. As these industries became less labor intensive and more

---

36. Gerald Seegers quoted in Vose, *Caucasians Only* 223.

37. "Historically the word 'redlining' originated with the alleged practice of some mortgage lenders of using a red crayon to define on a map the boundaries of areas within which they would not lend." This is the practice "of rejecting a loan applicant on the basis of an initial and costless categorization—such as property location or some obvious characteristic of the borrower such as color or sex" (Jack M. Guttentag and Susan M. Wachter, *Redlining and Public Policy* 11).

38. *Report of the National Advisory Commission on Civil Disorders* 2.

capital intensive, they hired fewer and fewer unskilled black workers. Many of these black workers would probably have been able to find employment in the suburbs *if* they could have found places to live, but the vast majority of whites were determined to keep blacks out of the suburbs.[39]

Further complicating the situation in northern cities was the emerging mechanization of southern agriculture that was beginning to replace thousands of black farm workers with tractors. Tens of thousands of these displaced rural workers, among the poorest and most uneducated in the country due to decades of racial exploitation of entire families, flooded into northern cities. But, unlike earlier southern black migrants whose lack of skills and formal education matched the demand for their labor, these displaced rural workers arrived during a period when such demand was rapidly declining. These latest black migrants—many poor, uneducated, and desperate—contributed to the ever-expanding black ghettoes, now teeming with even more poverty, unemployment, underemployment, crime, and violence, and characterized by an increasing resentment and hatred of the surrounding white society that many blacks knew to be at least partially responsible for maintaining their sordid conditions.[40] As the black ghettoes grew more menacing to white city officials and the surrounding white communities, whites began to rely more on institutionalized methods to check and control what they believed to be a threat to the social order.[41] The stage was set for the black urban explosions of the 1960s.

Changes in the Racial Status Quo: Challenges, Compromises, Resistance, and Denial

Even while institutionalized racism kept the vast majority of blacks locked in ghettoes with their terrible schools, confined black workers to the worst jobs, and in the South denied blacks both the right to vote and equal access to public accommodation, among other indignities, these forms of racism

---

39. *Report*, 251–65; Mark I. Gelfand, *A Nation of Cities: The Federal Government and Urban America, 1933–1965* 222–34; Joe T. Darden et al., *Detroit: Race and Uneven Development* 15–26, 137; Arnold R. Hirsch, *Making the Second Ghetto: Race and Housing in Chicago, 1940–1960* 68–99.

40. Harry C. Dillingham and David F. Sly, "The Mechanical Cotton-Picker, Negro Migration, and the Integration Movement" in *Human Organization* 25.4 (Winter, 1966): 344–51; William Julius Wilson, *The Truly Disadvantaged: The Inner City, the Underclass, and Public Policy* 34; Kenneth B. Clark, *Dark Ghetto: Dilemmas of Social Power* 81–110; *Report* 2, 274.

41. For decades predominantly white police forces performed the institutionalized function of maintaining control over urban black populations. See "The Police and the Community" in *Report* 295–318; David H. Bayley and Harold Mendelsohn, *Minorities and the Police: Confrontation in America* 109–92; Homer Hawkins and Richard Thomas, "White Policing of Black Populations: A History of Race and Social Control in America" in Cashmore and McLaughlin, eds., *Out of Order: Policing Black People.*

did not go unchallenged. From the late 1940s to the mid-1960s, every form and expression of historic white racism was challenged, and many were overcome. In 1947, Jackie Robinson's breaking the color barrier in major league baseball "shook American society as profoundly as the Supreme Court's decision to desegregate education a few years later."[42] In 1948, the Supreme Court declared racially restrictive convenants constitutionally unenforceable. That same year President Truman issued his Executive Order 9981 desegregating the United States Armed Forces, a major and historic step in challenging one of the bulwarks of institutionalized racism.[43]

Largely as the result of the sustained and uncompromising struggles of black organizations and their white allies, as well as the changing international climate that forced American leaders to demonstrate to an increasingly watchful world that America was doing its best to eliminate racial discrimination against its largest minority,[44] a steady stream of presidential, congressional, and judicial decisions, orders, and legislation "aimed at dismantling barriers to black participation appeared."[45] Among these were the following: The 1954 Supreme Court Decision in *Brown* v. *Board of Education of Topeka,* which ruled against segregating blacks and whites in public schools; President Eisenhower's 1955 Executive Order 1059, which set up the President's Committee on Government Employment Policy to fight discrimination in employment. This committee replaced the Fair Employment Committee established by President Truman in 1948. In 1955, the Interstate Commerce Commission issued an order banning segregation of passengers on trains and buses in interstate travel; two years later, the 1957 Civil Rights Act created a six-member presidential commission to investigate allegations of the denial of citizens' voting rights. In 1960, another Civil Rights Act was passed to strengthen the investigatory powers of the 1957 Civil Rights Commission. In 1961, President Kennedy established the Committee on Equal Employment Opportunity to combat discrimination in employment. That same year, the Justice Department moved against

---

42. Jules Tygiel, *Baseball's Great Experiment: Jackie Robinson and His Legacy* backcover.

43. Gerald David Jaynes and Robin M. Williams, Jr., eds., *A Common Destiny: Blacks in American Society* 64.

44. Black involvement in the United Nations and black organizations' petitions to the United Nations criticizing American racism (e.g., National Negro Congress in 1946, NAACP in 1947) forced white American leaders and government officials and leaders to acknowledge the damaging effects of American racism on the nation's image as a model democracy for the world to emulate. Racial discrimination and violence against black American citizens forced the State Department's "Voice of America" to include in its first broadcast to Communist Russia a report on a lynching of a young southern black being held on suspicion of murder. See Roy Wilkins with Tom Mathews, *Standing Fast: The Autobiography of Roy Wilkins* 198; John Hope Franklin and Alfred A. Moss, Jr., *From Slavery to Freedom: A History of Negro Americans* 408–510.

45. Jaynes and Williams, *Common Destiny* 64.

discrimination in airport facilities under the provisions of the Federal Airport Act and against discrimination in bus terminals under the Interstate Commerce Commission Act. A year later, President Kennedy issued Executive Order 11063 barring discrimination in public housing receiving federal funds. In 1964, the Civil Rights Act banned discrimination in public accommodation and employment. In 1965, the Voting Rights Act suspended literacy tests and sent federal examiners into many localities to protect the rights of black voters. And in 1968, fair-housing legislation prohibited discrimination in the sale or rental of housing.[46]

One has to wonder why over two decades of presidential executive orders, congressional and judicial decisions and orders, involving so much energy and time, were necessary just to ensure that black Americans had the same rights as white Americans. Why at that stage of American history was it so difficult for many whites to see their fellow black citizens as equal? White Americans did not need such governmental efforts on their behalf to exercise their basic rights, but far too many white Americans at the time (and even many at the present time) could not abandon their sense of white superiority. Sadly, all these efforts fell short in one way or another because of white resistance.

As we have seen, beginning with Roosevelt's executive order against discrimination in employment and notwithstanding the endorsement of his high office, many whites on every social level refused to relinquish their traditional racial privileges. No less a famous American than President Dwight D. Eisenhower, in office at the time of the 1954 Supreme Court Decision on school desegregation, the most monumental judicial decision affecting basic human rights in American society in over a half-century, and a man who became famous as one of the greatest generals in the Second World War, fighting against one of the worst violators of human rights in modern history, no less a man, refused to support the decision. "No help would come from the White House," Harvard Sitkoff, a leading scholar in the field of modern American relations stated. "The President of the United States . . . declined to join the battle against segregation. He refused to endorse or support the *Brown* ruling."[47] Not only did he not endorse or support the *Brown* decision but President Eisenhower also often remarked: "I don't believe you can change the hearts of men with laws or decisions." He was so upset with the decision that he told one of his aides:

> I am convinced that the Supreme Court decision set back progress in the South at least fifteen years. . . . It's all very well to talk about school integration—if you remember you may also be talking about social *dis*integration. Feelings are deep on this. . . . And the fellow who tries to tell me that you can do these things by force is just plain nuts.[48]

---

46. Jaynes and Williams, *Common Destiny* 65.
47. Harvard Sitkoff, *The Struggle for Black Equality, 1954–1980* 25.
48. Quoted in Sitkoff, *Struggle* 25.

Eisenhower would have preferred education over what he perceived to be unreasonable force, but as Sitkoff pointed out, the president "would not educate." Instead, President Eisenhower "rejected all pleas that he tour the South seeking compliance, or call a conference of Southern moderates, or appeal on television to the nation for understanding. He simply did not favor school desegregation, much as he had never approved desegregation of the armed forces."[49] Furthermore, he regretted appointing Earl Warren (the Chief Justice who rallied support among the justices for the 1954 decision to be unanimous) to the Supreme Court, as "the biggest damfool mistake I ever made."[50] Chief Justice Warren also had his own regrets. In his memoirs, Warren expressed disappointment in President Eisenhower's lack of support for the *Brown* decision, going so far as to suggest that if the president had placed the weight of his great popular appeal on the side of the *Brown* decision "we would have been relieved, in my opinion, of many of the racial problems which have continued to plague us."[51] But President Eisenhower was more concerned about the white South than about the long history of segregated education in the South that had underdeveloped generations of black children. Instead, he told the chief justice that white southerners "are not bad people. All they are concerned about is to see that their sweet little girls are not required to sit in school alongside some big overgrown Negroes."[52] In that statement alone, President Eisenhower, almost two centuries removed from the time of Jefferson, echoed the latter's (and many white males') greatest and most persistent fear of what might result from any challenge to the racial status quo.

Had he chosen to do so at the time, President Eisenhower could have paved the way for racial justice, equality, and racial unity, which, in turn, would have saved the country much time and energy spent on addressing the racial conflicts in the South during the Civil Rights Movement. Instead, he chose not to endorse a vision of a more racially equal America. His choice to back away from racial justice no doubt sent a clear message to many white Americans that it was all right to resist the decision of the Supreme Court to desegregate. Since he had already gone on record in opposition to the desegregation of the armed services, President Eisenhower's words and deeds legitimatized an era of white resistance to racial equality, racial unity, and social progress. Several years later, during the Fall of 1957, this trend of white resistance returned to haunt him. Governor Orval Faubus of Arkansas defied a federal court's order to desegregate Central High School in Little Rock. White mobs rushed to the city to prevent nine black youths

49. Sitkoff, *Struggle* 25.

50. Eisenhower quoted in Sitkoff, *Struggle* 25.

51. Warren quoted in J. Harvie Wilkinson, III, *From* Brown *to* Bakke: *The Supreme Court and School Integration, 1954–1978* 24.

52. Eisenhower quoted in Wilkinson, *From* Brown *to* Bakke 24.

from integrating the school. The scene of thousands of whites milling around a few black youth, who were also prevented from entering the school by the National Guard, attracted worldwide attention. President Eisenhower was forced to assume leadership in this racial crisis. He sent federal troops to the city to "uphold national supremacy, defend Presidential authority, and enforce the law of the land. In so doing, Eisenhower became the first President since Reconstruction to use armed troops in support of Negro rights."[53]

While the Warren Court did pave the way for racial justice through its historic, landmark decision, it adopted a gradualist policy of the implementation of its decision that lasted more than a decade. It took a mass movement, the Civil Rights Movement, finally to overcome some of the gradualist tendencies of the three branches of government.[54]

The Civil Rights Movement triggered a groundswell of white violence, murder, and intimidation in the South. In the process, however, the movement also generated one of the most impressive displays of interracial unity and fellowship that the modern world had ever witnessed. Unfortunately, when the struggle against institutionalized racism and its effects moved to the North, a new kind of white resistance surfaced. Many northern whites tended to support desegregation in the South but shied away from desegregation in the North. With the onset of bussing as a means of school integration in the North, particularly during the 1970s, northern whites began to realize their payments on historic racism were finally due. Bussing children to achieve racial integration became the most explosive issue of the 1970s and led to much confusion, pain, and anguish among blacks and whites alike.[55] Like southern white resistance to changes in the racial status quo, northern white resistance was no less racist in nature and purpose; most were primarily concerned with maintaining a racial comfort zone in which they could dictate the nature and pace of racial changes.

Starting with the white backlash of the late 1960s that continued into the 1970s, many whites began to grow weary of the protracted struggle over racism. Other issues began competing with racial issues. The black urban rebellions had frightened many whites who then fled to the suburbs and turned their backs on the problems of the increasingly black central cities. A tendency emerged among many of these whites to blame increasing black poverty, crime, and violence on blacks themselves. This "blaming the victim"[56] syndrome provided an emotionally comforting escape for many whites who wanted to disassociate themselves from the historic burden of

53. Sitkoff, *Struggle* 32–33, 41–197.

54. Wilkinson, *From* Brown *to* Bakke 131–249; Gary Orfield, *Must We Bus? Segregated Schools and National Policy* passim.

55. Sitkoff, *Struggle* 220–23. Several studies on white racial attitudes and the "white backlash" are still a bit contradictory. See, Jaynes and Williams, *Common Destiny* 120–21.

56. William Ryan, *Blaming the Victim.*

racism.[57] Much like the historic pattern of white collective guilt over slavery among some planters—guilt that was dissipated by proslavery apologists who shifted the blame of slavery onto the slaves themselves—from the 1970s to the present time, many whites began assuming a form of collective denial of the legacy of racism. With the advent of affirmative-action policies and programs to address the lingering effects of institutionalized racism, these whites and their apologists have postulated a theory of reverse discrimination[58] that has gained credence in many respectable circles. It goes without saying that these developments do not bode well for racial unity.

Black Awareness, Urban Rebellions, Political Empowerment, and Separation

White resistance, compromise, and denial had a devastating effect on black people and greatly complicated efforts at achieving a racially integrated society. Many blacks resented white resistance to their legitimate claims for racial justice and equality. The protracted delays of the Supreme Court and the lack of support from many white leaders eroded the trust of young blacks who had been taught to believe in racial integration. These young blacks, especially black college students, began questioning the value of racial integration, shifting their attention to emerging black nationalistic movements that emphasized black cultural values and separation from whites. The icons of the Civil Rights Movement, such as Martin Luther King, James Farmer, Thurgood Marshall, and others who had fought racial segregation for decades, began losing their influence among these young black radicals. No longer were these young people interested in integrating into what they considered to be a corrupt white society. New cultural heroes began emerging—Malcolm X, Huey Newton, LeRoi Jones, Stokely Carmichael, and Rapp Brown, among others. These new heros did not share the values of the traditional civil-rights establishment. As the last days of the Civil Rights Movement began to fade in the rising heat of the anti-war movement and the white backlash of the late 1960s and early 1970s, blacks had already entered what historian Alton Hornsby characterized as "an age of disillusionment."[59] The sad irony of this "age of

---

57. Jaynes and Williams, *Common Destiny* 150; Norman C. Amaker, *Civil Rights and the Reagan Administration* 115–30; Nathan Glazer, *Affirmative Discrimination: Ethnic Inequality and Public Policy* 77–222; Nijole V. Benokraitis and Joe R. Feagin, *Affirmative Action and Equal Opportunity: Action, Inaction, Reaction* 171–86.

58. One widespread criticism of affirmative action is that it has resulted in "reverse-discrimination"—that is, in hiring and promoting women and minorities over presumably better qualified white males. See Benokraitis and Feagin, *Affirmative Action* 84.

59. Alton Hornsby, Jr., *The Black Almanac* 120–227; Benjamin Muse, *The American Negro Revolution: From Nonviolence to Black Power* 230–54, 299; Sitkoff, *Struggle* 167–97; Franklin and Moss, *From Slavery* 458–66.

disillusionment," the years between 1964 and 1973, was that 1964 witnessed not only the beginning of black urban rebellions but also the awarding of the Nobel Peace Prize to Martin Luther King, Jr., "the champion of non-violent resistance to racial oppression. . . ."[60]

Throughout the 1960s, black urban rebellions in the North and South shook the nation to its core. The Civil Rights Movement had no answers or solutions for this phase of the legacy of racism. While the movement itself had led the way in overcoming legal barriers to racial equality and had won impressive victories for blacks in integrating southern public schools and public accommodations and, most important, in securing passage of the 1965 Voting Rights Act that opened the way for the most significant political empowerment of southern blacks in history, it could not address the festering complex social and structural problems affecting the majority of poor and desperate blacks in the declining central cities of both the North and South. Historic racism combined with structural changes in the urban economy had created a desperate situation for these blacks, who were later to be characterized as the "underclass."[61]

As more and more whites fled to the suburbs and as more blacks began turning inward, replacing the Civil Rights Movement's ideology of integration with "black power," "black community control," and general black empowerment, less time and energy were spent worrying about racial integration. As blacks became majorities in major cities of the nation, they began electing black mayors and city councillors. In 1967, Richard G. Hatcher and Carl B. Stokes, of Gary, Indiana, and Cleveland, Ohio, respectively, became the first elected black mayors of major cities in the United States. But as before in this age of mixed blessings and tragic historical contradictions and gross ironies, this was also the year of the worst urban riot or rebellion in U.S. history, the Detroit riot.[62]

As more black mayors were elected by increasingly black majorities and with the help of some very dedicated whites, suburban whites became increasingly isolated from the black-controlled cities with their escalating problems of poverty, crime, and violence. Blacks conversely began thinking increasingly of suburban whites as the enemy who abandoned the city rather than live under black political power. No love was lost in many cities as these two polarized communities went their separate ways. Detroit is a good example of this racial polarization; as Detroit became blacker and poorer, white suburbanites regularly criticized the city, especially to new white arrivals. As one such "new white arrival," Robert McCabe, president of Detroit Renaissance, explained in 1985, "I'd find people who had their

---

60. Hornsby, *Black Almanac* 120.
61. For a working definition of the black underclass, see Wilson, *Truly* 6–9.
62. Jaynes and Williams, *Common Destiny* 69.

tremendous sense of pride that they haven't been in downtown Detroit in 15 years and don't intend to go."[63] Recognizing this historic pattern of white racism, many black city officials have long since given up on suburban whites as incorrigible racists and instead have concentrated on building and consolidating black political and economic power in the space that they control. With such conditions prevalent around the country, there seems little hope for bringing blacks and whites together. The tragedy is that both black-majority cities and white-majority suburbs do not and cannot long exist or develop to their fullest potential without regional equity and racial unity.

Contemporary Racial Problems

During the last decade or so, we have faced both new and old racial problems. White resistance to affirmative action has triggered black resentment. Conflicts between blacks and Jews (old and trusted allies during many battles against racism) have caused much bitterness and vitiated the very core of the traditional black–white alliance that produced the greatest progress in race relations in twentieth-century American history. Interracial violence in cities like Detroit and New York, between Middle-Eastern merchants and blacks, and Korean merchants and blacks, respectively, complicated the already protracted black–white racial conflicts. Racial conflicts on college campuses reflect the racial tensions in the larger society.[64] Countless people are searching for answers and solutions to America's most persistent social problem. Many have given up hope of ever finding answers or solutions, but there can be no lasting social peace or progress without social justice and racial unity and harmony. Here again, the tragedy is that far too many white– and black–Americans do not realize that there really is no choice: either they learn to live together for the benefit of the *entire* society, or they continue the protracted divisive struggle of racism and racial conflict with inevitably negative results.

---

63. *Detroit News*, January 8, 1985.

64. Jonathan Kaufman, *Broken Alliance: The Turbulent Times Between Blacks and Jews in America* passim; Lowell Cauffiel, "Conflict of Cultures: Blacks and Chaldeans," *The Detroit News*, April 14, 1983, 1a, 11a; Don Terry, "Diplomacy Fails to End Boycott of Korean's Store," *New York Times*, July 16, 1990, B1.

Part III

The Interracial Struggle for Racial Justice, Unity, and Fellowship

7

The Other Tradition in American Race Relations

I have a dream that one day on the red hills of Georgia, sons of former slaves and sons of former slave-owners will be able to sit down together . . . in Alabama, little black boys and black girls will be able to join hands with little white boys and white girls as sisters and brothers. I have a dream today! . . . With this faith we will be able to transform the jangling discords of our nation into a beautiful symphony of brotherhood.

With this faith we will be able to work together, to pray together, to struggle together, to go to jail together, to stand up for freedom together, knowing that we will be free one day.

—Martin Luther King, Jr.

Understanding the Other Tradition

The long and terrible overshadowing tradition of racism and racial conflict in the United States has prevented many concerned people from examining the other tradition of American race relations that has embodied the best of American thinking and vision concerning a multiracial society. While far from what we in the 1990s would call "progressive" race relations, this tradition not only challenged the more popular tradition of white racism during each stage of its development but also at the same time held before the eyes of the larger society the vision of a multiracial society based upon racial justice, unity, and cooperation. It did not emerge fully defined; rather, it stumbled along, sometimes losing its way, and always struggling to overcome the influences of the stronger tradition of racism. Yet, it is this other tradition that has paved the way to a greater vision of a society free of racism and full of human love and fellowship.

This positive tradition started in part with religious communities such as the Quakers in the eighteenth century and can be seen operating today among a wide range of interracial groups and organizations. Many of the contemporary organizations, movements, and religions have infused this tradition with their own individual "spirit" and philosophy, without which infusion this tradition would have long since died out. For example, while the Quakers most certainly ignited and sustained much of this tradition during the early years of slavery, other groups and organizations, such as the early biracial National Association for the Advancement of Colored People (NAACP) and the National Urban League (NUL), tapped into the tradition and carried it forward well into the twentieth century. The American Bahá'í community, whose central teachings emphasize racial unity, fellowship, and love, infused a powerful and longlasting spirit into this tradition that is still at work throughout the nation in hundreds of communities. And, of course, the Civil Rights Movement and the Reverend Dr. Martin Luther King, Jr.'s philosophy of love and fellowship opened up wider possibilities of multiracial unity and cooperation for an entire generation of blacks and whites.

Notwithstanding the periodic racial conflicts in our cities, on campuses, and elsewhere—incidences that receive most if not all of the media coverage—this other tradition has never ceased. Badly overshadowed by the more dramatic tradition of racism and racial conflict, this other tradition is slowly making itself felt in many areas of society, in music, art, politics, religion, education, friendship and family networks, and religious communities. It is this tradition that has the power truly to transform our society and to create lasting bonds of genuine love and fellowship among our racially and culturally diverse people.

Acknowledging this other tradition of race relations should not be seen as denying the still very serious racial problems that face the United States and the world. Rather, it should be seen as an exploration of those racial experiences in American history that can best teach us how to create racial unity based upon justice, love, and fellowship. We already know a lot about racism and racial conflicts. We know why many whites have traditionally hated and feared nonwhites. We know why, based on the tradition of white racism, many nonwhites dislike and mistrust whites. We also know the tremendous historical and social costs racism and racial conflicts have exacted from the larger society over the centuries. If we know anything about racism and racial conflict, it is this: social progress for the entire society has always been retarded when these two forces have held sway. Racism created the enslavement, segregation, and ghettoization of blacks as well as the conquest and demoralization of Native peoples; now, the present social and economic plight of these two groups has retarded both their and the larger society's social progress. Where racial justice, love, and fellowship have prevailed, all members of society have progressed. To be convinced, we have only to examine those situations in American history where these positive social factors have prevailed. Therefore, we explore and study the other more positive, uplifting tradition of American race relations to understand better what we need to do to create conditions conducive to racial justice, unity, and fellowship. This approach to American race relations has been inspired in part by the late psychologist Abraham Maslow, who transformed the field of psychology by his emphasis on studying "good people" instead of limiting himself to the Freudian model with its emphasis on studying "sick people."[1]

This other tradition will provide us with a knowledge base for building a "good" multiracial society. It embodies the greatest potential for understanding the historical relationship between racial justice, unity, love, and fellowship, on the one hand, and social progress on the other.

Seeds of the Tradition: Antislavery Advocates and the Growth and Development of Interracial Cooperation in the Struggle for Racial Justice

No other white religious or secular organization, institution, or group was as committed to ridding itself of slavery as were the early American Quakers. George Fox, the founder of the Society of Friends, known as the Quakers, wrote to Quaker missionaries in the New World concerning the issue of slavery. In 1657, he warned them against enslaving blacks and Indians. While not attacking slavery as such, he made it clear that all people were equal in the sight of God.[2] This would become the first step in a great tradition of American race relations. William Edmundson, an Irish Quaker, became the first Quaker during the American Colonial Period to attack slavery. Writing in 1675 to the Friends in several slaveholding colonies, Edmundson criticized the ownership of slaves among the Quakers. Before long the Quakers became the leading voice opposing slavery. Their best-known statement against slavery was produced in 1688 in Germantown and is known as "The Germantown Protest." This statement was drafted by Dutch-speaking Quakers who opposed slavery because of their own persecution in the sixteenth century. This statement did not appear in print until 1844.[3] From the Germantown Protest to the early nineteenth century, the Quakers stood virtually alone among American religious groups in circulating published criticisms of slavery.[4]

Colonial Quakers had such strong feelings against African slavery that by 1776 they had "effectively abolished it—among themselves."[5] Influenced in large part by John Woolman, who in 1743 "suddenly recognized his aversion to human slavery when he was asked to write a bill

---

1. Edward Hoffman, *The Right To Be Human: A Biography of Abraham Maslow* 150–75, passim.
2. Wood, *Arrogance* 277.
3. Wood, *Arrogance* 278.
4. Wood, *Arrogance* 278.
5. Jordan, *White Man's Burden* 114.

of sale for a Negro,"[6] these early Quakers became the first among white Americans who refused to compromise their spiritual principles to support and maintain the enslavement of black people. Woolman, however, went further than most Quakers, who as a group were morally far ahead of their white contemporaries. He deeply empathized with the plight of black slaves, an empathy that represented one of the first genuine examples of racial bonding with black humanity, so different from the apologetic racism of people like Thomas Jefferson. Woolman had this to say of black slavery:

> . . . let us calmly consider their Circumstance; and, the better to do it, make their Case ours. Suppose then, that our Ancestors and we had been exposed to constant Servitude, in the more servile and inferior Employments of Life . . . that while others, in Ease, have plentifully heaped up the Fruit of our Labour, we had receiv'd barely enough to relieve Nature, and being wholly at the Command of others, had generally been treated as a contemptible, ignorant Part of Mankind: Should we, in that Case, be less abject than they now are? [7]

Unlike those in the tradition of American racism, Woolman highlighted the "crushing effects of slavery upon the enslaved. . . ."[8] He could have stopped there, with empathy for the slaves, but he was moved to explore how whites first victimized and dehumanized blacks and then held in contempt what they themselves had created. Woolman recognized how slavery produced white racial attitudes and beliefs.[9]

Anthony Benezet, another Quaker and a close friend of Woolman, was "the most prolific of all Quaker antislavery writers. . . ."[10] More important, however, Benezet played a major role in expanding the concern for blacks beyond merely seeking justice for slaves to working on their behalf once they were freed. From 1750 to 1770, within his home, Benezet operated an evening school for black children. In June of 1758, he wrote a letter to John Smith criticizing the unfair treatment of the Minisink Indians at the hands of both Quakers and non-Quakers. As historian Forrest G. Wood said of Benezet, "To this Quaker, every human was a child of God."[11]

Quakers continued to play a key role in the struggle against slavery well into the middle of the nineteenth century. Levi Coffin, a Quaker, became one of the most effective white workers on the Underground Railroad, which depended heavily on interracial cooperation and trust.

6. Jordan, *White Man's Burden* 114.

7. Quoted in Jordan, *White Man's Burden* 114.

8. Jordan, *White Man's Burden* 114.

9. Jordan, *White Man's Burden* 115.

10. Wood, *Arrogance* 279.

11. Wood, *Arrogance* 279–80.

Located in southern Indiana, Coffin assisted more than three-thousand slaves to escape to the North.[12]

The Quakers were not perfect by any means. Their founder, George Fox, while cautioning Quakers about the effects of slavery, accepted Negro slavery as "an institution that could be rationalized by the ancient dualisms of body and soul," matter and spirit.[13] However, other Quakers more than compensated for the shortcomings of their coreligionists. Without their contribution, the tradition of interracial cooperation within the antislavery movement would have been much less successful.

Between the 1830s and the start of the Civil War, the antislavery movement provided the major impetus for interracial cooperation. Notwithstanding the ideological conflicts that sometimes emerged between white abolitionists and black abolitionists, the movement itself constituted the most advanced form of interracial cooperation up to that time in American history. Whites and blacks risked their lives assisting slaves to freedom. Whites who worked on the Underground Railroad had very little to gain, and their lives and property to lose. Blacks expanded whites' vision of what America could become when free of slavery and racism and infused with interracial vigor. Whites and blacks, men and women forged a new interracial identity as they worked both together and independently to end slavery. Whatever the shortcomings in their relationships at that stage of interracial cooperation, it was a small price to pay for the contribution of their joint efforts to move America a little closer to a multiracial society based on justice, love, and fellowship.[14]

During the Civil War, black soldiers and white officers in the Union Army found themselves involved in an interracial alliance that had the potential either to strengthen or weaken the tradition of interracial cooperation for racial justice. Many white officers held the same racist views of blacks as did the white southerners they were fighting, and their views of the purpose of the war were quite different from those of the black men under their command: whites were fighting to reunite the country, while blacks were fighting to end the enslavement of their people. While not always mutually exclusive, these two racial visions posed difficult problems for interracial cooperation. Yet, in the long run, due to shared dangers, daily interaction, and genuine mutual concerns, a significant degree of racial bonding occurred among the men. This bonding sensitized many white officers to the humanity of black people and provided blacks, many

---

12. Franklin and Moss, *From Slavery* 170–71; Larry Gara, *The Liberty Line: The Legend of the Underground Railroad* 94–95.

13. Quoted in Wood, *Arrogance* 77.

14. Vincent Harding, *There is a River: The Black Struggle for Freedom in America* 124–29; Benjamin Quarles, *Black Abolitionists* 49–50, 56, 235; Robert L. Allen, *Reluctant Reformers: Racism and Social Reform Movements in the United States* 31–49.

of whom had been slaves, with an opportunity to interact with some white officers who genuinely believed in racial justice and equality. This interracial cooperation (unfortunately forged on some of the bloodiest battlefields of the war) revealed both to the men and to the larger society an example of interracial cooperation unprecedented in American history.[15]

The Tradition and New Challenge during the Post-Slavery Period

The emancipation of southern black slaves in January of 1863 represented the finest fruit of the long tradition of struggle for racial justice. Not even the facts that the Emancipation Proclamation was in large part a war measure, was opposed in some powerful and influential circles both in the United States and abroad, and was originally linked to the idea of colonization of emancipated slaves beyond the limits of the United States could taint its historic meaning for those who had struggled for so long to end the enslavement of black people.[16] To many white abolitionists the end of slavery meant the end of the struggle for racial justice. Others, however, realizing that freeing slaves was only a first step in the long journey towards racial justice and unity, continued to expand the agenda of the racial justice tradition. They realized the Emancipation Proclamation did not grant blacks the rights and protections of citizens. Therefore, they began struggling for the passage of the Thirteenth Amendment, which outlawed slavery, and the Fourteenth and Fifteenth Amendments, which made blacks citizens and gave black males the right to vote. Not all white abolitionists agreed with this expanded agenda because it forced the question of the extent to which abolitionism advocated and supported full racial equality for the emancipated blacks. Those white abolitionists who had the larger vision and the longer view on the tradition of racial justice would not even stop with the passage of the three Amendments. They were among those hundreds of whites and blacks who went to the South to teach and provide economic assistance to the former slaves.[17]

By 1870 this tradition of struggle for racial justice and the fostering of interracial cooperation was beginning to wane among even its most ardent supporters. The Radical Republicans and former abolitionists felt they had done all they could for the cause by attaining the passage of the Fourteenth and Fifteenth Amendments. As far as they were concerned, they had paid their dues. The antislavery societies closed down and advised their members to continue the tradition of struggling for racial justice by working either as

---

15. Joseph T. Glatthaar, *Forged in Battle: The Civil War Alliance of Black Soldiers and White Officers* 99–169.

16. John Hope Franklin, *The Emancipation Proclamation* 68–69, 81, 129–30.

17. Allen, *Reluctant Reformers* 47.

individuals or with new organizations to eliminate racism in both the South and the North. Some began working on integrating schools, a struggle that would last almost a century in many areas of the country.[18] Less than a decade later, the country was back to business as usual, and the tradition of racial justice, unity, and cooperation was under siege. Various forms of interracial cooperation emerged between the end of Reconstruction and the first decade of the twentieth century. However, most of them tended either to have short lifespans or to use interracial cooperation as a means to maintain new forms of white racial dominance. For example, the southern Populist movement succeeded for a while in creating interracial unity and cooperation between black farmers and white farmers. Georgia Populist leader Tom Watson recognized how racism kept the black and the white farmers fighting each other while the ruling élite exploited them both. Writing in 1892, Watson explained the basis of this mutual oppression:

> You are kept apart that you may be separately fleeced of your earnings. You are made to hate each other because upon that hatred is rested the keystone of the arch of financial despotism which enslaves you both. You are deceived and blinded that you may not see how this race antagonism perpetuates a monetary system which beggars both.[19]

Watson was one of the first white leaders in the South to attempt to articulate a social philosophy of interracial cooperation and unity, but he based it on the most tenuous of bonds: self-interest. "Gratitude may fail; so may sympathy and friendship and generosity and patriotism; but in the long run, self-interest *always* controls."[20] Mutual racial self-interest, Watson believed, was the rock upon which interracial cooperation and unity could best be built and sustained:

> Let it once appear plainly that it is to the interest of a colored man to vote with the white man, and he will do it. Let it plainly appear that it is to the interest of the white man that the vote of the Negro should supplement his own, and the question of having that ballot freely cast and fairly counted, becomes vital to the *white man*.[21]

According to Watson, the People's Party (Populism's political arm) constituted the best instrument through which this interracial self-interest could express itself. But Watson, as Allen has pointed out so well, was only interested in interracial cooperation and unity as a means of "paternalistic

---

18. Allen, *Reluctant Reformers* 47.
19. Quoted in Norman Pollack, ed., *The Populist Mind* 371–72.
20. Quoted in Pollack, *Populist Mind* 369.
21. Quoted in Pollack, *Populist Mind* 369.

pragmatism." Since blacks were a significant portion of the southern population and could not be ignored, they had to be accommodated. White racial self-interest in such circumstances, therefore, dictated that blacks be included in the movement. While "White Southern Populists attacked certain racist practices detrimental to the growth of their political power, . . . they did not challenge the underlying ideology of white supremacy—and in the long run this was to prove their undoing."[22]

The southern Populist form of interracial cooperation and unity represented one of the weakest of all historical forms of such unity and cooperation. Had white Populists and black Populists been able to develop a deeper, stronger bond based on genuine concern for each other's common humanity, they might have sustained their unity. But partisan power politics determined the nature of interracial cooperation and unity during much of this period. By 1896 Populism had passed from the scene, and when Tom Watson reemerged in 1904, he was advocating the disfranchisement of southern blacks.[23]

For a while Tom Watson had tapped into the positive tradition of American race relations, that of interracial struggle for racial justice, even if wrapped in racial political expediency. Was not the Emancipation Proclamation such a racial political expediency as well, one that fortunately turned out well in the end? What is important is that at this stage of American race relations, after centuries of black slavery when many white Americans still found it difficult to conceive of a multiracial democracy or of sharing political power with ex-slaves—or blacks who had never been slaves for that matter—any formula of interracial cooperation and unity would do. Watson and the southern Populists tried to build a political movement upon a form of racial mutual self-interest. This effort failed because the tradition of white supremacy proved much stronger than the watered-down tradition of racial political expediency that Watson and the southern Populists attempted to substitute for the more spiritually powerful tradition of the interracial struggle for racial justice, unity, and fellowship.

Other white social movements also failed to develop genuine interracial cooperation and unity because of the tendency to compromise spiritual principles for short-term political, economic, and social gains for whites only. Two other examples from the nineteenth century should suffice to make this point. In the mid-1880s, from among the largest post-Civil War labor organizations, only the Knights of Labor showed genuine willingness to include black workers in their union. Black workers flocked to the Knights. In the South, there were both integrated and segregated Locals. During this period close to sixty-thousand blacks became members of the

22. Allen, *Reluctant Reformers* 53.
23. Allen, *Reluctant Reformers* 79.

Knights. The Knights of Labor's motto, "An injury to one is a concern to all," seemed for a short while to be the answer to both class and race oppression. Labor historian Philip S. Foner, commenting on Knights of Labor's commitment to racial justice and unity, said:

> At its height and at its best, the Knights had acted upon the words of Frederick Douglass in 1883: "The labor unions of the country should not throw away this colored element of strength. . . . It is a great mistake for any class of laborers to isolate itself and thus weaken the bond of brotherhood between those on whom the burden and hardships of labor fall."[24]

In 1886, a white member of the Knights of Labor wrote in his book entitled *The Great Labor Question, or The Noble Mission of the Knights of Labor*: "Perhaps one of the noblest acts of the Knights of Labor is that of rising above the prejudices of thousands and millions of people that were engendered against the negro race when they were in bondage."[25] "At its best" the Knights stood squarely in the heart of the best and highest tradition of American race relations and its "noblest act" of "rising above the prejudices" of millions of whites reflected the best of that "great tradition." But like the Populists, the Knights did not sufficiently inoculate themselves against the virus of racism. ". . . [T]he Knights contributed immensely toward a brief era of good feelings between black and white workingmen, even in the South." However, Foner continues, "From those heights the Knights of Labor steadily declined, year after year weakening the fraternal bonds it had built, until at the end it became an apologist for white supremacy."[26]

The tradition was powerful when grounded in the principles of true racial unity. However, racial compromise and expediency, elements of the tradition of racism, eroded these principles and in the long run retarded both the growth and development of racial justice, cooperation, unity, and fellowship as well as social progress for society at large. By compromising the full expression of the best tradition of American race relations, these organizations prevented the full flowering of human potential latent in the multiracial composition of American society.

The first decade of the twentieth century witnessed what one historian of the NAACP has called the "Reincarnation of the Abolitionists."[27] Called into action by the increasingly racist social and political climate, the NAACP formed in 1909 from the merger of two major groups: the all-black Niagara Movement led by William Edward Burghardt Du Bois, and a group of concerned whites led by Mary White Ovington, a young white

---

24. Foner, *Organized Labor* 63.
25. Quoted in Foner, *Organized Labor* 63.
26. Foner, *Organized Labor* 63.
27. B. Joyce Ross, *J.E. Spingarn and the Rise of the NAACP, 1911–1939* 16–19.

social worker. In 1909 both groups met in New York in a National Negro Conference. Within a year, they formed the NAACP, which was destined to become the oldest civil rights movement in the United States. A year later, another biracial organization, the National League on Urban Conditions among Negroes (Urban League) emerged, as part of the tradition of racial justice, cooperation, and unity. While the NAACP's role was limited to the struggle to secure civil and political rights for blacks, the Urban League's role was to focus on the economic uplifting of black workers in urban areas. In 1911, they arrived at a tacit agreement that each would work in its own area of concern.[28] Meanwhile, on an international scale, there was a growing interest in the topic of race.

The First Universal Races Congress, 1911, London
An Early Effort to Understand the Significance of Race in the Modern World

Long before the late Martin Luther King, Jr. spoke of eliminating "the last vestiges of racism" as the "moral imperative of our age," the great black American scholar W. E. B. Du Bois, writing in 1903, placed it on the social agenda of the twentieth century: "The problem of the twentieth century is the problem of the color-line,—the relation of the darker to the lighter races of men in Asia and Africa, in America and the islands of the sea."[29] Du Bois wrote these words from his office at Atlanta University where he was then a professor, already on his way to becoming one of America's greatest writers and scholars in the field of race relations. He would spend his entire life struggling against racism in America and abroad. When he died in the early 1960s, disillusioned and bitter in self-exile in Ghana, West Africa, racism, "the hound of hell," was still dogging the tracks of our civilization.

W. E. B. Du Bois's deep concern for racial justice for the darker peoples of the world led him and his NAACP co-worker Mary White Ovington to attend the Universal Races Congress held in 1911 in London, England. Franz Boas, the famous anthropologist, and Charles A. Eastman, an American Indian scholar, were among the other Americans who attended this historic international gathering. According to the organizers, the object of the Congress was "to discuss, in the light of science and the modern conscience, the general relations subsisting between the peoples of the West and those of the East, between so-called white and so-called coloured peoples, with a view to encouraging between them a fuller understanding, the most friendly feelings, and a heartier co-operation."[30] Thoughtful and

---

28. Langston Hughes, *Fight for Freedom: The Story of the NAACP* 17–21, 31, 186–87.

29. W. E. B. Du Bois, *The Souls of Black Folk* 13.

30. G. Spiller, ed., *Papers on Inter-Racial Problems: Communicated to the First Universal Races Congress Held at the University of London, July 26–29, 1911* v.

concerned men and women around the world had come to the conclusion that action must be taken to address the problems of race. European racial dominance over millions of nonwhite natives could lead only to racial hatred and conflict. Clearly, the world could not progress with millions of nonwhites oppressed in body and spirit by white governments that placed the social and economic progress of the white race above the rights and dignity of nonwhite races.

The First Universal Races Congress occurred during a decade characterized by what one scholar has described as "the proliferation of international conferences and agencies, and the intensification of movements for national dignity and independence—as revolutions from China to Mexico and the great 'dress rehearsal' in 1905 that shook the Czar's Empire."[31]

Racial developments of various historic import also marked this decade. Uprisings in Africa, notably on the French Ivory Coast and the one racial event that traumatized the white world and forced it to confront both its racial arrogance and its vulnerability—the Japanese defeat of Russia. A little over a decade earlier, blacks from various parts of the African Diaspora had met in London, convening the first Pan African Congress. Du Bois attended this Congress as its secretary.[32]

While race was the key concern of the Universal Races Congress, world peace also occupied a central place on the agenda. However, Gustav Spiller, one of the major organizers of the Congress and the spiritual leader of the London Ethical Culture Movement and author of several books on education and psychology, and Du Bois, then a leading expert on American race relations and social conditions among black Americans, were in the minority of those who linked race to peace.

In his paper "The Problem of Race Equality," Spiller argued that "if the brotherhood of man is to become a reality, as poets and prophets have fondly dreamed, and if the great nations of the world, irrespective of race, are to create a World Tribunal and a World Parliament, it is indispensable that the leading varieties of mankind shall be proved substantially equals."[33] In an unsigned commentary on the Congress published in *The Crisis* during the Fall of 1911, Du Bois painted a visionary picture of the potential of the Congress: "When fifty races look each other in the eye, face to face, there rises a new conception of humanity and its problems. . . . On the whole the view of the race problems of the world as revealed in the Congress was strongly reassuring; but the reason of this was clear. It was because the men themselves were there."[34]

31. Herbert Aptheker, introduction to G. Spiller, *Inter-Racial Problems* 5.
32. Aptheker in Spiller, *Inter-Racial Problems* 5.
33. In Spiller, *Inter-Racial Problems* 30.
34. "The Races Congress," *The Crisis* (September, 1911): 207, 209; quoted by Apetheker in Spiller, *Inter-Racial Problems* 5.

The presence of people from all racial backgrounds at the Congress impressed Du Bois, but more important was the presence of representatives from many of the oppressed racial groups speaking on behalf of their own people. "In their absence," Du Bois pointed out, "a terrible indictment against 'lazy' Negroes, 'dishonest' Chinese, and 'incompetent' Asiatics could have been framed; but in the face of gentlemen from various human races of all shades and cultures. . ." some white Americans and Europeans found the burden of affirming their racism a bit more difficult.[35]

Obviously pleased with the major thrust of the Congress and the racial climate at the social events where racial unity and fellowship prevailed, Du Bois commented, "It seems no exaggeration to say that a few world congresses like this would do more for the unity of mankind and reasonable sympathy between races, [and] . . . the stopping of war, slavery and oppression than any other single movement."[36]

The Bahá'í approach to the problems of race was one of several presented at the Congress. However, the Bahá'í view placed more emphasis on racial unity and harmony. Unable to attend himself, 'Abdu'l-Bahá (1844–1921), the son of Bahá'u'lláh (the prophet-founder of the Bahá'í Faith) and the appointed leader of that religion from 1892 to 1921, sent a message to the gathering in which he explained the importance and beauty of diversity in the human family. He asked the gathering to consider the varieties of flowers in a garden and how they "seem but to enhance the loveliness of each other," and "when differences of colour, ideas, and character are found in the human Kingdom, and come under the control of the power of Unity, they too show their essential beauty and perfection." 'Abdu'l-Bahá explained in his letter that rivalry among "the different races of mankind was first caused by the struggle for existence among the wild animals. This struggle is no longer necessary: nay, rather! interdependence and co-operation are seen to produce the highest welfare in nations. The struggle that now continues is caused by prejudice and bigotry."[37] According to 'Abdu'l-Bahá, there was only one way to address such problems:

> To-day nothing but the power of the Divine Word, which embraces the Reality of all things, can draw together the minds, hearts, and spirits of the world under the shadow of the heavenly Tree of Unity.
>
> The Light of the Word is now shining on all horizons. Races and nations, with their different creeds, are coming under the influence of the Word of Unity in love and in peace. . . .

35. "The Races Congress" 208.
36. "The Races Congress" 208.
37. Quoted in Spiller, *Inter-Racial Problems* 156.

The call to arbitration, to peace, to love, and to loyalty is the call of Baha'u'llah. His standard floats since fifty years, summoning all of whatever race and creed.[38]

"This Congress is one of the greatest of events," 'Abdu'l-Bahá proclaimed in his letter. "It will be for ever to the glory of England that it was established at her capital. It is easy to accept a truth; but it is difficult to be steadfast in it; for the tests are many and heavy."[39] Realizing how difficult it would be to carry out such a task, to go beyond the reading of scholarly papers and idealistic statements, of which the world had had its fill, 'Abdu'l-Bahá urged the Congress not to become just a "thing of words." "O ye people! cause this thing to be not a thing of words, but of deeds. Some Congresses are held only to increase differences. Let it not be so with you. Let your effort be to find harmony. Let Brotherhood be felt and seen among you; and carry ye its quickening power throughout the world. It is my prayer that the work of the Congress will bear great fruit."[40]

As the key organizer of this historic event, Gustav Spiller must have been optimistic about future congresses. He drafted and sent to delegates a printed memorandum marked confidential, in which he urged them "to consider the Congress as the springboard from which might eventuate a world-wide 'Association for the Promotion of Inter-Racial Concord'." He encouraged the delegates when they returned home to hold public meetings and to establish local branches of the proposed Association. Several months later, at least one such meeting was held in New York addressed by Felix Adler and W. E. B. Du Bois. But, as historian Herbert Aptheker said so well in his excellent commentary on this noble effort by Spiller, ". . . the realities of economics, of imperial conflicts, and of strategic considerations—on the whole conspicuously absent in the deliberations of the Congress—worked their inexorable way and 1914 marked not the holding of the Second Universal Races Congress, but rather the commencing of World War I!"[41]

Notwithstanding the tragic interruption of war, the prayers of 'Abdu'l-Bahá and the optimism of W. E. B. Du Bois were not in vain. As Aptheker expressed: "Nevertheless the First Universal Races Congress did represent some of the noblest ideals of Humanity; it did bring together men and women of all climes and all colors; it did project the vital vision of a world comity of Peoples and it did serve as educator and inspirer of thousands seeking a fraternal and creative and peaceful way of life."[42] In 1912,

---

38. Quoted in Spiller, *Inter-Racial Problems* 156.
39. Quoted in Spiller, *Inter-Racial Problems* 157.
40. Quoted in Spiller, *Inter-Racial Problems* 157.
41. Aptheker in Spiller, *Inter-Racial Problems* 14.
42. Aptheker in Spiller, *Inter-Racial Problems* 14–15.

'Abdu'l-Bahá visited North America where he gave many talks on the relationship between racial unity, love, and fellowship.[43] Du Bois never forgot this First Universal Races Congress. Fifty years later, he wrote about it in his autobiography: "It was a great and inspiring occasion bringing together representatives of numerous ethnic and cultural groups and bringing new and frank conceptions of scientific bases of racial and social relations of people."[44]

Against the backdrop of racism in America, the NAACP and NUL represented two of the best models of the tradition of racial justice, cooperation, unity, and fellowship. Free of the racial compromise and expediency of the Populists and Knights of Labor, the major goals of the NAACP and the NUL centered around the political, social, and economic advancement of black people. The goals and objectives of both organizations stimulated formal and informal interaction between blacks and whites. This contributed to building trust, fellowship, and lasting friendships among members. This is not to say that conflicts related to race, ideology, and tactics did not occur within these two pioneer biracial organizations. For example, the resignation of W. E. B. Du Bois in 1934 and the subsequent conflicts between young black radicals and older white liberals over tactics caused much concern but did not destroy future interracial cooperation within the organization. During the Civil Rights Era, NAACP units "formed interracial picket lines of both young and old,"[45] and both black- and white-NAACP lawyers worked together to secure racial justice. Out of this devotion to racial justice emerged genuine bonds of friendship and love that demonstrated to a skeptical world the power of a tradition devoted to racial justice, unity, cooperation, and fellowship. However, the bonds were constantly being tested by both internal and external social forces. In the summer of 1964 long-time NAACP lawyer Jack Greenberg and some blacks in Mississippi clashed over his role as a white in the Civil Rights Movement. According to Kaufman, during the 1970s some black lawyers resented Greenberg's role as head of the NAACP Legal Defense Fund.[46]

While the NAACP presented a model of interracial cooperation and unity in the struggle for racial justice for blacks, their work was complemented by the National Urban League, which represented a model of interracial cooperation for the economic uplifting of blacks in urban communities. Inspired by the spirit of the progressive movement, black and

---

43. Allan L. Ward, *239 Days: 'Abdu'l-Bahá's Journey in America* 40; 'Abdu'l-Bahá, *The Promulgation of Universal Peace*.

44. W. E. B. Du Bois, *The Autobiography of W. E. B. Du Bois* 263.

45. Hughes, *Fight for Freedom* 187.

46. Hughes, *Fight for Freedom* 122–23; Ross, *J.E. Spingarn* 186–245; Kaufman, *Broken Alliance* 109.

white social reformers struggled separately and jointly to help southern black migrants survive in the industrial North. But not until the founding of the NUL in New York in 1911, through the merger of three other related organizations—the Committee on Urban Conditions among Negroes in New York, the National League for the Protection of Colored Women, and the Committee for Improving Industrial Conditions among Negroes—did a really effective national program dedicated to black urban survival emerge.[47] While the NUL failed to solve many of the major problems plaguing black urban America, it did provide a safety net without which many black workers and their families would not have survived. Much like the NAACP, it brought together dedicated social reformers and professionals to address the problems of urban blacks. The NUL embodied many of the tradition's best aspects of interracial cooperation, as it gradually developed a nationwide network of blacks and whites from which it could tap resources to solve black urban problems. This network included capitalist–philanthropists such as Julius Rosenwald; John D. Rockefeller, Jr.; Ruth Standish Baldwin; Alfred T. White; and a generation of very bright and professionally trained black social workers.[48] As in most other evolving biracial organizations during this period, interracial cooperation and unity often became tied to larger social and economic agendas of the more powerful white players. Two scholars writing in the 1930s understood this relationship when they wrote: "Many of the largest industrial concerns came to regard the local league as a useful agency for procuring labor and as a conservative stabilizing force in the colored community, and contributed substantially to its support."[49] However often these kinds of obviously exploitative elements might have crept into the work of the NUL with powerful economic forces, they did not alter the essential purpose and objectives of generations of black and white social workers who carried on the tradition of interracial cooperation and unity in their work.[50]

Throughout the 1930s, several reform and labor movements preached interracial solidarity. Socialists, Communists, and the Congress of Industrial Organizations (CIO) began working in various ways and (for as many reasons and motives) for interracial unity. The labor movement, of which the CIO was the most progressive on racial issues, had come to realize the power of racial cooperation and unity. Unfortunately, they had not learned very much since the days of the Knights of Labor: their interest in unity between blacks and whites was largely limited to class issues. Blacks were

---

47. Nancy J. Weiss, *The National Urban League: 1910–1940* 41–46.

48. Weiss, *National Urban League* 41–46; L. Hollingsworth Wood, "The Urban League Movement," *The Journal of Negro History* 9.1 (January, 1924): 119–20.

49. Sterling D. Spero and Abram L. Harris, *The Black Worker* 141.

50. Several good local examples of this long tradition of interracial cooperation can still be seen in such local Urban League branches as Lansing and Detroit in Michigan.

seen as essential to the unionization of the mass-production, industrial plants. But the vast majority of white workers were not interested in racial unity beyond the shop floor. However, in fairness to the CIO, many of its international unions, such as the United Auto Workers, made major contributions to the long struggle for racial justice, cooperation, and unity. Not unlike other biracial organizations of the twentieth century, they built long-term bonds and alliances that greatly expanded and strengthened the tradition of racial unity and cooperation.[51]

During the next several decades, the tradition of racial justice, cooperation, unity, and fellowship clashed on many fronts with the tradition of racial hatred, conflict, and polarization. From the 1940s to the late 1960s, the latter tradition fought the former tradition in every area of social, political, and economic life. It was a war for the heart and soul of America. At the height of the Civil Rights Movement, blacks and whites reached one of the highest stages of interracial cooperation, unity, and spiritual fellowship ever achieved in the history of American race relations. But under the stress, conflicts, and confusion of the time, it all came apart, evaporated in pain and anguish and distrust. What was once called the "beloved community" faded away as many blacks and whites went their separate ways, concerned only with their separate agendas. Once again, something basic was missing: a spiritual force strong enough to sustain the long and difficult process of building genuine interracial fellowship. At the present time, there are still organizations and groups working for racial justice, cooperation, unity, and fellowship, but there are few interracial communities that have been established for the sole purpose of the unification of the human race and that see racial justice, cooperation, unity, and fellowship as essential elements of this process.

---

51. Sumner M. Rosen, "The CIO Era, 1935–55," in Jacobson, *The Negro* 188–208.

8

Towards a Model of Racial Unity
A Case Study of
Bahá'í Teachings and Community Practices

My hope is that the white and the black will be united in perfect love and fellowship, with complete unity and brotherhood. Associate with each other, think of each other, and be like a rose garden. Anyone who goes into a rose garden will see various roses, white, pink, yellow, red, all growing together and replete with adornment. Each one accentuates the beauty of the other. . . .

I hope you will continue in unity and fellowship. How beautiful to see blacks and whites together! I hope, God willing, the day may come when I shall see the red men, the Indians, with you, also Japanese and others. Then there will be white roses, yellow roses, red roses, and a very wonderful rose garden will appear in the world.
—'Abdu'l-Bahá, *Promulgation of Universal Peace*

One other pattern deserves mention. Though the process of achieving racial harmony involves all the races in the human family, it is to the unity of black and white that American Baháʾís are asked to give special attention. The legacy of distrust between these two races casts a shadow that only the light of unity can dispel. Consequently, the power of unity between black and white serves to draw all the other racial and cultural minorities into its embrace. We cannot afford to ignore the special blessings that come from fostering the unity of black and white.
—National Race Unity Committee,
Baháʾís of the United States, *The Power of Unity*

As we have seen, the history of the interracial struggle for racial justice, unity, and cooperation in the United States has experienced both great advances and equally great setbacks. Somehow even the most ardent and ambitious movements for racial justice have tended to burn out, to regress into racism and compromise, or to abandon outright the vision of a just, loving multiracial society. As a result, they have tended to turn inward to concentrate on more "practical" social programs. Not even veteran civil-rights organizations such as the NAACP and the Congress on Racial Equality (CORE) have been spared the grinding and demoralizing effects of the protracted interracial struggle to achieve a multiracial society based upon justice, love, trust, and cooperation. Given the long and noble tradition of the interracial struggle to achieve a just and loving society, what went wrong? Has racism been so virulent that it has poisoned the entire body politic and spiritual core of present-day American society? Is it possible that racism and racial conflicts are social maladies we will just have to learn to live with, or just "manage"?

There are some very basic historical reasons why the various movements, organizations, and individuals that have contributed so much to the tradition of racial justice, unity, and cooperation have not been able to effect a longer lasting, positive transformation of American race relations. One reason is the historically persistent and adaptive nature of racism among many Americans and their inability or unwillingness to see such racism as a chronic social, psychological, and spiritual illness that retards their own healthy growth and development as well as that of racial minorities and the larger society. In addition, the deep-seated mistrust, suspicion, and bitterness among black Americans that flow from the history of racism will have to be eliminated. Another reason is the repeated failure and unwillingness of many well-meaning individuals, organizations, and movements within the noble tradition of the interracial struggle for racial justice, unity, cooperation, and fellowship, to explore the vast potential of spiritual approaches to the problem. As a result, those persons, groups, and organizations that have contributed so much to the tradition have been unable to infuse in the tradition the necessary spirit and vision to effect a lasting transformation in racial attitudes and behavior. The erratic advances and reverses in the history of American race relations are due in large part to this lack of a unifying spirit and vision of racial love and fellowship that can bond people and set their hearts and souls on fire to create a truly harmonious multiracial community.

The Bahá'í Teachings on Racial Unity: A Significant New Approach to American Race Relations

Long-term racial transformation can only occur within a community dedicated to interracial love, fellowship, and unity. Nothing less will suffice. A community of loving, caring, nurturing human beings will not only be able to address the issue of racial justice but will also move far beyond that stage to more transcendent stages of interracial love, unity, and fellowship. Such an interracial community would create a synergistic interracial force that would in turn not only transform race relations but also transform countless other social relationships in the United States. The entire social and economic order of the United States would be transformed if blacks and whites became spiritually unified. In addition, this spiritual unity would contribute to the spiritual unification of the entire planet. As 'Abdu'l-Bahá (1844–1921), the son of the founder of the Bahá'í Faith and its head from 1892–1921, explained during his visit to the United States in 1912, "When the racial elements of the American nation unite in actual fellowship and accord, the lights of the oneness of humanity will shine, the day of eternal glory and bliss will dawn, the spirit of God encompass, and the divine favors descend."[1]

The Bahá'í teachings on racial unity emanate from the wealth of teachings by Bahá'u'lláh (1817–92), the prophet-founder of the Bahá'í Faith, on the unity of the human race. The principle of unity stands at the very heart of Bahá'u'lláh's revelation and Bahá'í community life:

Ye are all the leaves of one tree and the drops of one ocean.[2]

O CHILDREN OF MEN! Know ye not why We created you all from the same dust? That no one should exalt himself over the other. Ponder at all times in your hearts how ye were created. Since We have created you all from one same substance it is incumbent on you to be even as one soul, to walk with the same feet, eat with the same mouth and dwell in the same land, that from your inmost being, by your deeds and actions, the signs of oneness and the essence of detachment may be made manifest. Such is My counsel to you, O concourse of light! Heed ye this counsel that ye may obtain the fruit of holiness from the tree of wondrous glory.[3]

He Who is your Lord, the All-Merciful, cherisheth in His heart the desire of beholding the entire human race as one soul and one body.[4]

'Abdu'l-Bahá explained the meaning of unity in these words:

What is real unity? When we observe the human world, we find various collective expressions of unity therein. For instance, man is distinguished from the animal by his degree, or kingdom. This comprehensive distinction includes all the posterity of Adam and constitutes one great household or human family, which may be considered the fundamental or physical unity of mankind.

1. 'Abdu'l-Bahá, *Promulgation of Universal Peace* 57.
2. Bahá'u'lláh, *Tablets of Bahá'u'lláh Revealed after the Kitáb-i-Aqdas* 129.
3. Bahá'u'lláh, *The Hidden Words of Bahá'u'lláh* 20.
4. Bahá'u'lláh, *Gleanings from the Writings of Bahá'u'lláh* 214.

Furthermore, a distinction exists between various groups of humankind according to lineage, each group forming a racial unity separate from the others. There is also the unity of tongue among those who use the same language as a means of communication; national unity where various peoples live under one form of government such as French, German, British, etc.; and political unity, which conserves the civil rights of parties or factions of the same government. All these unities are imaginary and without real foundation, for no real result proceeds from them. The purpose of true unity is real and divine outcomes. From these limited unities mentioned only limited outcomes proceed, whereas unlimited unity produces unlimited result. For instance, from the limited unity of race or nationality the results at most are limited. It is like a family living alone and solitary; there are no unlimited or universal outcomes from it.

The unity which is productive of unlimited results is first a unity of mankind which recognizes that all are sheltered beneath the overshadowing glory of the All-Glorious, that all are servants of one God; for all breathe the same atmosphere, live upon the same earth, move beneath the same heavens, receive effulgence from the same sun and are under the protection of one God. This is the most great unity, and its results are lasting if humanity adheres to it; but mankind has hitherto violated it, adhering to sectarian or other limited unities such as racial, patriotic or unity of self-interests; therefore, no great results have been forthcoming. Nevertheless, it is certain that the radiance and favors of God are encompassing, minds have developed, perceptions have become acute, sciences and arts are widespread, and capacity exists for the proclamation and promulgation of the real and ultimate unity of mankind, which will bring forth marvelous results. It will reconcile all religions, make warring nations loving, cause hostile kings to become friendly and bring peace and happiness to the human world. It will cement together the Orient and Occident, remove forever the foundations of war and upraise the ensign of the Most Great Peace.[5]

The lack of this "most great unity" has prevented the world from solving many of its most intractable problems. Along with the need for unity among all the peoples of the world is the need for true love among human beings. "The disease which afflicts the body politic is lack of love and absence of altruism," 'Abdu'l-Bahá explained. "In the hearts of men no real love is found, and the condition is such that, unless their susceptibilities are quickened by some power so that unity, love and accord may develop within them, there can be no healing, no agreement among mankind." It is clear, then, according to 'Abdu'l-Bahá, that "love and unity are the needs of the body politic today. Without these there can be no progress or prosperity attained. Therefore, the friends of God must adhere to the power which will create this love and unity in the hearts of the sons of men."[6]

It is difficult for even the most secure and well-meaning social reformers and the average concerned citizen to grasp this simple truth: love,

---

5. *Promulgation* 190–91.
6. *Promulgation* 171.

fellowship, and unity are inseparable from the social advancement of the entire human race. "It is certain that the greatest of instrumentalities for achieving the advancement and the glory of man, the supreme agency for the enlightenment and the redemption of the world," 'Abdu'l-Bahá counselled, "is love and fellowship and unity among all the members of the human race. Nothing can be effected in the world, not even conceivably, without unity and agreement, and the perfect means for engendering fellowship and union is true religion."[7]

In this very secular world with its overreliance on science, politics, war, and revolution as key instrumentalities of social change, this emphasis on "true religion" as "the perfect means for engendering fellowship and union" is often summarily dismissed as too simpleminded and naïve. But few can deny at this stage of human history that the world is undergoing a process of fragmentation on every level of social, political, and economic life, or that even the present hopeful signs of world unification cannot be sustained without some unifying force capable of not only overcoming the countless divisions among humankind but also elevating it to higher levels of unity and cooperation. "Naught but the celestial potency of the Word of God, which ruleth and transcendeth the realities of all things, is capable of harmonizing the divergent thoughts, sentiments, ideas, and convictions of the children of men," 'Abdu'l-Bahá explained, "Verily, it is the penetrating power in all things, the mover of souls and the binder and regulator in the world of humanity."[8]

This spiritual power spoken of in the Bahá'í writings is none other than that "force" spoken of in all the great spiritual traditions of the world. We have seen it operating throughout the history of humankind, called different names by different religions. The world has seen and felt the influence of this "penetrating power" that has moved souls and bonded divergent peoples and nations. However much some arrogant secular minds might want to deny it, this powerful spiritual force has influenced the history of humankind in ways that we have only just begun to understand. All the great prophets spoke of this force, and all the great spiritual movements testified to the elevating power of this penetrating force. As in other religious traditions, the Bahá'í Faith describes this spiritual force as the "Holy Spirit," and Bahá'ís believe that this is "the penetrating power" which is capable of creating love and fellowship among all the members of the human race. 'Abdu'l-Bahá has said:

> Bahá'u'lláh teaches that the world of humanity is in need of the breath of the Holy Spirit, for in spiritual quickening and enlightenment true oneness is attained with God and man. The Most Great Peace cannot be assured through

---

7. 'Abdu'l-Bahá, *The Secret of Divine Civilization* 73.
8. 'Abdu'l-Bahá, *Selections from the Writings of 'Abdu'l-Bahá* 292.

racial force and effort; it cannot be established by patriotic devotion and sacrifice; for nations differ widely and local patriotism has limitations. Furthermore, it is evident that political power and diplomatic ability are not conducive to universal agreement, for the interests of governments are varied and selfish; nor will international harmony and reconciliation be an outcome of human opinions concentrated upon it, for opinions are faulty and intrinsically diverse. Universal peace is an impossibility through human and material agencies; it must be through spiritual power. There is need of a universal impelling force which will establish the oneness of humanity and destroy the foundations of war and strife. None other than the divine power can do this; therefore, it will be accomplished through the breath of the Holy Spirit.[9]

According to the Bahá'í writings, ". . . the Holy Spirit is like unto the life in the human body, which blends all differences of parts and members in unity and agreement" and "establishes such a unity in the bodily organism that if any part is subjected to injury or becomes diseased, all the other parts and functions sympathetically respond and suffer, owing to the perfect oneness existing."[10]

One can hardly imagine the power of such a degree of sympathy among all the members of the human race to contribute to the social and economic well-being of the human family. Such a power would be capable of releasing vast stores of creative energy into every area of human life, healing and elevating the entire human race. It could do all this simply by the process of spiritual unity. "Just as the human spirit of life is the cause of coordination among the various parts of the human organism, the Holy Spirit is the controlling cause of the unity and coordination of mankind." Elaborating further, 'Abdu'l-Bahá comments, "That is to say, the bond or oneness of humanity cannot be effectively established save through the power of the Holy Spirit, for the world of humanity is a composite body, and the Holy Spirit is the animating principle of its life."[11]

Bahá'ís firmly believe in the spiritual power of the Holy Spirit to unite all people in love and fellowship. According to their Writings, ". . . the foundation of real brotherhood . . . the source of real kindness and unselfish devotion is none other than the breaths of the Holy Spirit." No other influences, according to the Bahá'í writings, are capable of such a difficult task. "Without this influence and animus it [real brotherhood] is impossible. We may be able to realize some degrees of fraternity through other motives," 'Abdu'l-Bahá stated, "but these are limited associations and subject to change. When human brotherhood is founded upon the Holy Spirit, it is eternal, changeless, unlimited."[12]

---

9. *Promulgation* 108–9.
10. *Promulgation* 321.
11. *Promulgation* 321.
12. *Promulgation* 392.

In 1936, almost a hundred years after the founding of the worldwide Bahá'í Faith, Shoghi Effendi (1897–1957), the appointed Guardian of the Faith from 1921–1957, described how a "universal" and "transcending love" among Bahá'ís of diverse backgrounds had "burned away their prejudices" and "made them lovers of mankind." Clearly the Bahá'í belief in the transforming power of the Holy Spirit was at work within their community:

> The Faith of Bahá'u'lláh has assimilated, by virtue of its creative, its regulative and ennobling energies, the varied races, nationalities, creeds and classes that have sought its shadow, and have pledged unswerving fealty to its cause. It has changed the hearts of its adherents, burned away their prejudices, stilled their passions, exalted their conceptions, ennobled their motives, coördinated their efforts, and transformed their outlook. While preserving their patriotism and safeguarding their lesser loyalties, it has made them lovers of mankind, and the determined upholders of its best and truest interests. . . . This universal, this transcending love which the followers of the Bahá'í Faith feel for their fellow-men, of whatever race, creed, class or nation, is neither mysterious nor can it be said to have been artificially stimulated. It is both spontaneous and genuine. They whose hearts are warmed by the energizing influence of God's creative love cherish His creatures for His sake, and recognize in every human face a sign of His reflected glory.[13]

Bahá'ís throughout the world are involved in building an international community of diverse peoples, many from previously mutually antagonistic backgrounds. Once these people become Bahá'ís, they are encouraged to accept all peoples regardless of race, class, or religious differences. So unlike the traditional religious and secular organizations, the Bahá'í teachings do not compromise on the principle of love, unity, and fellowship among its diverse members. At a time when most of the world frowned upon marriage across racial, religious, and cultural boundaries, the Bahá'í teachings encouraged it as one of the highest expressions of unity and love among diverse peoples. 'Abdu'l-Bahá warmly encouraged interracial marriage: "In marriage the more distant the blood-relationship the better, for such distance in family ties between husband and wife provides the basis for the well-being of humanity and is conducive to fellowship among mankind."[14]

In a world religion as diverse as the Bahá'í Faith, Bahá'ís from varied cultural, religious, and racial backgrounds needed constant encouragement to understand and appreciate the social ramifications of the spiritual teachings of their Faith. Since the Bahá'í teachings embraced intermarriage, rejected by some traditional religions of which they had once been members, many Bahá'ís needed guidance and encouragement on how best

---

13. Shoghi Effendi, *The World Order of Bahá'u'lláh* 197–98.
14. 'Abdu'l-Bahá quoted in Bonnie Taylor, ed., *The Power of Unity: Beyond Prejudice and Racism* 55.

to apply the Bahá'í teachings on unity to the traditional problems of intermarriage. Addressing the matter of intermarriage between Zoroastrian and Hindu Bahá'ís, Shoghi Effendi gave this advice:

> Also with regard to the problem of inter-marriage between the Zoroastrian and Hindu Baha'is, this is a highly delicate and vital question, as important as the problem of the black and white in America. The friends should all realize that racial considerations do not, in the light of the Baha'i Teachings, constitute any hindrance to any kind of intercourse between the believers. The Hindu and Zoroastrian Baha'is should forget their former and traditional prejudices whether religious, racial or social, and commune together on a common basis of equality, love and devotion to the Cause. While the goal is quite clear yet, wisdom and caution are needed in order to carry this ideal into full practice.[15]

'Abdu'l-Bahá had already demonstrated the Bahá'í teachings reflecting this "ideal" when in 1912 he united a black man and a white woman in marriage and praised their union as a means for promoting "love and affection between the black and the white":

> O ye two who have believed in Him!
> . . . I pray God that ye may at all times be in the utmost love and harmony, and be a cause for the spirituality of the human world. This union will unquestionably promote love and affection between the black and the white, and will affect and encourage others. These two races will unite and merge together, and there will appear and take root a new generation sound in health and beauteous in countenance.[16]

In a letter written on his behalf in 1957 to the American Bahá'í Interracial Teaching Committee, Shoghi Effendi told them, "The Bahá'ís should welcome the negroes to their homes, make every effort to teach them, associate with them, even marry them if they want to." He then reminded them of 'Abdu'l-Bahá's encouragement of interracial marriage. "We must remember that 'Abdu'l-Bahá Himself united in Bahá'í marriage a colored and a white believer. He could not do more."[17]

The Bahá'í teachings on racial justice, unity, fellowship, and love have provided the American Bahá'í community with priceless encouragement and guidance throughout its history. No other religious community in American history can lay claim to such a rich tradition of explicit teachings on how to create and maintain a multiracial fellowship. At a time when most Christian denominations were either silent or apologetic about their

---

15. Quoted in *Dawn of a New Day: Messages to India 1923–1957* 198.
16. 'Abdu'l-Bahá quoted in Taylor, *Power of Unity* 55.
17. Quoted in Gayle Morrison, *To Move the World: Louis G. Gregory and the Advancement of Racial Unity in America* 294.

segregationist practices—practices that still prevail today among the vast majority of American Christians—the American Bahá'í community was being encouraged and guided by the Bahá'í teachings on racial unity. Without such explicit and emphatic guidance on racial unity provided by the central figures of the Bahá'í Faith and later by the appointed Guardian and still later by the world-governing body of the Bahá'í Faith, the Universal House of Justice, the American Bahá'í community would have gone the way of the American churches, which compromised on racial justice, fellowship, and unity to the point where they have currently become the tragic example of one of the most racially segregated institutions in present-day America. Specific Bahá'í teachings and instructions on racial issues saved the American Bahá'í community from the historic fate of the American Christian community.

We have already discussed the Bahá'í teachings on the unity of the human race, the core belief of the Bahá'í Faith, and noted how Bahá'ís believe that such unity can only come about through the instrumentality of some spiritual force, such as "the Holy Spirit." Furthermore, we have seen how such a belief in the organic unity of the human race accepts and encourages intermarriage among all peoples. Yet, such beliefs have not proceeded without challenges and resistance within the Bahá'í community, particularly within the American Bahá'í community during its long struggle to overcome the influence of racism and racial conflicts among its members. This resistance was overcome due to the clear and emphatic teachings and guidance on race relations provided by the Bahá'í writings.

The most important among the Bahá'í teachings on race have dealt with black–white relations in America. "Intense is the hatred, in America, between black and white, but my hope is that the power of the Kingdom will bind these two in friendship, and serve them as a healing balm." 'Abdu'l-Bahá said, "Let them look not upon a man's colour but upon his heart. If the heart be filled with light, that man is nigh unto the threshold of His Lord; but if not, that man is careless of His Lord, be he white or be he black."[18]

Many people of both races simply did not believe that blacks and whites could ever become united. But American Bahá'ís were expected to trust in the power of the Holy Spirit. "To bring the white and the black together is considered impossible and unfeasible, but the breaths of the Holy Spirit will bring about this union." Bahá'ís were expected to trust in this spiritual force working through the Holy Spirit to create harmony between black and white: ". . . the enmity and hatred which exist between the white and the black races is very dangerous and there is no doubt that it will end in bloodshed unless the influence of the Word of God, the breaths of the Holy Spirit and the teachings of Bahá'u'lláh are diffused amongst them and harmony is established between

---

18. 'Abdu'l-Bahá, *Selections* 113.

the two races." According to 'Abdu'l-Bahá, "They must destroy the foundation of enmity and rancor and lay the basis of love and affinity. The power of the Teachings of Bahá'u'lláh will remove this danger from America."[19]

Modeling the Bahá'í Teachings on Racial Unity, Love, and Fellowship: 'Abdu'l-Bahá's Influence on the History of Black–White Relations in the United States

The early American Bahá'í community was mainly composed of white Americans who were just beginning to understand the tremendous social and historical significance of the Bahá'í teachings on racial unity. It would take them many decades to understand fully and to apply these teachings to their community life. Fortunately for the American Bahá'í community and American race relations, 'Abdu'l-Bahá visited North America in 1912 and both lectured on and demonstrated the Bahá'í teachings on racial unity and love. His contribution to the betterment of race relations has yet to be properly placed in the annals of American race relations scholarship, but any objective scholar of American race relations studying the period between 1912–1921 would have to take into account the role played by 'Abdu'l-Bahá in affecting the direction of American race relations.

There are several major areas in which 'Abdu'l-Bahá left his mark on American race relations during this period: He infused contemporary discussions on American race relations with the Bahá'í teachings on racial unity, love, and fellowship and thus elevated that discussion to the highest intellectual and spiritual plane in its history. He gave Americans, Bahá'ís and non-Bahá'ís alike, a new spiritual language and racial images with which they could visualize the highest expressions of racial unity. 'Abdu'l-Bahá then modeled the Bahá'í teachings on racial unity, love, and fellowship in such dramatic and loving ways as to leave an indelible imprint on the minds and spirits of those who heard him. After he returned home to what was then Palestine, he encouraged a white American Bahá'í woman to organize a race amity conference that started a Bahá'í tradition still carried on today and is the American Bahá'í community's undisputed contribution to the best tradition of American race relations.

As already mentioned, 'Abdu'l-Bahá had sent a message to the 1911 Universal Races Congress in London in which he explained the importance of the diversity of the human family and compared humankind to a flower garden adorned with different colors and shapes that "enhance the loveliness of each other." The next year, in 1912, 'Abdu'l-Bahá spoke at Howard University, the premier black university in Washington, D.C. According to one of his companions who kept diaries of 'Abdu'l-Bahá's Western tours and

---

19. 'Abdu'l-Bahá quoted in *Power of Unity* 31.

lectures, wherever 'Abdu'l-Bahá witnessed racial diversity, he was compelled to call attention to it. During 'Abdu'l-Bahá's talk at Howard University in April of 1912, this companion reported: ". . . here, as elsewhere, when both white and colored people were present, Abdul Baha seemed happiest."[20]

As he looked over the racially mixed audience at Howard, 'Abdu'l-Bahá remarked: "Today I am most happy, for I see here a gathering of the servants of God. I see white and black sitting together."[21] After two talks the very next day, 'Abdu'l-Bahá was visibly tired as he prepared for the third talk. He was not planning to talk long. But here again, when he saw blacks and whites in the audience, he became inspired.[22] "A meeting such as this seems like a beautiful cluster of precious jewels—pearls, rubies, diamonds, sapphires. It is a source of joy and delight." 'Abdu'l-Bahá then went on to elaborate on the theme of racial unity to an audience that probably had never heard such high praise for a gathering that many white Americans would have frowned upon and just as many black Americans would have avoided. "Whatever is conducive to the unity of the world of mankind is most acceptable and praiseworthy. . . . Therefore, in the world of humanity it is wise and seemly that all the individual members should manifest unity and affinity." Returning once again to his constant use of positive racial images woven into the new language of racial unity and fellowship, he painted a picture for his audience: "In the clustered jewels of the races may the blacks be as sapphires and rubies and the whites as diamonds and pearls. The composite beauty of humanity will be witnessed in their unity and blending."[23] To still another racially mixed audience, 'Abdu'l-Bahá commented: "As I stand here tonight and look upon this assembly, I am reminded curiously of a beautiful bouquet of violets gathered together in varying colors, dark and light."[24]

Realizing the depth of American racism from both his conversations and correspondences with black and white American Bahá'ís years before he visited the United States. 'Abdu'l-Bahá did not miss any opportunity to demonstrate to all Americans, black and white, high and low, young and old, the Bahá'í approach to the racial problems in the United States.[25] While visiting the Bowery Mission area in New York, some poor boys visited 'Abdu'l-Bahá in his room. As the boys filed into the room 'Abdu'l-Bahá greeted each one. The last boy to enter the room was a very dark African–American. Because he was the only black boy in the group he

20. Maḥmúd quoted in Allan L.Ward, *239 Days: 'Abdu'l-Bahá's Journey in America* 40.
21. 'Abdu'l-Bahá, *Promulgation* 44.
22. H. M. Balyuzi, *'Abdu'l-Bahá: The Center of the Covenant of Bahá'u'lláh* 181–82.
23. 'Abdu'l-Bahá, *Promulgation* 56–57.
24. 'Abdu'l-Bahá, *Promulgation* 49.
25. *Cf.* Shoghi Effendi's letters in *Power of Unity*.

probably felt that 'Abdu'l-Bahá and his host would not accept him. But as an observer reported:

> When 'Abdu'l-Bahá saw him His face lighted up with a heavenly smile. He raised His hand with a gesture of princely welcome and exclaimed in a loud voice so that none could fail to hear; that here was a black rose.
> The room fell into instant silence. The black face became illumined with a happiness and love hardly of this world. The other boys looked at him with new eyes. I venture to say that he had been called a black—many things, but never before a black rose.[26]

As in the talks to racially mixed audiences, 'Abdu'l-Bahá's repeated comparisons of beautifully diverse flowers and jewels to an equally beautiful mixture of peoples, particularly black and white, transformed the traditional racist color symbolism and imagery into the symbolism and imagery of racial unity. In short, 'Abdu'l-Bahá presented black and white Americans with "new eyes" and a new spiritual language with which to visualize, and therefore to achieve, a spiritual fellowship. By calling upon black and white Americans to see themselves in a new light, as different colored flowers and jewels complementing each other, 'Abdu'l-Bahá enabled them to counter and transcend the racist cultural tendencies so ingrained in the American national character with a flow of radiant imagery and symbolism of racial diversity.

While in the United States 'Abdu'l-Bahá's every act seemed to be calculated to demonstrate the Bahá'í teachings on the supreme importance of love and unity between all members of the human race, especially blacks and whites. Perhaps at no other time and place during his visit to the United States did 'Abdu'l-Bahá demonstrate in so dramatic yet so characteristically gentle and unassuming a way the Bahá'í teachings and principles of racial unity than at a luncheon held in his honor in Washington, D.C. The luncheon had been arranged by two Bahá'ís, Ali-Kuli Khan, the Persian chargé d'affaires, and Florence Breed Khan, his wife. Some of the guests were members of Washington's social and political élite. Before the luncheon 'Abdu'l-Bahá sent for Louis Gregory, a well-known black Bahá'í. They chatted for a while, and when lunch was ready and the guests were seated, 'Abdu'l-Bahá invited Louis Gregory to the luncheon. The assembled guests, including the Bahá'ís, were no doubt surprised not only by 'Abdu'l-Bahá's inviting a black person to an upperclass social affair but even more by the affection and love shown by 'Abdu'l-Bahá for Gregory when he gave the latter the seat of honor on his right. A biographer of Louis Gregory writes of this event: "Gently yet unmistakably, 'Abdu'l-Bahá had assaulted the

---

26. Howard Colby Ives, *Portals to Freedom* 65.

customs of a city that had been scandalized only a decade earlier by President Roosevelt's dinner invitation to Booker T. Washington."[27]

Given the facts that during 'Abdu'l-Bahá's visit to the United States many blacks and whites did not accept interracial marriage and that there were many states which outlawed the practice or did not recognize such unions, 'Abdu'l-Bahá never wavered in his insistence that black Bahá'ís and white Bahá'ís should not only be unified but also should intermarry. Once while he was home in Palestine, he discussed the matter of interracial marriage with several black and white Western Bahá'ís and explored the sexual myths and fears at the core of American racism. His solution was to encourage interracial marriage. Once again as the supreme model of the Bahá'í teachings and principles, he brought together a black American Bahá'í, Louis Gregory, and an English Bahá'í, Louisa Mathew. It was the first black–white interracial marriage between Bahá'ís and became known as the marriage that was personally encouraged by 'Abdu'l-Bahá. This demonstration of Bahá'í teachings and principles proved difficult to accept for some Bahá'ís who doubted that such a union could last in a segregated society, but the marriage lasted until their deaths close to four decades later. Throughout this period the Gregorys became the ultimate American Bahá'í symbol of racial unity, love, and fellowship.[28]

Historians of American race relations in the early twentieth century will one day examine the influence of 'Abdu'l-Bahá's 1912 visit to the United States on certain aspects of American race relations, as well as examine the impact of Bahá'í-initiated race amity conferences on the history of race relations. 'Abdu'l-Bahá had warned American Bahá'ís that bloodshed would take place if America did not solve the racial crisis.

Years later, from his home in Palestine, 'Abdu'l-Bahá initiated a plan to address the racial crisis in America. His plan was to organize "a series of large, well-publicized interracial meetings, conducted not to protest any specific grievance or to seek improvement of the lot of American blacks in some particular way, but to proclaim the oneness of mankind and to promote 'racial amity' between black and white Americans." The first of these conferences took place in 1921 in Washington, D.C., followed by others. Decades later, race amity or race unity conferences would become the hallmark of the American Bahá'í community's contribution to American race relations.[29] And this was all due to the manner in which 'Abdu'l-Bahá modeled the Bahá'í teachings on racial unity, love, and fellowship.

---

27. Morrison, *To Move the World* 53.
28. Morrison, *To Move the World* 63–72, 309–10.
29. Morrison, *To Move the World* 132.

Bahá'í Community Practices: The Struggle for Racial Unity, Love, and Fellowship

The American Bahá'í community has been involved in a long struggle to realize the great potential 'Abdu'l-Bahá envisioned for it before, during, and after his visit to the United States. He worked very hard to help the American Bahá'ís realize the connection between racial unity and social progress. He gave them a new spiritual language with which to articulate a new vision of race relations. He demonstrated how a true Bahá'í should approach America's racial problems—even going so far as to encourage the first interracial marriage between a black and a white in the American Bahá'í community.

However, the road to racial unity and harmony has been a long challenging one for the American Bahá'í community. For decades, even while some Bahá'ís labored in the difficult field of race relations, others, particularly whites, struggled with the racial feelings they had inherited from the larger racist society. White Bahá'ís and black Bahá'ís had both their own separate and joint spiritual battles to fight so as to create a Bahá'í community worthy of the teachings and principles of Bahá'u'lláh and the vision of 'Abdu'l-Bahá. Even after the visit and modeling of racial unity, love, and fellowship by 'Abdu'l-Bahá, some white Bahá'ís in Washington, D.C. still considered racially integrated meetings as "the one serious obstacle to the growth of the Cause"[30] in that city. In the end, however, motivated by the spiritual teachings, these same white Bahá'ís decided to live up to the high ideals of the Bahá'í teachings on racial unity. The process by which they arrived at this dramatic transformation demonstrated the spiritual power latent in their belief in Bahá'u'lláh's revelation. Morrison says it best in her book *To Move the World*:

> . . . the racial problems in Washington, D.C., from 1914 to 1916 cannot be seen simply as an example of a religious community failing to live up to its ideals. Rather, these early Bahá'ís are revealed as having been immature, deprived of their accustomed leadership, on their own and groping toward the light of understanding. The decision to follow either the Bahá'í way or the way of the world was theirs to make, without even a further word of prompting from 'Abdu'l-Bahá. Thus—however many unresolved feelings may have remained on both sides for many years to come—the 1916 resolution to end the white-only meeting and demonstrably reunite their efforts proved the sincerity of their commitment to a changing order.[31]

White Bahá'ís would have to struggle for decades to overcome the influence of racial segregation on the delicate, still-forming community life

---

30. E. Belmont quoted in Morrison, *To Move the World* 74.
31. Morrison, *To Move the World* 81.

of their religion. While the vast majority of American whites experienced no such challenges to their segregated meetings and hence felt few moral qualms about them—many believing that segregation was sanctioned by God and the Bible[32]—white Bahá'ís had clear and explicit guidance in the Bahá'í holy writings and teachings, as well as equally clear and explicit instructions and guidelines from Shoghi Effendi, that racial segregation was morally wrong and a direct violation of the Bahá'í teachings. Furthermore, white Bahá'ís were instructed to live up to the Bahá'í teachings on racial unity, love, and fellowship. Only the most spiritually courageous white Americans with a deep belief in the world-embracing principles of Bahá'u'lláh were willing to make such a commitment.

Blacks had been involved in the American Bahá'í community since the 1890s[33] and had to suffer through what Morrison referred to as the white Bahá'ís' "groping toward the light of understanding." Often, this meant that black Bahá'ís had to carry the burden of transcending the racism of the white Bahá'ís in order to live up to their role and tasks of creating racial unity within the larger society. This was very difficult because black Bahá'ís, seeing the Bahá'í Faith through the eyes of an oppressed racial minority, expected white Bahá'ís to transcend their racism. When white Bahá'ís failed to live up to the Bahá'í teachings on racial unity, black Bahá'ís felt betrayed. For example, in 1937, when one of the two most prominent black Bahá'ís in Chicago, Ellsworth Blackwell, was "barred from serving as a guide at the [Bahá'í] Temple because of his race," he wrote a letter to Shoghi Effendi in which he said in part:

> From my knowledge of the [Bahá'í] Teachings it appears to me that the Principles of Bahaullah are being violated within His Temple by the Believers. The only apparent excuse for their policy is that the presence of Colored guides would offend people of the White race. As you no doubt realize the aforementioned large touring groups are composed of all nationalities and races. Are we supposed to alter the Principles to accom[m]odate the prejudices of the people outside the Cause, particularly within our own institutions? And, may I ask, when are we to begin to live the Teachings of Bahaullah?[34]

Fortunately for all concerned, the appropriate Bahá'í local and national institutions responded very well to what had been the residual effect of a past policy of racial segregation. The earlier policy of barring black Bahá'ís from serving as guides was eliminated as a result of consultation on the issue in the light of 'Abdu'l-Bahá's repeated warnings about the American racial crisis.

---

32. Everett Tilson, *Segregation and the Bible* 15–28.

33. See Gwen Etter-Lewis, unpublished paper on black Bahá'í women.

34. Mark Lloyd Perry, "The Chicago Bahá'í Community, 1921–1939." Unpublished dissertation, University of Chicago, 1986, 299–300; also published as "Pioneering Race Unity: The Chicago Bahá'ís, 1919–39" in *World Order* 20.2 (Winter 1985–86): 41–60.

Shoghi Effendi recognized the humiliation, pain, and anguish black Bahá'ís were experiencing as the result of white Bahá'ís' racial attitudes. In a letter to Sadie Oglesby, a black Bahá'í woman, sent on his behalf, he said that he was "well aware that the conditions within the ranks of the believers in respect to race prejudice is [*sic*] far from being as it should be. However he feels very strongly that it presents a challenge to both white and coloured believers." Shoghi Effendi, then gave the following advice to his black fellow Bahá'ís: ". . . it is incumbent upon the negro believers to rise above this great test which the attitude of some of their white brethren may present. They must prove their innate equality not by words but by deeds. They must," Shoghi Effendi stressed, "accept the Cause of Bahá'u'lláh for the sake of the *Cause*, love it, and cling to it, and teach it, and fight for it as *their* own Cause, forgetful of the shortcomings of others. Any other attitude is unworthy of their faith." He then reminded the black believers how Bahá'u'lláh had praised blacks: "Proud and happy in the praises which even Bahá'u'lláh Himself has bestowed upon them, they must feel He revealed Himself for them and every other down-trodden race, loves them, and will help them to attain their destiny." Pointing to the fact that "the whole race question in America is a national one and of great importance," Shoghi Effendi expressed the concern that "the negro friends must not waste their precious opportunity to serve the Faith, in these momentous days, by dwelling on the admitted short comings of the white friends. They must arise and serve and teach, confident of the future they are building, a future in which we know these barriers will have once and for all been overcome!"[35]

Shoghi Effendi's letter emphasized the role black Bahá'ís had to play in the spiritual unification of America. As he explained to another believer: "The more Negroes who become Bahá'ís, the greater the leaven will be within their own race, working for harmony and friendship between these two bodies of American citizens: the white and the colored."[36] In addition to the role they could play "as leaven . . . within their own race, working for harmony and friendship between. . . . white and black," Shoghi Effendi pointed to still another contribution blacks could make: "The qualities of heart so richly possessed by the Negro are much needed in the world today—their great capacity for faith, their loyalty and devotion to their religion when once they believe, their purity of heart. God has richly endowed them, and their contribution to the Cause is much needed. . . ."[37]

For all these reasons, Bahá'ís in the United States had to help each other to build a model community reflecting racial unity, love, and

---

35. Quoted in Morrison, *To Move the World* 296.

36. On behalf of Shoghi Effendi, letter dated 18 December 1943 to an individual believer, quoted in *The Power of Unity* 107.

37. Helen Hornsby, comp., *Lights of Guidance* 532.

fellowship. As the years passed, they have struggled with this "most challenging issue." They have not always been able to avoid all the "pitfalls" along the "long and thorny road," but they have continued to try. In 1986, the National Race Unity Committee of the Bahá'ís of the United States took the Bahá'í community another step along this path with the following insightful and challenging words:

> Our American Bahá'í community may soon possess a majority of members who are from minority populations in the United States. Inevitably, our culture as a Bahá'í community must also change. Such a change will manifest itself initially through an increasing appreciation for the cultural offerings—music, food, festivities, manners of speech and dress—of blacks, Hispanics, Native Americans, Persians, Southeast Asians, and others in the Bahá'í community. But ultimately we must become multicultural so that our community life acquires a character that is flexible, versatile, creative, and blessed with a wide repertoire of cultural responses to daily Bahá'í life. These patterns of our collective life also deserve our attention because they serve to become magnets for the spiritual energy that quickens our community life. As 'Abdu'l-Bahá guides us: "It is impossible to unite unless united.". . .
>
> The National Race Unity Committee is eager for the friends to meditate on the question of unity, to develop a longing to see it manifest in all its beauty in their lives and in their communities. . . .[38]

In the final pages of *The Promise of World Peace*, a statement on peace from the Universal House of Justice, the supreme governing body of the Bahá'í Faith, addressed "To the Peoples of the World," is the following statement: "If the Bahá'í experience can contribute in whatever measure to reinforcing hope in the unity of the human race, we are happy to offer it as a model for study."[39] Perhaps the same should be said of the American Bahá'í community's experience in its long struggle to create racial unity, love, and fellowship among fellow Americans.

The Most Challenging Issue: Spiritual Guidelines for Achieving Racial Unity, Love, and Fellowship within the American Bahá'í Community

One of the most far-reaching statements on American race relations as related to the Bahá'í community was published in 1939 in a book entitled *The Advent of Divine Justice*.[40] The section on race relations, called, "The Most Challenging Issue," constitutes one of the most insightful statements on American racial problems in the history of American race relations

---

38. *The Power of Unity* x–xi.
39. Universal House of Justice, *The Promise of World Peace* 36–37; "To the Peoples" 24.
40. Shoghi Effendi, *The Advent of Divine Justice* 33–41.

literature. Written by Shoghi Effendi, who for decades had been guiding the American Bahá'í community down the "long and thorny road" of racial conflicts, "The Most Challenging Issue" has become the most well-known and often-quoted formulation of the roles of black Bahá'ís and white Bahá'ís in the resolution of racial problems both within and outside the American Bahá'í community.

"As to racial prejudice, the corrosion of which, for well nigh a century, has bitten into the fiber, and attacked the whole social structure of American society, it should be regarded as constituting the most vital and challenging issue confronting the Bahá'í community at the present stage of its evolution." Such a challenging statement by the spiritual head of the Bahá'í Faith on an issue upon which no major secular or religious American leader had ever taken so bold a stand at once made clear to every Bahá'í the "vital and challenging" nature of the racial problem. This would not be an easy problem to solve. Shoghi Effendi knew only too well that Bahá'ís would have to prepare themselves for a grave challenge. "The ceaseless exertions which this issue of paramount importance calls for, the sacrifices it must impose, the care and vigilance it demands, the moral courage and fortitude it requires, the tact and sympathy it necessitates," Shoghi Effendi explained, "invest this problem, which the American believers are still far from having satisfactorily resolved, with an urgency and importance that cannot be overestimated." Every member of the American Bahá'í community was called upon to work on the problem. "White and Negro, high and low, young and old, whether newly converted to the Faith or not, all who stand identified with it must participate in, and lend their assistance, each according to his or her capacity, experience, and opportunities, to the common task of fulfilling the instructions, realizing the hopes, and following the example, of 'Abdu'l-Bahá."[41] 'Abdu'l-Bahá embodied the spiritual qualities Bahá'ís were instructed to emulate if they desired to be good Bahá'ís. By emulating 'Abdu'l-Bahá, both black Bahá'ís and white Bahá'ís would be more spiritually attuned to racial unity, love, and fellowship. As explained by Shoghi Effendi, neither black Bahá'ís nor white Bahá'ís for whatever reason could place the burden of resolving the racial problem on the other group. "Whether colored or noncolored, neither race has the right, or can conscientiously claim, to be regarded as absolved from such an obligation, as having realized such hopes, or having faithfully followed such an example." Bahá'ís, Shoghi Effendi warned, still had a long road to travel: "A long and thorny road, beset with pitfalls, still remains untraveled, both by the white and the Negro exponents of the redeeming Faith of Bahá'u'lláh. On the distance they cover, and the manner in which they travel that road," Shoghi Effendi cautioned, "must depend, to an extent

---

41. Shoghi Effendi, *Advent* 33–34.

which few among them can imagine, the operation of those intangible influences which are indispensable to the spiritual triumph of the American believers and the material success of their newly launched enterprise."[42]

Shoghi Effendi called upon the American Bahá'í community to "call to mind, fearlessly and determinedly, the example and conduct of 'Abdu'l-Bahá while in their midst. Let them remember His courage, His genuine love, His informal and indiscriminating fellowship, His contempt for and impatience of criticism, tempered by His tact and wisdom." They were to "revive and perpetuate the memory of those unforgettable and historic episodes and occasions on which He so strikingly demonstrated His keen sense of justice, His spontaneous sympathy for the downtrodden, His ever-abiding sense of the oneness of the human race, His overflowing love for its members. . . ." Any discrimination "against any race, on the ground of its being socially backward, politically immature, and numerically in a minority, is a flagrant violation of the spirit that animates the Faith of Bahá'u'lláh. The consciousness of any division or cleavage in its ranks is alien to its very purpose, principles, and ideals."[43]

Once Bahá'ís have "fully recognized the claim of its [the Bahá'í Faith's] Author, and, by identifying themselves with its Administrative Order, accepted unreservedly the principles and laws embodied in its teachings," Shoghi Effendi explained, "every differentiation of class, creed, or color must automatically be obliterated, and never be allowed, under any pretext, and however great the pressure of events or of public opinion, to reassert itself."[44]

The very act of becoming a Bahá'í commits one to live by the Bahá'í teachings on racial unity. There is no way around this. The Bahá'í teachings were clear; no bias of any sort was allowed, no matter how "great the pressure of events or of public opinion." This statement was written in 1938 when segregation in the schools and racially restrictive covenants were sanctioned by the United States Constitution, and the Federal Housing Administration unabashedly supported segregated housing. Baseball, the most popular sport in America, had not yet been desegregated, and the Armed Services of the United States, soon to go into the Second World War, still boasted a racially segregated system. How were the American Bahá'ís expected to resist such an array of the most powerful forces and institutions in the United States that were solidly behind the racial status quo? Shoghi Effendi not only expected them to stand firm on the Bahá'í teachings and principles related to racial unity and fellowship but also in certain situations as a means to achieve certain goals to discriminate in favor of minorities within the Bahá'í communities:

---

42. Shoghi Effendi, *Advent* 34.
43. Shoghi Effendi, *Advent* 34–35.
44. Shoghi Effendi, *Advent* 35.

If any discrimination is at all to be tolerated, it should be a discrimination not against, but rather in favor of the minority, be it racial or otherwise. Unlike the nations and peoples of the earth, be they of the East or of the West, democratic or authoritarian, communist or capitalist, whether belonging to the Old World or the New, who either ignore, trample upon, or extirpate, the racial, religious, or political minorities within the sphere of their jurisdiction, every organized community enlisted under the banner of Bahá'u'lláh should feel it to be its first and inescapable obligation to nurture, encourage, and safeguard every minority belonging to any faith, race, class, or nation within it. So great and vital is this principle that in such circumstances, as when an equal number of ballots have been cast in an election, or where the qualifications for any office are balanced as between the various races, faiths or nationalities within the community, priority should unhesitatingly be accorded the party representing the minority, and this for no other reason except to stimulate and encourage it, and afford it an opportunity to further the interests of the community.[45]

Shoghi Effendi's application of Bahá'í teachings and principles to minority issues within the Bahá'í community represented a profound and unprecedented model of how communities should treat their minorities so as to enable them better to serve and contribute to the larger social order. One can only imagine the tremendous social and economic progress the United States could have made if local and national leaders had applied Shoghi Effendi's suggestions to racial problems. Had white America seen as "its first and inescapable obligation to nurture, encourage, and safeguard" Native peoples, blacks, and other racial minorities, the country would have been light years ahead in material and spiritual progress. The policy of discriminating in favor of the minority so as to "stimulate and encourage it, and afford it an opportunity to further the interests of the community" could have only been conceived by one who believes in the organic unity of the human race. Outside of such a context of spiritual unity, the policy would be interpreted as a form of "reverse discrimination." Tainted by the pervasive influence of racism and unable or unwilling to think of racial minorities as members of "their [white] communities," many white Americans would fail to see how such an application of positive discrimination on behalf of racial minorities could benefit them and the larger community as well. That Shoghi Effendi understood and shared this application of Bahá'í teachings to the racial problems in the American Bahá'í community is testimony to the profound relevance of these teachings to American race relations. But there was much more in "the Most Challenging Issue."

Continuing, Shoghi Effendi explained how in light of this principle the Bahá'í community should go out of its way to arrange its affairs to encourage minorities to participate in all areas of its community life:

---

45. Shoghi Effendi, *Advent* 35.

In the light of this principle, and bearing in mind the extreme desirability of having the minority elements participate and share responsibility in the conduct of Bahá'í activity, it should be the duty of every Bahá'í community so to arrange its affairs that in cases where individuals belonging to the divers minority elements within it are already qualified and fulfill the necessary requirements, Bahá'í representative institutions, . . . may have represented on them as many of these divers elements, racial or otherwise, as possible. The adoption of such a course, and faithful adherence to it, would not only be a source of inspiration and encouragement to those elements that are numerically small and inadequately represented, but would demonstrate to the world at large the universality and representative character of the Faith of Bahá'u'lláh, and the freedom of His followers from the taint of those prejudices which have already wrought such havoc in the domestic affairs, as well as the foreign relationships, of the nations.[46]

Shoghi Effendi understood the pervasive nature of American racism and how it could poison Bahá'í community life, particularly at a time when European and American racism was rampant. The American Bahá'í community was instructed by Shoghi Effendi to adopt the watchword "freedom from racial prejudice" to aid them in their struggles against racism. A watchword can be a motto, a cry, or a slogan, but it usually means something that embodies a principle:

Freedom from racial prejudice, in any of its forms, should, at such a time as this when an increasingly large section of the human race is falling a victim to its devastating ferocity, be adopted as the watchword of the entire body of the American believers, in whichever state they reside, in whatever circles they move, whatever their age, traditions, tastes, and habits. It should be consistently demonstrated in every phase of their activity and life, whether in the Bahá'í community or outside it, in public or in private, formally as well as informally, individually as well as in their official capacity as organized groups, committees and Assemblies.[47]

Here again, Shoghi Effendi clearly set the guidelines for combatting racism and promoting the Bahá'í principle and model of racial unity. Living in a state that practiced racism did not excuse Bahá'ís from working on their racial attitudes and behavior. If they belonged to social circles that discriminated against blacks or other racial minorities, they were obviously violating the principles of the Bahá'í Faith. Whatever their "age, traditions, tastes, and habits," they were obligated to work on freeing themselves from racial prejudices. Furthermore, Shoghi Effendi told them to demonstrate freedom from racial prejudice consistently in every phase of their lives, both

---

46. Shoghi Effendi, *Advent* 35–36.
47. Shoghi Effendi, *Advent* 36.

inside and outside the Bahá'í community. Being free from racial prejudice only within the Bahá'í community was far from sufficient. The Bahá'í teachings, as explained by Shoghi Effendi and applied by him to American racial problems, demanded much more from Bahá'ís, especially whites, who had much racial and cultural prejudice that had to be eliminated.

What more could the American Bahá'ís do to rid themselves of racial prejudice after demonstrating the Bahá'í teachings in their public and private lives? They should, Shoghi Effendi wrote, "deliberately" cultivate freedom from racial prejudice "through the various and everyday opportunities, no matter how insignificant, that present themselves, whether in their homes, their business offices, their schools and colleges, their social parties and recreation grounds, their Bahá'í meetings, conferences, conventions, summer schools and Assemblies."[48] Addressing their national governing body, Shoghi Effendi told American Bahá'ís that freedom from racial prejudice "should, above all else, become the keynote of the policy of that august body which, in its capacity as the national representative, and the director and coordinator of the affairs of the community, must set the example, and facilitate the application of such a vital principle to the lives and activities of those whose interests it safeguards and represents."[49]

After explaining why and how the American Bahá'í community should work on freeing itself from racial prejudice, Shoghi Effendi quotes 'Abdu'l-Bahá:

> Bahá'u'lláh hath said . . . that the various races of humankind lend a composite harmony and beauty of color to the whole. Let all associate, therefore, in this great human garden even as flowers grow and blend together side by side without discord or disagreement between them.[50]

'Abdu'l-Bahá also pointed out that "Bahá'u'lláh also once compared the colored people to the black pupil of the eye surrounded by the white. In this black pupil is seen the reflection of that which is before it, and through it the light of the spirit shineth forth."[51] Of all Bahá'u'lláh's statements on racial unity, this is probably the one most favored by black American Bahá'ís because of the very positive symbolism given to blackness. In a culture where whiteness has always been the unquestioned symbol of spiritual purity and blackness the symbol of the lack of spiritual purity, Bahá'u'lláh's teachings on race transformed the negative meaning of black–white symbolism infused in Western culture by centuries of ethnocentrism and racism into a black–white symbol of spiritual unity. This meaning was not lost upon

---

48. Shoghi Effendi, *Advent* 36.
49. Shoghi Effendi, *Advent* 36–37.
50. In Shoghi Effendi, *Advent* 37.
51. In Shoghi Effendi, *Advent* 37.

American Bahá'ís. Those who reflected upon it could not help but be transformed: blacks could see themselves in a new spiritual light as the "black pupil" reflecting "that which is before it," and through which "the light of the spirit shineth forth." They could in fact rejoice in this affirmation of their spirituality embodied in such a powerful color symbolism by the founder of the Faith. White Bahá'ís could free themselves of all the negative cultural connotations Western religious thought had attributed to the symbolism of blackness. Both black Bahá'ís and white Bahá'ís could also rejoice in the fact that for the first time in Western religious thought there was now a color symbolism that did not cast black and white as spiritual opposites but as spiritual complements to each other.

To assist Bahá'ís in carrying out their dual roles of applying Bahá'í principles to the solution of the problems of racism and racial conflicts, both within their community and in the larger society, Shoghi Effendi provided the following instructions and guidelines. First he reminded them that "tremendous effort is required by both races if their outlook, their manners, and conduct are to reflect, in this darkened age, the spirit and teachings of the Faith of Bahá'u'lláh. Casting away once and for all the fallacious doctrine of racial superiority," he said, "with all its attendant evils, confusion, and miseries, and welcoming and encouraging the intermixture of races, and tearing down the barriers that now divide them, they should each endeavor, day and night, to fulfill their particular responsibilities in the common task which so urgently faces them." While working jointly on this "common task," he reminded them to remember 'Abdu'l-Bahá's warnings about racial conflicts in America. "Let them, while each is attempting to contribute its share to the solution of this perplexing problem," Shoghi Effendi wrote, "call to mind the warnings of 'Abdu'l-Bahá, and visualize, while there is yet time, the dire consequences that must follow if this challenging and unhappy situation that faces the entire American nation is not definitely remedied."[52] He then outlined guidelines for Bahá'ís to work within in their joint efforts to remedy the racial problems facing their country. Addressing his white fellow Bahá'ís, Shoghi Effendi wrote:

> Let the white make a supreme effort in their resolve to contribute their share to the solution of this problem, to abandon once for all their usually inherent and at times subconscious sense of superiority, to correct their tendency towards revealing a patronizing attitude towards the members of the other race, to persuade them through their intimate, spontaneous and informal association with them of the genuineness of their friendship and the sincerity of their intentions, and to master their impatience of any lack of responsiveness on the part of a people who have received, for so long a period, such grievous and slow-healing wounds.[53]

52. Shoghi Effendi, *Advent* 39–40.
53. Shoghi Effendi, *Advent* 40.

Turning next to his black fellow Bahá'ís, Shoghi Effendi said:

> Let the Negroes, through a corresponding effort on their part, show by every means in their power the warmth of their response, their readiness to forget the past, and their ability to wipe out every trace of suspicion that may still linger in their hearts and minds.[54]

Having given both black Bahá'ís and white Bahá'ís separate but complementary guidelines for their joint task, Shoghi Effendi then addressed them as members of a spiritual community upon which the ultimate resolution of American racial problems depended:

> Let neither think that the solution of so vast a problem is a matter that exclusively concerns the other. Let neither think that such a problem can either easily or immediately be resolved. Let neither think that they can wait confidently for the solution of this problem until the initiative has been taken, and the favorable circumstances created, by agencies that stand outside the orbit of their Faith. Let neither think that anything short of genuine love, extreme patience, true humility, consummate tact, sound initiative, mature wisdom, and deliberate, persistent, and prayerful effort, can succeed in blotting out the stain which this patent evil has left on the fair name of their common country. Let them rather believe, and be firmly convinced, that on their mutual understanding, their amity, and sustained cooperation, must depend, more than on any other force or organization operating outside the circle of their Faith, the deflection of that dangerous course so greatly feared by 'Abdu'l-Bahá, and the materialization of the hopes He cherished for their joint contribution to the fulfillment of that country's glorious destiny.[55]

The Bahá'í Community Response to "The Most Challenging Issue"

The above spiritual guidelines for the achievement of racial unity within the American Bahá'í community and the larger society represented the most revolutionary race-relations program yet devised in any multiracial society. The Guardian of the Bahá'í Faith, Shoghi Effendi, had identified the race issue as the "most challenging issue" facing American Baha'is. His messages and the Bahá'í teachings contained clear guidelines for the achievement of racial unity, love, and fellowship within the American Bahá'í Community as well as for the healing of the racial problems of the larger society. The Guardian had instructed that each Bahá'í should deliberately cultivate freedom from racial prejudice.

Bahá'ís were given both a map through the present and future minefields of racial turmoil and a set of spiritual guidelines for building a multiracial

---

54. Shoghi Effendi, *Advent* 40.
55. Shoghi Effendi, *Advent* 40–41.

community based on the Bahá'í teachings. "The most challenging issue" is the unique Bahá'í formulation of the problem of racism and its solution.

Despite the relatively advanced stage of race relations in the American Bahá'í Community, attitudes and behaviors were still lagging behind professed beliefs. Many Bahá'ís were focussed on less controversial issues such as world peace. One commentator noted that between 1936 and 1939 the Bahá'í community had retreated "from active concern for racial amity . . . ."[56]

The National Spiritual Assembly (NSA) of the Bahá'ís of the United States and Canada[57] understood the challenge as a fundamentally spiritual one. In 1939, the newly elected NSA called for "a new and higher standard of loyalty to the principle of the Oneness of Mankind" and insisted that "the horizon of our Bahá'í love is to be extended, and our understanding of the true nature of Bahá'í unity is to be deepened and demonstrated in action." The NSA and the Bahá'í administrative bodies would have to set the example, as they had "the obligation to encourage and protect the members of the racial, religious and class minorities comprising the American Bahá'í Community." The Guardian had instructed that qualified minority group members should, in fact, receive preference for offices within the Bahá'í Faith. As well, the NSA noted that the application of the new standard "involves the participation of, and the sharing of responsibility by, these minority elements. . . ."[58]

To begin this new stage in race relations, the NSA appointed a five-member Race Unity Committee (RUC) that included two long-time champions of racial amity and unity, Louis Gregory, the best-known African–American Bahá'í and the foremost advocate for racial unity in the American Bahá'í Community, and Dorothy Beecher Baker, a northern white who was the great-granddaughter of Harriet Beecher Stowe and a member of the NSA.

In his advocacy for racial unity, Gregory had observed that the motives of influential white Bahá'ís tended not to be questioned as readily as those of "even the most tactful and distinguished black."[59] His long and often painful and frustrating experience with the pendulum-like nature of race relations within the Bahá'í' community enabled Gregory to understand and to accept this developmental stage, not unlike similar developmental stages of race relations within the larger society. Gregory was not disappointed in Baker. He watched his Bahá'í sister "emerge as a leading advocate of increased efforts for racial justice and understanding."[60] In 1950 Gregory

---

56. Morrison, *To Move* 257.
57. This Assembly became two distinct Assemblies (NSA of the Bahá'ís of Canada; NSA of the Bahá'ís of the United States) in 1948.
58. *Bahá'í News* (April, 1939): 1–2.
59. Quoted in Morrison, *To Move* 275.
60. Morrison, *To Move* 275.

would write, "I regard her as the foremost Baha'i of the western world."[61]

In a series of articles in *Bahá'í News* the RUC set out to raise the consciousness of the American community regarding "the most challenging issue." Pointing out that we all have prejudices to one degree or another, the committee reminded Bahá'ís of the Guardian's exhortations and urged: "We must exert ourselves ceaselessly; we must sacrifice ourselves; we must use care and vigilance, moral courage and fortitude, tact and sympathy in solving this problem." The committee then announced that it would make an effort to "present materials which will help us to understand and appreciate minority groups many of which are suffering very unjustly today. It is the hope of the Race Unity Committee that freedom from racial prejudice may really become the watchword of the entire body of the American believers."

In the same issue, the Bahá'í Child Education Committee reviewed and highly recommended Bruno Lasker's book *Race Attitudes in Children*. The book described how children learn and express racial attitudes toward a variety of racial and ethnic groups, and the committee warned Bahá'í parents that "these subtle social weapons are all around your child. No suasion of parent or teacher can alone effect protection. Constant recourse to the Holy Utterances can protect him. Every child has a clean beginning. He is, at first, not soiled by prejudices." The committee referred readers to passages in *The Advent of Divine Justice* and stated that "every Bahá'í parent sees again in them the need of waging honest war against the hosts of prejudice. . . ." It suggested children memorize the following quotations, first pointing out that "they will make your children proud of the garment of unity which is their great distinction. Keep the garment always shining and new with a few of these thoughts. . . ."[62]

Close your eyes to racial differences, and welcome all with the light of oneness.[63]

God maketh no distinction between the white and the black. If the hearts are pure both are acceptable unto Him.[64]

In the estimation of God there is no distinction of color; all are one in the color and beauty of servitude to Him.[65]

For the accomplishment of unity between the colored and white will be an assurance of the world's peace.[66]

---

61. Quoted in Morrison, *To Move* 276.
62. *Bahá'í News* (January, 1940): 10–12.
63. Bahá'u'lláh, quoted in *Advent* 37.
64. 'Abdu'l-Bahá, quoted in *Advent* 37.
65. 'Abdu'l-Bahá, quoted in *Advent* 37.
66. 'Abdu'l-Bahá, quoted in *Advent* 39.

Let all associate, therefore, in this great human garden even as flowers grow and blend together side by side without discord or disagreement between them.[67]

This handful of dust, the world, is one home. Let it be in unity.[68]

Know ye not why We created you all from the same dust? That no one should exalt himself over the other.[69]

. . . regard ye not one another as strangers. Ye are the fruits of one tree, and the leaves of one branch.[70]

Light is good in whatsoever lamp it is burning. A rose is beautiful in whatsoever garden it may bloom, A star is as radiant whether it shines from the East or the West.[71]

This committee's response was particularly important because it set the standards for the education of the next generation of American Bahá'ís, preparing them to play a leading role in building a racially harmonious society. This generation would have to be prepared for another round of American racial turmoil.

The American Bahá'í community had long ago realized the importance of linking knowledge of minority group history and culture to the eradication of racism and the development of racial unity. Several early Bahá'í race amity conferences in the 1920s and 1930s had presented scholars and leaders representing the history and culture of racial minorities.[72] These conferences were a key element in the process of educating the Bahá'í community members, who, like most other Americans, knew very little about minority history and culture. Without such knowledge, some Bahá'ís tended to cling to comfortable racist beliefs, myths, and stereotypes that rationalized the racist practices so common in the United States at the time.

In 1940 the RUC's article "Books on Race Relations" emphasized the vital link between the knowledge of minority history and culture, and the work for racial unity:

The need for racial unity is perhaps more apparent today than at any other time in the world's history, Bahá'ís everywhere are engaged in working for true

---

67. 'Abdu'l-Bahá, *Promulgation of Universal Peace* 69.
68. Bahá'u'lláh, cited in *Bahá'í News* (January, 1940): 12.
69. Bahá'u'lláh, *Hidden Words* 20.
70. Bahá'u'lláh, *Gleanings* 218.
71. 'Abdu'l-Bahá, cited in *Bahá'í News* (January, 1940): 12.
72. Louis G. Gregory, "Racial Amity in America: An Historical Review," *The Bahá'í World* 7: 652–66; Louis G. Gregory, "Light on Basic Unity," *Star of the West* 22.7 (October, 1931): 220–23.

brotherhood among all the races of the world. In our work we discover that one of the biggest obstacles to understanding between the various races is ignorance of each other. The White race knows very little about the actual accomplishments of the Negro race. The Yellow race is uninformed about the achievements of the White race.

The RUC noted that contemporary scholars of race relations were already making the connection between racial unity and knowledge of different cultures. "We must study the background, history, progress, accomplishments, and peculiar problems of every race. Only then can we achieve a deep and lasting appreciation for each other. Only then will we have a strong foundation on which to build race unity."[73]

The RUC listed some of the best books in the field of race relations at the time, including one entitled, *Negro Americans, What Now?* written by James Weldon Johnson, the famous African–American writer, who spoke at one of the first Bahá'í race amity meetings in New York in 1924.[74] In its review of Johnson's book, the RUC notes that "the author calls attention to the fact that white people must be educated to an understanding of their Negro brothers." The RUC quotes Johnson:

> The ignorance of white people concerning us constitutes one of our greatest obstacles.—The greater part of white America thinks of us in stereotypes; most of these stereotypes coming to them second-hand by way of the representation of Negro life and character on the stage and in certain books.
> . . . White people must be educated. They must be taught the truth about us. . . . [They] must . . . be made thoroughly conscious of the handicaps, injustices, and wrongs under which Negro Americans struggle. . . . And [they] must learn not only about the material but also about the artistic and spiritual contributions that Negro Americans have made to our common cultural store.[75]

The RUC reviewed a few other books on African–Americans and then concluded with this message to Bahá'í readers: "It is the hope of the Race Unity committee that every Bahá'í will be stimulated to read some of these books."[76]

Educating the American Bahá'í community about the history and cultures of minority groups and the nature of prejudices became a major method of consciousness-raising during this period of Bahá'í race unity work. Anti-Semitism was also a concern among the American Bahá'í community. The RUC mentioned several books that would assist Bahá'ís in addressing the issue of anti-Semitism and urged Bahá'ís to consult their

---

73. *Bahá'í News* (February, 1940): 10.
74. Gregory, "Racial Amity" 657.
75. *Bahá'í News* (February, 1940): 10.
76. *Bahá'í News* (February, 1940): 11.

local libraries and to "read as widely as possible on this subject so that your understanding of its many problems may grow."[77]

By September, 1940, the RUC was able to get a reading of the response of the American Bahá'í community to the Guardian's "most challenging issue" message in *The Advent of Divine Justice*. The RUC reported: "Bahá'í communities everywhere . . . are attempting to spread the Bahá'í Faith to minority groups living in their vicinity. Recently we have learned of the acceptance of two members of the Indian race by the Milwaukee Assembly." The Guardian cabled the assembly expressing his delight and assuring them of his prayers. Other Bahá'í communities were welcoming other Native–American peoples as the race unity movement began to sweep the country.[78]

The RUC urged Bahá'ís to make race unity a topic of the consultation period at one of the Nineteen-day Feasts,[79] suggesting that the Bahá'í groups discuss whether they had considered "major gifts of the great American minorities . . ." whether they had made special efforts to approach minorities, and asking them to consider the essential difference between the Bahá'í ideal of unity and other efforts in that direction. It asked for feedback on each community's plans and activities "so that we may share them with the entire Bahá'í community."

The RUC concluded by quoting from the Guardian's "most challenging issue" message:

> As to racial prejudice, the corrosion of which, for well nigh a century, has bitten into the fibre, and attacked the whole social structure of American society, it should be regarded as constituting the most vital and challenging issue confronting the Bahá'í community at the present stage of its evolution. The ceaseless exertions which this issue of paramount importance calls for, the sacrifices it must impose, the care and vigilance it demands, the moral courage and fortitude it requires, the tact and sympathy it necessitates, invest this problem, which the American believers are still far from having satisfactorily resolved, with an urgency and importance that cannot be over-estimated.[80]

Although such exhortations seemed intended to help Bahá'í communities develop more advanced and progressive methods of addressing minority issues, in essence, the RUC was repeating the earlier Bahá'í race amity committee's tactics. For example, the suggestion that Bahá'í communities make special appeals to minority organizations had been pioneered in 1910 when Louis Gregory invited two Bahá'ís, one, a white American, and the other, a Middle-Easterner, to speak at a gathering of the Bethel Literary and

---

77. *Bahá'í News* (April, 1940): 7.
78. *Bahá'í News* (September, 1940): 6.
79. *Bahá'í News* (October, 1940): 9.
80. *Bahá'í News* (October, 1940): 9.

Historical Society, the oldest and leading African–American organization in Washington, D.C. The two Bahá'í speakers focused on "The Race Question from the Standpoint of the Baha'i Revelation."[81] Two years later during his trip to North America, 'Abdu'l-Bahá also spoke to this and other African–American organizations, including Howard University, then the premier African–American educational institution in the country.[82] These Bahá'í linkages with the African–American community were further expanded during the race-amity stage of Bahá'í race-relation history during the 1920s when Bahá'ís carefully cultivated ties and linkages with African–American leadership, scholars, organizations, and institutions.[83]

The early years of race amity work during the 1920s witnessed Bahá'ís working with several organizations, such as the NAACP and the Urban League, which obviously shared the Bahá'í belief in racial unity even while pursuing their own unique social agendas. The first race amity conferences during the 1920s exposed Bahá'ís to some of the greatest African–American writers and scholars, such as W. E. B. Du Bois and James Weldon Johnson.[84] During the summer of 1931, a conference on racial amity held at Green Acre Bahá'í summer school in Eliot, Maine, featured as one of its speakers, William Leo Hansberry, Howard University history professor, who spoke on "The Negro Civilization in Ancient Africa." Such efforts by Bahá'ís to educate themselves about little-known facts about Africa and to organize a receptive setting in which such facts could be presented by an African–American scholar helped lay the foundation for their future work in this area.

Returning to 1940, an example of the Bahá'í community's continuing tradition of reaching out to racial and religious minorities and demonstrating racial unity was the Temple Model Exhibit at the American Negro Exposition held in Chicago during the summer and fall of 1940. Two Bahá'ís, one black and one white, discussed the Bahá'í Faith and its principles. Afterwards, the Bahá'ís received the following letter from the African–American Emancipation Commission: "Your exhibit at the Exposition has caused favorable comment, particularly because of the very fine representatives that have been in attendance there. The American Negro Exposition is very anxious that your Faith present a program developing your fundamental beliefs. . . ."[85] Such efforts would expand as Bahá'ís became more attuned to the need to reach out to minority communities.

---

81. Morrison, *To Move* 32.

82. Gregory, "Racial Amity" 654; Allan L. Ward, *239 Days: 'Abdu'l-Bahá's Journey in America* 40; 'Abdu'l-Bahá, *Promulgation* 44–46.

83. Gregory, "Racial Amity" 657; Gregory, "Light on Basic Unity" 220–22; "Interracial Amity Activities," *Bahá'í News* (April, 1933): 6.

84. Gregory, "Light on Basic Unity"; Gregory, "Racial Amity" 656–57.

85. *Bahá'í News* (October, 1940): 9.

By far the most dramatic response to the Guardian's "most challenging issue" message came from the National Spiritual Assembly in November, 1940, when it met in Atlanta, Georgia, for its first meeting ever in the deep South. Its action demonstrated how far the spiritual leadership of the national Bahá'í community would go to put into practice the Bahá'í teachings on racial unity as outlined in the Guardian's clear instructions, showing both reluctant white Bahá'ís and racial minorities within the Bahá'í community that the NSA would not compromise Bahá'u'lláh's teachings on the oneness of the human race.

The NSA's choice of Atlanta was particularly timely because the predominantly white Bahá'í community in Atlanta was uninterested in practicing racial unity or in accepting black Bahá'ís into the fold. Not even the visit of the most popular and much-loved black Bahá'í in the West, Louis G. Gregory, moved the prosegregation faction of the Atlanta Bahá'ís to attend the meeting arranged for him in that city. At the time, Gregory was a member of the NSA and had arrived early to meet with the local Bahá'ís. However, when Dorothy Baker, also a member of the NSA and chairperson of the RUC, arrived and asked for a meeting, everyone, including the prosegregation faction attended. She took this opportunity to inform the gathering that she was "the great granddaughter of Henry Ward Beecher, one of the outstanding preachers who advocated the emancipation of the Negro in the pre-Civil War days." She then went on to "make it clear that the Baha'i community could never restrict anyone because of color. . . ."[86] The NSA made its position on racial unity clear during its visit in Atlanta through the racially integrated meetings that were held both for Bahá'ís only as well as for the general public. For example, meetings at the Biltmore Hotel were racially integrated. As a result, at one of the public meetings, most of the audience was black, causing some concern among the whites. One observer commented, "This meeting was . . . criticized by some persons of the white race but the colored people who were present were very appreciative to see the oneness of mankind being practiced."[87]

Future scholars of race relations within the American Bahá'í community will probably note this visit of the NSA as a watershed in American Bahá'í history both in the South and the nation. Morrison correctly summed up the historical significance of this event: "By meeting in Atlanta the National Spiritual Assembly helped to reinforce the movement toward racial unity among the Bahá'ís there. The whites were put on notice, even at the risk of their withdrawal from the Faith, that they had to come to terms with the principle of oneness in both their Bahá'í community life and in their approach to the public."[88]

---

86. Olga Finke, "Atlanta Bahá'í History: 1909–1944" (Archives of the Local Spiritual Assembly of the Bahá'ís of Atlanta, Georgia): 24–25. Quoted in Morrison, *To Move* 282.

87. Finke, "Atlanta Bahá'í History" 25.

88. Morrison, *To Move* 283.

Obviously, this choice of meeting-place was a direct challenge to those white Bahá'ís who chose to stand by their Bahá'í principles. As Morrison again points out, "It was no small thing to ask of them, requiring as it did courage to challenge the mores of a divided society and to expose oneself to hostility."[89] Both black and white Bahá'ís had their faith tested in Atlanta and other areas of the deep South during this period. Olga Finke, a white Bahá'í in Atlanta, was warned to leave the city after Louis G. Gregory visited her. In 1947, the local Ku Klux Klan " 'broke up an interracial Bahá'í meeting in Atlanta'."[90] However, because the Bahá'ís took an uncompromising position on racial integration and unity, they laid the foundation for the growth of the Bahá'í Faith in Atlanta and the rest of the South, ". . . if not at first among the white population, which was not yet ready to accept change, then among the blacks, for whom change was grievously overdue." And the NSA's uncompromising position on race made all the difference.[91]

Their bold and uncompromising stand on the race issue in Atlanta at a time when few predominantly white religious or secular organizations in the country were taking such a stand brought great praise from Shoghi Effendi. Here was a sterling example of what he had asked this body to do in addressing the race issue. A few months after its Atlanta visit, the NSA received a letter from Shoghi Effendi, written on his behalf by his secretary, praising them for their efforts. The letter stressed that "a special effort . . . should now be made to lay a foundation of unity between the white and colored Bahá'ís and weld the groups [in the region] into communities capable of forming Assemblies representative of both races."[92]

Notwithstanding the impact of the NSA's visit to Atlanta during the Fall of 1940 and the praise it received from Shoghi Effendi, teaching the Bahá'í Faith in the South still met formidable resistance both within and outside the Bahá'í community. Writing to an individual Bahá'í two years later, in 1942, Shoghi Effendi, through his secretary, commented upon the problems and challenges of teaching the Bahá'í Faith to blacks and whites in the South: "Regarding the whole manner of teaching the Faith in the South: the Guardian feels that, although the greatest consideration should be shown the feelings of white people in the South whom we are teaching, under no circumstances should we discriminate in their favor, consider them more valuable to the Cause than their Negro fellow-southerners, or single them out to be taught the Message first."

Evidently, there was still a tendency in the South to cater to the racial feelings of whites at the expense of blacks, in order to expand the religion.

89. Morrison, *To Move* 283.
90. Finke quoted in Morrison, *To Move* 283.
91. Morrison, *To Move* 283.
92. Quoted in Morrison, *To Move* 284.

But Shoghi Effendi was uncompromising. He refused to accept such an approach or policy for whatever short-term benefit it might bring. "To pursue such a policy, however necessary and even desirable it may superficially seem, would be to compromise the true spirit of our Faith, which permits us to make no such distinctions in offering its tenets to the world. The Negro and white races should be offered, simultaneously, on a basic of equality, the Message of Bahá'u'lláh."[93]

Understanding the legal discrimination as well as the delicate nature of race relations in the South, Shoghi Effendi offered some advice: "This does not mean that we should go against the laws of the state, pursue a radical course which will stir up trouble, and cause misunderstanding. On the contrary, the Guardian feels that, where no other course is open, the two races should be taught separately until they are fully conscious of the implications of being a Bahá'í, and then be confirmed and admitted to voting membership." This approach to teaching blacks and whites separately could have been misconstrued by those who did not understand that it was a means to an end, as the Guardian's letter made clear. "Once, however, this has happened, they cannot shun each other's company, and feel the Cause to be like other Faiths in the South, with separate white and black compartments. . . ." Shoghi Effendi reminded the reader that 'Abdu'l-Bahá had set "the perfect example" for Americans on the issue of race and had not shown any "favoritism to the white people as opposed to their dark-skinned compatriots." Then, Shoghi Effendi addressed the heart of black–white relations in the American Bahá'í community and the larger society: the whites' sometimes unconscious feelings of racial superiority that made them seek control in all situations involving non-whites. "No matter how sincere and devoted the white believers in the South may be, there is no reason why they should be the ones to decide when and how the Negro Southerner shall hear of the Cause of God; both must be taught by whoever rises to spread the Message in those parts."[94]

These events and the correspondence from Shoghi Effendi clearly show that the American Bahá'í community was experiencing a process of uneven development in the area of race relations. However, unlike other communities, it had the Guardian's spiritual guidance to keep it on track.

In 1943, the campaign for racial unity within the American Bahá'í community was bolstered when the NSA reminded the American Bahá'ís of "the connection between the struggle for race unity and the cause of international peace" and made racial unity the theme for nationwide proclamation near the end of a seven-year teaching plan.[95] The next year,

93. Quoted in Morrison, *To Move* 291.
94. Quoted in Morrison, *To Move* 291.
95. Morrison, *To Move* 284. There were three seven-year plans. The plan mentioned in the text was the first one. It was "launched with three major goals: (1) to establish at least

the NSA continued its bold and courageous leadership in the area of race unity by addressing a letter to President Franklin D. Roosevelt, who, in the face of black protests in 1941, had issued an Executive Order banning employment discrimination. The NSA commended the president for his "firm and powerful support of the principle of justice in race relations in connection with labor policy . . . and . . . attitude of understanding and sympathy toward the economic and social hardships sustained by our Negro citizens. . . ." The NSA told the president that what he had done was appreciated by all American Bahá'ís and that the "Bahá'ís have for many years been conscious and aware of the vital importance of race unity as a foundation for world order, and have established race unity spiritually and socially in their own community. . . ."[96]

As chairperson of the RUC, Dorothy Baker played an increasingly vital role in broadening the scope of the committee. For example, in 1941, she toured the South extensively to survey the state of race relations there. The results of the survey suggested how much race relations work Bahá'ís would have to do in the South. "The vast majority of the people," the survey found, "have no thought about minority groups. To them it seems that matters of race should be handled only with extreme delicacy. Their ideas and system are a combination of paternalism and the feudalism of a past age. The problem is so close to them that they cannot see it in perspective."[97]

Baker took notice in her survey of the shortcomings of the so-called liberal southern white mood exemplified by the "Southern Interracial Commission and the liberal attitudes of many southern colleges and universities." According to Baker, while these southern white organizations and institutions "advocate social reform and a bi-racial culture . . . any plan or suggestion for the races to meet upon an equal social plane causes a panic among them."[98] However, Baker's survey did uncover some people and groups who, though few in numbers, were like the Bahá'ís. "They see that even the rise of a bi-racial culture will not end perpetual conflict, unless there is a strong spiritual bond and a pattern for future society adopted."[99]

As it concluded its 1941 public programs, the RUC reported that "work with the great Negro minority of America has also gone steadily forward. The Bahá'í Faith has been presented this year to nineteen Negro schools

---

one local spiritual assembly in every state of the United States and every province of Canada; (2) to make certain that at least one Bahá'í teacher was residing in each Latin American republic; and (3) to complete the exterior design of the first Bahá'í House of Worship in North America. . . ." This plan was successfully completed in May of 1944. See William S. Hatcher and J. Douglas Martin, *The Bahá'í Faith: The Emerging Global Religion* 68.

96. *Bahá'í News* (April–May, 1945): 12.

97. *Bahá'í News* (June, 1941): 6.

98. *Bahá'í News* (June, 1941): 6.

99. *Bahá'í News* (June, 1941): 6.

and colleges, as well as to a number of adult Negro organizations." The RUC expressed its deep appreciation for the "noble and inspiring cooperation of the friends at large with these activities."[100]

Reports from Bahá'í local spiritual assemblies (LSAs) in December, 1942, indicated that many Bahá'í communities had accepted the RUC's invitation. Bahá'ís in San Francisco organized a Chinese evening that attracted fifty-eight people, including "five Chinese, five Negroes and one Mexican." The Bahá'ís in Philadelphia reported that they entertained at their center ". . . a group of very progressive Negro college boys and girls known as the 'West Phil. Civic Club' " and had high hopes that they would meet with this group in the future. In Urbana, Illinois, the Bahá'ís presented a twelve-minute radio broadcast, "The Question of Prejudice," which attracted the attention of the black community. The Bahá'ís received requests for copies of the talk and the *Illinois Times* in Danville, Illinois, printed the talk on its front page. Bahá'í communities in Phoenix, Milwaukee, Arlington, East Orange, Ann Arbor, Los Angeles, and Chicago, were all engaged in or planning some form of race unity work.[101] Clearly, the influence of the "most challenging issue" was awakening the American Bahá'í community.

As the American Bahá'í community became more involved in race unity work, Bahá'ís felt the need to be better acquainted with those Bahá'í sacred writings that bore directly on those racial issues confronting them. A partial list was published in the November, 1942, issue of *Bahá'í News*.

During the Fall of 1944, a report in *Bahá'í News* claimed: "The past year has reported the most progress in race unity since the movement began." Responding to appeals from the NSA, fifty-seven centers reported on race unity activities such as presentations to colleges, American Indians, and Eskimos, both in Alaska and Seattle. At the annual national Bahá'í convention, a reporter commented enthusiastically: ". . . the Convention itself was the greatest demonstration of race unity that history records, with so many traditionally discordant elements melted into oneness by the attracting power of the love of God. It was also the sign of the unity of religions and none the less, an index of world unity."[102]

Bahá'í communities continued their race unity activities led in part by the RUC, which in turn proceeded under the guidance of Shoghi Effendi. The Guardian's periodic, gentle but firm advice continued to keep the American Bahá'í community on course during its struggles to build a racially harmonious spiritual community. In December, 1945, Shoghi Effendi sent a letter through his secretary to the RUC pointing out that "to abolish prejudice against any and every race and minority group, it is obviously

---

100. *Bahá'í News* (September, 1941): 8.
101. *Bahá'í News* (December, 1942): 3–4.
102. *Bahá'í News* (September, 1944): 7.

proper for them to include in particular any group that is receiving especially bad treatment—such as the Japanese–Americans are being subjected to."[103] During World War II, anti-Japanese racism was widespread, and thousands of Japanese–Americans were interned in concentration camps.[104] Shoghi Effendi further specified that racial unity work should include the Mexicans, Chinese, and Native-Americans, in whom he was particularly interested. "He has always been very anxious to have the Indians taught and enlisted under the banner of the Faith, in view of the Master's ('Abdu'l-Bahá) remarkable statements about the possibilities of their future and that they represent the aboriginal American population."[105]

Of course, the key racial problem in America related to white discrimination against African–Americans. As Shoghi Effendi made clear in this letter: "The Negroes, likewise, are, one might say, a key problem and epitomize the feelings of color prejudice so rife in the United States. That is why he has so constantly emphasized the importance of the Bahá'ís actively and continuously demonstrating that in the Faith this cruel and horrible taint of discrimination against, and contempt for, them does not exist but on the contrary is supplanted by a feeling of esteem for their great gifts and a complete lack of prejudice in every field of life." Shoghi Effendi instructed the RUC that they should include in their work "as far as is possible, contacts with all minority groups, and wherever there is a particularly stout prejudice against a special group—such as . . . the Japanese in the Western states and the Negroes in the Southern [states] . . . efforts should be made to counteract it by showing publicly the Bahá'í example of loving tolerance and brotherly association."[106]

The RUC ended its work perhaps prematurely when during the 1947 National Bahá'í Convention it recommended its own demise. Several factors had contributed to this decision. According to Morrison, it was explained as a concern to "make the oneness of mankind an integral part of every facet of Bahá'í activity, rather than to compartmentalize it. . . ." However, Morrison points out, the RUC was going the way of previous Bahá'í committees on race. "Once again, after a period of concerted activity, the view that specific race unity activities emphasize differences more than unity seems to have predominated."[107] The historical ramifications of this decision would be clear decades later, as the community found itself revisiting some of the same old problems of

103. *Bahá'í News* (October, 1946): 3–4.

104. Bill Hosokawa, *Nisei: The Quiet Americans* 207–38; Ronald Takaki, *Strangers from a Different Shore: A History of Asian Americans* 379–405.

105. *Bahá'í News* (October, 1946): 4.

106. *Bahá'í News* (October, 1946): 4.

107. Morrison, *To Move* 290.

overcoming white resistance and black bitterness on what Shoghi Effendi had called the "long and thorny road, beset with pitfalls. . . ."[108]

The above divergence of views on how best to address the race problem in relation to the Bahá'í principle of the oneness of the human race was not new in the development of the American Bahá'í community's racial consciousness. It represented the constant tension between levels and stages of commitment to the instructions of 'Abdu'l-Bahá and Shoghi Effendi on how best to eliminate racism and build racial unity within both the American Bahá'í community and the larger American society. While some Bahá'ís felt uncomfortable about focusing upon the racial issue and had managed either to ignore or deny its significance, thus reconciling the Bahá'í teachings on the oneness of the human race with traditional policies of racial segregation, others, both black and white, were struggling with the Bahá'í insistence on acceptance and encouragement of interracial marriage. Shoghi Effendi's "most challenging issue" message forced many of these Bahá'ís to examine their fundamental racial feelings and beliefs. It left no room for compromise or denial. It was a clear and unequivocal mandate on how black and white Bahá'ís should relate to each other in their mutual responsibility for the resolution of the racial issue both within the American Bahá'í community and the larger society.

The RUC's discontinuation as an independent committee focusing exclusively on race and the incorporation of its responsibilities into the Bahá'í National Teaching Committee at a time when racism was still rampant in the United States could only result in a decline of interest in race issues in the American Bahá'í community at that stage of its development. Without the Race Unity Committee, Morrison notes, ". . . the most challenging issue was allowed to slip from the place of prominence that Shoghi Effendi and 'Abdu'l-Bahá had given it."[109]

Even so, the American Bahá'í community continued to grow and develop due to the Bahá'ís' commitment to what they accepted as a spiritual covenant between them and Bahá'u'lláh. This belief in the sacredness of the covenant created the receptivity of many American Bahá'ís to another round of advice and instruction on the racial issue in America from the Guardian of the Bahá'í Faith.

Shoghi Effendi's Messages on Race to the United States Bahá'í Community in the 1950s

In 1953, the American Bahá'í community received another infusion of guidance from the Guardian on the racial issue at the historic All-American Conference in Chicago celebrating the centenary of the birth of

---

108. Shoghi Effendi, *Advent of Divine Justice* 34.
109. Morrison, *To Move* 290.

Bahá'u'lláh's revelation, the dedication of the completed Bahá'í Temple in Wilmette, Illinois, and the start of a ten-year teaching and consolidation plan. Dorothy Baker, just returned from the Bahá'í World Centre, told the 2,000 Bahá'ís in attendance that the Guardian had said "one driving thing over and over—that if we did not meet the challenging requirement of raising to a vast number the believers of the Negro race, disasters would result. And . . . that it was now for us to arise and reach the Indians of this country. In fact he went so far as to say on two occasions that this dual task is the most important teaching work on American shores today."[110]

Baker related that Shoghi Effendi also discussed the historical and spiritual significance of the rise of dark-skinned peoples throughout the world. He told Baker that the dark-skinned people "would have an upsurge that is both spiritual and social. The spiritual upsurge will rapidly bring them great gifts because this is an act of God, and it is so intended. And all the world's prejudiced forces will not hold it back one hair's breadth."[111] The Bahá'ís, unlike the vast majority of Western white nations who were resisting the rising of the dark-skinned peoples, "will glorify it and understand it. The social repercussions of race suppressions around the world will increase at the same time, and, frightened, the world's forces will see that the dark-skinned peoples are really rising to the top—a cream that has latent gifts only to be brought out by divine bounties."[112]

Shoghi Effendi's powerful message reflected his profound insight into the historical and spiritual meaning of the rise of many Third World colonial and liberation movements. He well understood how the old world order, dominated for centuries by European peoples, was destined to be transformed by the rising up of peoples of color. Already by 1953, vast numbers of dark-skinned peoples were positioning themselves to throw off decades and centuries of racial oppression. Indians, Africans, and other dark-skinned people, including African–Americans, were in various stages of rising up against years of white racial domination. One scholar of the international ramification of race would go so far as to say: "In a world where the white rich seek to preserve an order against which the coloured poor rebel, the central fact of the future will increasingly emerge as the struggle between them. . . . The two colours are physically clashing in a dozen parts of the world already, whether through riots in the slums of American cities or the engagement of guns in South Vietnam and Angola." But, more importantly, he concluded, ". . . the occasions for clash must multiply, and the war grow ever more intense, unless the circumstances which provoke the antagonisms of race are themselves removed."[113]

---

110. Quoted in Morrison, *To Move* 292.
111. Quoted in Morrison, *To Move* 292.
112. Quoted in Morrison, *To Move* 292.
113. Ronald Segal, *The Race War* 1–63.

Once again the failure of the American Bahá'í community to reach the African–American and Native–American peoples in significant numbers compelled Shoghi Effendi to instruct them to establish special committees to do so. According to Baker, some Bahá'ís present at the meeting when Shoghi Effendi gave these instructions were concerned about "the kind of psychology that might ensue if you had a committee just to reach the Negroes." However, Shoghi Effendi had already heard these traditional excuses. They represented a pattern of avoidance and denial, even unwillingness to follow his and 'Abdu'l-Bahá's explicit instructions on the race issue. Dorothy Baker reported that Shoghi Effendi "scoffed" at these excuses "in a precious, twinkling kind of way, and firmly reiterated that without such special attention we simply had not done it—and that the important thing is to *do* it."[114]

Dorothy Baker continued her report to the conference by recalling that Shoghi Effendi then instructed the American Bahá'í community to establish two committees, one to teach African–Americans and the other to teach Native–Americans. What is to key to remember is how Shoghi Effendi characterized the nature of the effort to be undertaken, namely: "to reach the Negro minority of America with this great truth in vast numbers. Not just little publicity stunts. . . ."[115]

Shoghi Effendi's instructions to the predominantly white American Bahá'í community to bring into their ranks "vast numbers" of African–Americans was problematic at this stage of race relations when many white Bahá'ís undoubtedly felt that they were doing enough just conducting and participating in periodic race unity programs and attending occasional African–American events. Most certainly this level of Bahá'í activity was not sufficient to reach large numbers of African–Americans.

It is clear from Shoghi Effendi's teachings that had vast numbers of African–Americans, Native–Americans, and other people of color become Bahá'ís along with their white brothers and sisters, the American Bahá'í community would have had the spiritual power to transform American race relations for centuries. The spiritual blending within a community based upon the principles of the oneness of the human race would have spared the United States the many "disasters," e.g., race riots, urban rebellions, alluded to by both 'Abdu'l-Bahá and Shoghi Effendi.

Shoghi Effendi's subsequent letters to American Bahá'ís conveyed a sense that he was growing impatient with resistance to his explicit instructions and guidance on racial issues. Notwithstanding the increased interracial activity that followed the appointment of the Interracial Teaching Committee (ITC) in 1953, in 1957 Shoghi Effendi sent a letter through his

---

114. Dorothy Baker quoted in Morrison, *To Move* 293.
115. Dorothy Baker quoted in Morrison, *To Move* 293.

secretary to the committee: "White American Bahá'ís, he feels, although they have very much less prejudice than the American people, are nevertheless tainted to some extent with this national evil, perhaps wholly unconsciously so. Therefore, it behooves every believer of white extraction to carefully study his own attitude, and to see whether he is condescending in his relations with his fellow-Bahá'ís of [N]egro extraction. . . ."[116]

In keeping with his concerns for bringing large numbers of African–Americans, most of whom were at the time concentrated in the South, into the American Bahá'í community, Shoghi Effendi instructed the Bahá'ís to change their teaching methods, which up to that time had been designed to teach in ways that did not offend white racial sensibilities. "The attitude toward teaching the Faith in the southern states of the United States should be entirely changed," Shoghi Effendi told them. "For years, in the hope of attracting the white people, in order to 'go easy' with them and not offend their sensibilities, a compromise has been made in the teaching work throughout the South. The results have been practically nil. The white people have not responded worth mentioning, to the Faith, and the colored people have been hurt and also have not responded." Shoghi Effendi then advised the American Bahá'ís what should be done to remedy this situation. "He feels it is time that the Bahá'ís stopped worrying entirely about the white element in a community, and that they should concentrate on showing the [N]egro element that this is a Faith which produces full equality and which loves and wants minorities."[117]

Shoghi Effendi's characterization of white racial prejudice as a "national evil" and his appeal to every white Bahá'í to "carefully study his own attitude, and to see whether he is condescending in his relations with his fellow-Bahá'ís of [N]egro extraction . . ." did not mean that black and white American Bahá'ís were not still expected to work jointly on the racial problem: "Let neither think the solution of so vast a problem is a matter that exclusively concerns the other. . . ." However, in subsequent letters and messages to individuals, committees, and the American Bahá'í community in general, the increasing focus on white racial attitudes is clear. For example, in 1954, the same year that witnessed the historic landmark Supreme Court decision ending the Separate-but-Equal doctrine, Shoghi Effendi, in a letter to the American Bahá'í community, wrote: ". . . a revolutionary change in the concept and attitude of the average white American toward his Negro fellow citizen" was the vital element in remedying racism as one of the "basic weaknesses in the social fabric of the nation. . . ."[118]

---

116. Quoted in Morrison, *To Move* 293.
117. Quoted in Morrison, *To Move* 294.
118. *Citadel of Faith* 126.

Unfortunately, the concept and attitudes of the average white American toward black fellow citizens did not undergo much revolutionary change. This lack of willingness of average white Americans contributed in large part to the black urban rebellions of the 1960s, 1980s, and most particularly in the role that disenchanted black innercity residents and other marginalized groups in Los Angeles played in the 1992 riots in the wake of the Rodney King verdict.[119]

White American racism was but one manifestation of the global racism that had been a blight on humanity for centuries. Shoghi Effendi understood the global pervasiveness of white racism and sought to guide white Bahá'ís in overcoming its effects on the Bahá'í teaching efforts among peoples of color around the world. "The racial question all over Africa is very acute," he wrote to a British Bahá'í in August, 1951, "but, while being wise and tactful, believers must realise that their standard is far from that of the white colonials. They have not gone there to uphold the white man's supremacy, but to give the Cause of God to, primarily, the black man whose home is Africa."[120] The standards of the Bahá'í Faith to which Shoghi Effendi referred were the belief in and the practice of racial unity and the oneness of the human family. Such standards were in sharp contrast to the racial oppression of African peoples by European colonists. Shoghi Effendi's letter seems to suggest that perhaps some Bahá'ís had to be reminded not to "uphold the white man's supremacy" in Africa, a common practice among many European Christian missionaries in the region for decades.[121]

Invigorated by the messages of Shoghi Effendi, the American Bahá'í community embarked upon another stage in its march forward on the "long and thorny road" toward racial unity. Building on past achievements in race relations of the former RUC and a host of local Bahá'í communities, the Bahá'í Interracial Teaching Committee (ITC), in partnership with some local Bahá'í communities, began a systematic reaching out to African–Americans and Native–Americans.

---

119. For examples of how white racism continued to contribute to racial conflicts and violence in the 1980s, see *Confronting Racial Isolation in Miami: A Report of the United States Commission on Civil Rights.* For an excellent analysis of how the predominantly white jury perceived the Rodney King verdict, see "A Different Reality for Us," *U. S. News and World Report* (May 11, 1992): 36.

120. *The Unfolding Destiny of the British Bahá'í Community: The Messages from the Guardian of the Bahá'í Faith to the Bahá'ís of the British Isles* 460.

121. One example of how Christian missionaries upheld "the white man's supremacy" was in Central Africa. According to Robert I. Rotberg, a scholar of the region: "The missionaries urged Africans to copy the white man's ways. . . . many methods of coercion were used by the missionaries to obtain compliance with the modernizing demands; they denied a place upon the ladder of material advancement to those who refused to comply with missionary dictates" (*The Rise of Nationalism in Central Africa: The Making of Malawi and Zambia, 1873–1964* 9).

In November, 1954, the ITC joined the Birmingham, Alabama, Spiritual Assembly (LSA) in holding a public meeting on "Unity—The Keynote for Today." Dr. George Mitchell, regional director for the Southern Regional Council on Race Relations, discussed the economic and social aspects of the topic, while Mr. Ellsworth Blackwell, an African–American member of the National Spiritual Assembly and the Interracial Teaching Committee, presented the Bahá'í view. During the same month, the Bahá'ís of Albuquerque, New Mexico, joined with the southwest region of the NAACP in a Bahá'í-sponsored public meeting on "The Most Challenging Issue." In that same year, Bahá'ís participated in the Third Annual Conference of Branches of the NAACP, in Roswell, New Mexico. The Bahá'ís and the NAACP developed a very close relationship to the extent that some Bahá'ís in the state held executive positions in the NAACP branches. The Bahá'ís were so respected by the NAACP that a Bahá'í prayer was read at the opening of their first business session.[122]

Later in the year, the ITC reminded the American Bahá'í community of the Guardian's instructions concerning teaching minorities and urged them to study the messages again. The committee made an important suggestion: that public meetings be held "where the public, colored and white alike, can attend." The ITC explained that "while a special effort is made to attract the Negro, the Negro friends [Bahá'ís] must also put forth effort to invite and bring white friends to the meetings. . . ." The Bahá'ís should also, the ITC suggested, seek out contacts in similar organizations working for integration. The committee offered its assistance in both endeavors: "The Bahá'í Inter-Racial Committee is eager to assist any community or group in planning a program that will awaken the consciousness of the community to the importance of the principles of the Oneness of Humanity."[123]

American Bahá'ís and the Native–American

According to Bahá'í teachings, the black–white issue was pivotal for the solution of the racial problems in the United States, and by extension, in establishing world peace, but the role of Native–Americans in the fulfillment of America's spiritual destiny and the unification of the human race was no less significant. As noted earlier, 'Abdu'l-Bahá had pointed out to the American Bahá'í community the great role the Native–Americans would play in the unfolding of the New World Order.

During the 1920s when American Bahá'ís first read these words of 'Abdu'l-Bahá, most thought of Native-Americans in stereotypical terms soon to be institutionalized within American popular culture via "cowboy-and-Indian" movies. Much like white stereotypes about

---

122. *Bahá'í News* (January, 1955): 6.
123. *Bahá'í News* (September, 1955): 8.

African–Americans, racial stereotypes about Native peoples were historical and cultural by-products of centuries-old patterns of white racial dominance. The Bahá'í teachings on the role of the Native peoples not only rejected the stereotypical views but also emphasized the great need in the world for their special gifts and talents. As Shoghi Effendi explained in a 1957 letter to the National Spiritual Assembly of the Bahá'ís of Central America and Mexico, ". . . special attention most be focused on the work of converting the Indians to the Faith. The goals should be All-Indian assemblies, so that these much exploited and suppressed original inhabitants of the land may realize that they are equals and partners in the affairs of the Cause of God, and that Bahá'u'lláh is the Manifestation of God for them."[124]

The Bahá'í view of Native peoples in the Americas was far different from the traditional religious approach, which viewed them as wards and children to be rescued by so-called superior white religious organizations and which saw little to be gained from their culture. Shoghi Effendi told the Bahá'í community the Native peoples "should receive from the Bahá'ís a special measure of love, and every effort be made to teach them." Because, as Shoghi Effendi explained, "Their enrollment in the Faith will enrich them and us, and demonstrate our principle of the Oneness of Man far better than words or the wide conversion of the ruling races ever can."[125]

The Bahá'ís in the United States had been reaching out to Native peoples for years. In 1941, eighteen members of an Oneida tribe in Wisconsin were invited to the Bahá'í National Convention by Eli Whitney Pawlas, a member of the tribe, and by Clarence Niss, a white Bahá'í member of the Race Unity Committee. The presence of these Native peoples at the convention aroused great interest among the assembled Bahá'ís. Each Native person was introduced by name and given a gracious welcome. An observer of the event reported that the Oneidas "took a keen interest in what they saw and heard. It is hoped that these contacts will result in the spread of the Bahá'í Faith among a long neglected people, with heavenly results."[126]

By 1955, the Bahá'í community in the United States was making some impressive strides in its approach to Native peoples. Led by their American Indian Service Committee Bahá'ís made contact with eighteen Native–American tribes. Other major objectives of the current teaching and expansion plan were the translation of selections of the Bahá'í sacred writings into the Cherokee language, to be published in both Cherokee and English, and the "conversion of members of the leading Indian tribes. . . ."

124. *A Special Measure of Love: The Importance and Nature of the Teaching Work among the Masses, Messages from Shoghi Effendi and the Universal House of Justice* 19.

125. *Special Measure* 5.

126. *Bahá'í News* (June, 1941): 6.

Shoghi Effendi sent the 1955 Bahá'í national convention a message that further challenged the Bahá'ís in Indian service work. The message stated that "there should be added impetus in teaching the American Indian." According to the reporter, Shoghi Effendi pointed out to the American Bahá'í community how racism impeded the Bahá'í teaching efforts among minorities: "In America the Home Front teaching is staggering because of racial prejudice within Bahá'í communities themselves. Minorities are sensitive to this. It is the great weakness in America."[127]

The American Indian Service Committee informed Bahá'ís that one-third of Native peoples "live, work or go to school in towns across the country. Thus, most Bahá'ís have the opportunity to be neighbors and make friends with their Indian fellow-citizens: to demonstrate and then teach the Faith." The committee then presented a challenge to the American Bahá'í community in reaching out to the Native peoples: "Every believer, every group and every community has its part in this task."[128]

A brochure suggested methods of establishing first contacts with Native peoples and what Bahá'ís could do "to correct false conceptions concerning the Indian. . . ."[129] It would not be sufficient just to reach out to embrace the Native peoples as brothers and sisters in a common religious community; Bahá'ís also had to recognize and help facilitate the process by which Native peoples' great spiritual and cultural gifts, transformed and amplified by the spiritual teachings of Bahá'u'lláh, would enable them, in 'Abdu'l-Bahá's words, to "become so enlightened that the whole earth will be illumined."[130]

Throughout the 1950s and 1960s, Bahá'í communities in the vicinity of Native communities increased their efforts to serve, embrace, and welcome Native peoples into the Bahá'í community. In June, 1955, a conference in Bellingham, Washington, attended by blacks, whites, and Asians, featured a salmon bake on the Lummi Indian reservation.[131] During this period, the American Indian Service Committee of the American Bahá'í community assisted in meeting the medical needs of several Native communities. For example, in 1956, several Bahá'í medical professionals moved to Native reservations in Idaho, Montana, and New Mexico to serve the medical and educational needs there.[132]

The more Bahá'ís chose to live among the Native peoples, the more they came to appreciate the Bahá'í principle of the oneness of humanity. In the 1950s, an African–American Bahá'í family, Amos and Mary Gibson and their three children, moved to a Navajo reservation in Arizona. In 1956,

127. *Bahá'í News* (June, 1955): 16.
128. Reported in *Bahá'í News* (September, 1955): 8–9.
129. *Bahá'í News* (September, 1955): 9.
130. Quoted in Shoghi Effendi, *Advent* 55.
131. *Bahá'í News* (September, 1955): 9.
132. *Bahá'í News* (February, 1956): 10.

Amos and Mary wrote: "Here on the Navajo reservation we have met some new and different experiences. But we are more strongly impressed by the similarities which we believe are common to all mankind; a sense of pride in one's cultural heritage, a love for children, an eagerness for education, and a deep spiritual belief in a power far greater than man himself." The only regret the Gibsons had was that they had hesitated so long "considering family, home, jobs, health."[133] For the Gibsons and other Bahá'ís who chose to live and work among their Native–American spiritual brothers and sisters, the experience was well worth any inconvenience and brought them great spiritual rewards.

Bahá'í efforts to live among the Native peoples and to learn to appreciate and love them genuinely as spiritual members of a universal family contributed to the creation of deep and lasting spiritual bonds among Native–Americans, African–Americans, European–Americans, Asian–Americans, Hispanic–Americans, and other groups. The supreme purpose of this spiritual bonding was and remains the Bahá'í goal of the oneness of the human race. American history offers few other examples of such multiracial bonding.

One of the most touching stories of the growing love affair between the American Bahá'í community and the Native peoples occurred in 1956 during a visit by some Bahá'ís to the Hopi reservation in Northern Arizona. Among these Bahá'í visitors was a Bahá'í who had originally lived in Bombay, India. Through an interpreter, a venerable elder Hopi Chief told the Bahá'í visitors the story of the origins of the Hopi and of "an ancient stone tablet preserved at Hotevilla which carries the precepts of the Hopi way of life, and of the hope held by his people that the day is fast approaching when they can deliver it into the hands of the Massawa, the Great Spirit who was once in human form on this earth and who promised he would return to lead his people." One of the Bahá'ís responded with great compassion for the problems afflicting the Hopi (whose name means "the peaceful ones"), telling the Chief the story of Bahá'u'lláh's suffering and how he was forced to walk barefoot through the desert and endure imprisonment for bringing his message of peace to humankind. A Bahá'í who reported this story commented on the Hopi Chief's response: "There were tears in the old Chief's eyes as he listened to the story of the wrongs done to the Holy Ones of the Bahá'í Faith. Meanwhile, others came into the room and listened, quietly and attentively, to the telling of Bahá'u'lláh's message for all peoples and of the work of the Bahá'ís in fulfillment of the Hopi's [sic]." Later, a Hopi young man confided to the Bahá'í visitors that when he discussed the Bahá'í message with the oldest Hopi Chief, when the

---

133. *Bahá'í News* (April, 1956): 10.

Chief heard the name Bahá'u'lláh, he nodded and said, " 'Of course it is He to whom we have always been praying'."[134]

Bahá'ís in the United States and Canada continued their efforts to bond with the Native peoples. In 1956, Bahá'ís throughout southern California were invited to participate in a conference dedicated to urban Indians.[135] In 1957, two Bahá'ís established an "Indian Advancement Association" in Whitehorse, Yukon Territory, Canada.[136] In 1961, the Bahá'í teaching efforts on Native reserves in Canada, according to *Bahá'í News,* "attracted the attention of the London *Daily Mail,* which quoted Chief Samson Knowlton, a Bahá'í from the Peigan Reserve in Alberta: 'I think that by converting the Canadian tribes to the Bahá'í Faith, we can overcome the religious, political and tribal differences which for so long have split our people'." Chief Knowlton was then chairperson of the first Peigan Reserve Bahá'í Spiritual Assembly and an elected member of the Band Council for the Peigan Band of the Blackfoot Confederacy.[137]

During the same year, a group of Bahá'í Native peoples and whites visited a Canadian Native reserve. They brought with them letters of introduction to "the chiefs of all the Six Nations Reserves in Ontario and Quebec." Some of the reserves welcomed the Bahá'ís with a "special ceremony."[138] Bahá'í activities among Native peoples continued to make impressive headway. A 1962 report on Canadian Bahá'í teaching mentioned that "teaching among the Indians continues to be one of the highlights of Canadian Bahá'í activity." *Bahá'í News* reported that in September and October of 1961, "almost fifty new Indian believers were welcomed to the Faith." Most of these new Bahá'ís lived on reserves in Saskatchewan and in the Yukon Territory.[139]

One of the places where the spiritual bonding between the American Bahá'í community and the Native peoples was most evident was on the Great Navajo Indian Reservation in Arizona. In 1962, in Pine Spring, Arizona, a "Oneness of Mankind" conference, called by the Navajo hosts, "Different Races Gathering with Prayer," attracted peoples representing races, countries, and cultures from around the world. Four recently enrolled Navajo Bahá'ís played major roles in planning and conducting the conference. Bahá'ís from around the world could now see the first budding of the spiritual fruits, in faint but inevitable fulfillment of 'Abdu'l-Bahá's prediction that through the divine teachings the Native peoples would "shed light to all regions." Described by the Bahá'í American Indian Service Committee as "A Program of Love and Unity," the conference began with a

---

134. *Bahá'í News* (October, 1956): 11
135. *Bahá'í News* (May, 1956): 17.
136. *Bahá'í News* (February, 1957): 6.
137. *Bahá'í News* (August, 1961): 10.
138. *Bahá'í News* (August, 1961): 10.
139. *Bahá'í News* (January, 1962): 5.

prayer by an Iranian-born Bahá'í, Hand of the Cause of God[140] Zikru'lláh Khádem "who, as principal speaker, touched the hearts of the great audience through his loving spirit." The committee described the conference's program as like "a picture of a beautiful Navajo woman, who, having prepared her dyes from roots, herbs and minerals, and colored her wool, weaves into her rug the pattern of the unity of man."[141]

The guests shared the traditional sacred Navajo cake that was first blessed with traditional Navajo prayers. This conference of many races and cultures, inspired "many prayers and talks, all of them telling of the day when there will be the blending together of humanity in the sea of oneness." People from many races and cultures spoke on the theme of the oneness of the human family.

> We heard from the Navajo, the Hopi, the Ghanian [*sic*], the Chinese, the Eskimo, the Cherokee, the Aleut, the Taos, the Hawaiian, the Samoan, the Mexican, the Sioux, the Washoe, the African and the American—red, brown, white, black and yellow brothers and sisters. All spoke of the power of love to bring to the world the unity of mankind, their words being translated into Navajo. Young and old alike gave expressions of peace, love, oneness of mankind, humility and justice for all. What a joy it was to know "Ye are all the fruits of one tree."[142]

The oneness of humanity was manifested throughout the conference through a variety of intimate experiences:

> At suppertime families joined families and bread was broken in the beautiful mingling of races. The children joined in games. . . .
> There were Indian dances, friendship dances, fire dances, beautiful symbolic interpretive dances . . . everything inspired by the theme of the conference. The beauty of the words of Mr. Khádem stirred to tears more than a thousand souls as they listened to his message of God's love for all mankind. A Navajo policeman was heard to say, "I have to write a report about this meeting, but I don't know what to say. It's unexplainable! . . . I've never been to a meeting like this before."[143]

---

140. Bahá'u'lláh created the institution of the Hands of the Cause of God during the end of his ministry, "when He appointed four Hands of the Cause charged with the responsibility of teaching and promoting the interests of the Faith" (Taherzadeh, *The Covenant of Bahá'u'lláh* 1). In his will and testament, 'Abdu'l-Bahá described the obligations of the Hands of the Cause of God in relation to the Bahá'í community: "The obligations of the Hands of the Cause of God are to diffuse the Divine Fragrances, to edify the souls of men, to promote learning, to improve the character of all men, and to be, at all times and under all conditions, sanctified and detached from earthly things. They must manifest the fear of God by their conduct, their manners, their deeds and their words" (*Will and Testament of 'Abdu'l-Bahá* 13.
141. *Bahá'í News* (August, 1962): 10–11.
142. *Bahá'í News* (August, 1962): 11.
143. *Bahá'í News* (August, 1962): 11.

The Establishment of Race Amity Day
A Bahá'í Annual Observance

The oneness of humanity theme that had drawn Bahá'ís from all over the world to a Navajo reservation to pray, break bread, and celebrate their membership in one human family was at the same time inspiring other Bahá'ís across the United States to observe June 10th as Race Amity Day. In 1957, the National Spiritual Assembly, with the approval of the Guardian, had instituted this annual observance to be "comparable in importance with World Religion Day" and to be "observed on the second Sunday of June beginning June 9, 1957." Race Amity Day was established to be an exclusively Bahá'í-sponsored event different from Brotherhood Week and Negro History Week, events sponsored by other organizations in which Bahá'ís had participated. The purpose of Race Amity Day was to "celebrate the Bahá'í teaching of the Oneness of Mankind, the distinguishing feature of the Revelation of Bahá'u'lláh."[144]

Also in 1957, the Bahá'í Interracial Teaching Committee started holding a race amity meeting in conjunction with the annual observance of Negro History Week by the Association for the Study of Negro Life and History. Eighty-three Bahá'í communities in thirty-five states conducted some form of public meeting addressing the concerns of African–Americans and the Association distributed Bahá'í literature to its exclusive mailing list of distinguished African–Americans. In turn, the committee gave the Association 500 copies of *Race and Man,* a Bahá'í publication featuring discussions on race.[145]

The NSA pointed out that "far more than a mere numerical addition to the Bahá'í community is involved. The relationship of the white and Negro races in America is crucial in the national and indeed the international destiny."[146] The NSA then quoted an April 12, 1927, letter from Shoghi Effendi that bore directly on the subject:

> As this problem, in the inevitable course of events, grows in acuteness and complexity, and as the numbers of the faithful from both races multiplies [*sic*], it will become increasingly evident that the future growth and prestige of the Cause are bound to be influenced to a very considerable degree by the manner in which the adherents of the Bahá'í Faith carry out, first among themselves, and in their relations with their fellow-men, those high standards of interracial amity so fearlessly exemplified to the American people by . . . 'Abdu'l-Bahá.[147]

144. *Bahá'í News* (May, 1957): 1.
145. *Bahá'í News* (April, 1957): 6.
146. *Bahá'í News* (September, 1957): 1.
147. Quoted in *Bahá'í News* (September, 1957): 1.

The NSA ended its message with this urgent appeal: "Prayer, meditation, and consecrated action in this field of interracial teaching are indeed required!"[148]

Bahá'í Race Unity Work during the Turbulent 1960s

The annual Race Amity Day observance played a key role during the racially volatile period of the 1960s. Building on its long tradition of working for racial unity, justice, and amity, beginning with the first race amity conferences in the early 1920s, the American Bahá'í community became increasingly recognized for its unique and exclusive focus on racial amity and unity as the foundation for the solution of the racial crisis in the United States. While the 1960s in racial terms is most often characterized by scholars and lay persons alike as the decade of the Civil Rights Movement and black urban rebellions, it was also a decade during which scores of local Bahá'í communities (many of which were all-white) worked tirelessly for racial unity between blacks and whites.

As significant as the Civil Rights Movement and the black urban rebellions were in influencing American race relations and in raising public awareness of the urgency of addressing racial injustices, the annual Race Amity Day observances of the Bahá'í community during and after the 1960s kept before the American public a vision of a more transcendent and potentially transforming view of race. While sharing the fundamental view of the Civil Rights Movement that African–Americans' rights as citizens had been violated and that they deserved to be heard and their rights as citizens vindicated, the Bahá'í community through its annual Race Amity observances also sought to transform the historical relationship between blacks and whites, to elevate it to the level of a spiritual fellowship based on the recognition of the oneness of the human race.

Years after the first Bahá'í Race Amity Day observance, scores of Bahá'í communities throughout the country, through picnics, panel discussions, media events, and official proclamations had imprinted on the consciousness of thousands of Americans from many racial and cultural backgrounds the vision and model of a much higher level of interracial interaction: namely, that of genuine interracial love and harmony as reflected in the Bahá'í concept of racial unity. By 1960, several years after the initiation of the Race Amity Day observance, this annual observance was earning increasing recognition by governmental officials. For example, in 1967, eleven mayors and one governor officially proclaimed Race Unity[149] Day in the United States.[150]

---

148. *Bahá'í News* (September, 1957): 2.

149. For a discussion of the change from race *amity* to race *unity*, see Morrison, *To Move* 275ff.

150. *Bahá'í News* (August, 1966): 14–17.

The NAACP recognized the American Bahá'í community's long commitment to racial justice and unity in 1964 when it invited Dr. Rexford Parmelee, chairman of the Washington, D.C. Bahá'í Assembly, to "present greetings from the Bahá'ís of the United States" to its 55th National Convention. Dr. Sarah Martin Pereira, a second-generation African–American Bahá'í woman and one of several blacks on the National Spiritual Assembly of the Bahá'ís of the United States, read a message from the Bahá'í national body to Roy Wilkins, then Executive Secretary of the NAACP:

> The National Spiritual Assembly of the Bahá'ís of the United States extends to you a warm and sincere greeting, acknowledging the continuing success of your noble aims and lofty ambitions to achieve justice and equal opportunity for colored peoples. We feel we are a kindred spirit because our endeavors to further the cause of the oneness of mankind parallel yours. All organizations working for unity are of God and will one day share in the glory and the gratification of having striven earnestly and long for the promised day when the unification of mankind will become a cherished reality.[151]

A year later, the NSA requested Bahá'ís to participate in the march on Montgomery[152] and sent out two telegrams "making known the uncompromising stand of the Bahá'ís for unity of all mankind." One telegram went to President Lyndon B. Johnson:

ON EVE HISTORIC MARCH SIGNALLING END LIMITATIONS NEGRO VOTING SOUTHERN STATES, WE AFFIRM YOUR MORAL STAND FOR THE RIGHTS OF MAN. AMERICA'S WORLD LEADERSHIP DEPENDS UPON THESE COURAGEOUS STEPS TOWARD POLITICAL, SOCIAL AND PERSONAL FREEDOM. MAY GOD ALLOW YOU TO SPEAK FORTH WITH WISDOM AND ELOQUENCE, THAT YOU MAY BECOME, IN AMERICA AND IN THE WORLD, THE UPHOLDER AND DEFENDER OF THE VICTIM OF OPPRESSION, WHOEVER HE MAY BE.[153]

The other telegram went to the Southern Christian Leadership Conference: "YOUR MORAL LEADERSHIP HUMAN RIGHTS IN SOUTH PRAISEWORTHY HISTORY MAKING FREEDOM IN UNITED STATES. SENDING

---

151. *Bahá'í News* (September, 1964): 16.

152. The march on Montgomery, Alabama, was to celebrate the end of voting restrictions placed on southern blacks for decades. Marching on Montgomery also held symbolic significance for the nation and the world because it was the city of the famous 1955 bus boycott that catapulted the Reverend Dr. Martin Luther King, Jr. to international fame and opened the era of the Civil Rights Movement in the United States. For the history of the Montgomery bus boycott, see Chapter 5, "The Montgomery Bus Boycott" in Taylor Branch, *Parting the Waters: America in the King Years, 1954–63* 143–206.

153. *Bahá'í News* (June, 1965): 13.

REPRESENTATION MONTGOMERY AFFIRM YOUR CRY FOR UNITY OF AMERICANS AND ALL MANKIND."[154]

The Bahá'ís who responded to the NSA's appeal to participate in this historic 1965 march could not help but feel that they were reflecting 'Abdu'l-Bahá's and Shoghi Effendi's most heartfelt concern for the achievement of racial justice and unity in the United States:

> The Bahá'ís who marched will never forget these moving experiences. We were very happy to be among and share with others the wonderful realization of the oneness of mankind. Viewing the traumatic situation of America and the American Bahá'ís' participation in remedying the great sickness of their nation, we are reminded of the words of Shoghi Effendi, "The American believers, standard bearers of this world-wide community and torch-bearers of an as yet unborn civilization, have girt up their loins, unfurled their banners, and stepped into the arena of service. Their plan has been formulated. Their forces are mobilized. They are steadfastly marching towards their goal. . . . The generality of mankind, blind and enslaved, is wholly unaware of the healing power with which this community is endowed, nor can it as yet suspect the role which this same community is destined to play in its redemption."[155]

When the first of several black urban rebellions of the 1960s broke out in the Watts section of Los Angeles during the summer of 1965, a Bahá'í reporter for *Bahá'í News* wrote a moving article describing not only what happened but also how several white Bahá'ís responded. In describing the devastation in the wake of the urban disturbance, the reporter went to the very heart of the problem:

> An uneasy peace settled slowly on this densely-populated core of colored citizenry in the very center of the sprawling Los Angeles megalopolis. Its physical scars, ugly as they were, still were nothing in comparison with the deeper wounds in the hearts of a Negro populace understandably embittered, sullen, suspicious. The police, overwhelmingly white, had been dismally unconvincing as a guardian of peace and justice. Many residents, toughened by prior clashes with the law, and with the savagery that is born of the slums, had lashed out viciously at invader and neighbor alike. Could any other group of people be less convinced that mankind's destiny is unity? Would people, afraid to open their doors, open their hearts? The word of John Law had aroused resentment. The words of Bahá'u'lláh would arouse hope of justice and unity.[156]

For the fourth time[157] since 'Abdu'l-Bahá's 1912 warning about how the

---

154. *Bahá'í News* (June, 1965): 13.

155. Quoted in *Bahá'í News* (June, 1965): 13.

156. *Bahá'í News* (December, 1965): 21.

157. The 1965 Watts racial disorder, i.e., black urban rebellion, was preceded by more overtly racial conflicts between blacks and whites in East St. Louis in 1917, Chicago in 1919, and Detroit in 1943. See Joseph Boskin, *Urban Racial Violence in the Twentieth Century* 42–60.

unresolved racial problems in America would cause the streets of American cities to flow with blood, the American Bahá'í community faced the challenge of playing its vital role in contributing to the solution of America's racial crisis. A few brave Bahá'ís responded to the challenge. A white Bahá'í couple "faced the challenge of Watts with prayerful dedication and determination. Their efforts were the seeds of a campaign of love in a turbulent, hate-tormented area." They were soon followed by other Bahá'ís dedicated to building bridges and healing the wounds of racism. These were not guilt-ridden whites rushing into black ghettoes to give advice and charity only to retreat to their comfortable all-white suburbs. Several months later, there were eight black Bahá'ís in Watts[158] who could join the Bahá'í community in working for racial justice and unity.

While these Bahá'ís were attempting to live up to the mandate placed upon them by the sacred teachings of their religion, the Watts and subsequent black urban rebellions spoke clearly to what in many American Bahá'í minds and hearts was their own shortcoming in carrying out the instructions of 'Abdu'l-Bahá and Shoghi Effendi. Young African–American Bahá'ís, influenced in large part by the radical black-power movements of the decade and dissatisfied with the, at times, slow pace of racial changes within the American Bahá'í community, began demanding a more radical race-relations agenda from the larger Bahá'í community. Many of these African–American Bahá'í youth used Shoghi Effendi's assessment of the American Bahá'í community's role in solving the racial crisis, "The Most Challenging Issue," as their manifesto in forcing the racial issue upon the older generation of black and white Bahá'ís who had become somewhat comfortable with less controversial approaches to race.

Some of these younger African–American Bahá'ís were involved in various black radical organizations in black urban communities and on college campuses and often found it difficult to balance their devotion to a faith founded on universal principles of the oneness of the human race with a radical black ideology that advocated racial justice and black power and that believed "Black-is-Beautiful." As expected, tensions developed not only between the radical blacks and many older white Bahá'ís who had resisted putting into practice Shoghi Effendi's repeated instructions on the racial issue but also between these black youth and some of the older African–American Bahá'ís who had not moved beyond the initial stage of race relations within the American Bahá'í community. Only their common belief in the teachings of Bahá'u'lláh enabled them finally to work cooperatively on this persistent problem of racism and racial conflict both within and outside the American Bahá'í community.[159]

---

158. *Bahá'í News* (December, 1965): 21.

159. These events are drawn from the author's and other African–American Bahá'ís' experiences during the 1960s.

As the 1960s ended, a white backlash began. Not unlike previous periods of radical change in the racial status quo, a growing segment of the white population began mobilizing to offset the real and imagined gains achieved by African–Americans during the Civil Rights and Black Power Movements. Much as they had before, these white Americans were growing tired of the national focus on racial issues. The rise of neoconservatism in politics eroded much of the waning white public sentiment for the continuation of the struggle against racism.

Building a Multi-ethnic Religious Community during an Era of Resurgent Racism and Racial Conflict

From the late 1960s to the present, the forces of racism steadily gained ground in certain circles of influence, encouraged and supported by many leaders in high places who have unabashedly employed "racial policies" to acquire power and influence. Remedial programs such as affirmative action came steadily under fire from resurrected and refurbished theories of racial and cultural inferiority. As the struggle for racial justice and unity faded from the public memory, the American Bahá'í community continued its long, steady, and often lonely struggle to keep before the American public the vision of racial unity as the only real solution to a seemingly unsolvable problem.

One of its most impressive achievements blossomed during the early 1970s when thousands of African–Americans in rural South Carolina and many in other southern states joined the Bahá'í Faith.[160] It was this sudden and much welcomed entry of large numbers of southern blacks into the American Bahá'í Community that placed it vastly above the majority of multiracial religious communities in the United States. Unlike so many predominantly white religious communities in the United States that keep their racial minorities at arm's length, avoiding at all costs, an increase of minorities—especially African–Americans—in their congregations, most white Bahá'ís saw this increase in black Bahá'ís in the South as a partial fulfillment of the American Bahá'ís' spiritual destiny of uniting the races. In 1986, the Interracial Teaching Committee mentioned this great influx of southern rural blacks into the Bahá'í community in connection with other racial groups as an indication of the American Bahá'í community's becoming "a truly multiethnic community, with fully one-third of its membership black and rural, and a significant percentage from the Native American, Hispanic, Iranian, and Southeast Asian populations."[161] "Multi-ethnic" included many other groups as well: for example, in 1972, the American Bahá'í Northeast Oriental Teaching Committee, composed of Bahá'ís from Chinese, Japanese, Jewish, and African–American backgrounds, began its work "to bring the Faith of

---

160. *The American Bahá'í* (February, 1971): 1–4; (April, 1976): 1.
161. *Power of Unity* ix.

Bahá'u'lláh to the Oriental peoples of the Northeastern States so that through His power, their true station will be achieved."[162]

The American Bahá'í community's efforts among Asian populations throughout the United States continued during the 1980s. The teaching plan called for appointment of a Chinese Teaching Committee (done in 1985) and the development of Chinese-speaking teachers. The committee identified university campuses as the most receptive area for teaching, and Bahá'ís at a number of large universities engaged in a variety of activities to build relationships with Chinese friends.[163]

In 1985, Milwaukee Bahá'ís, in cooperation with the Midtown Neighborhood Association, a social-service agency, and the Hmong–American Friendship Association endeavored to serve the needs of the Hmong people in the neighborhood by opening the Bahá'í center on weekends for adult English classes and after school for culture and language classes for children ages 8-13. The Bahá'ís in turn were invited by the directors of the Hmong associations to attend culture and language classes. The Bahá'ís' hope was that soon they and "the Hmongs and Laotians would be able to take part in some kind of joint social event to facilitate understanding, friendship and an exchange of information among the groups."[164]

During this period in southern California, a Bahá'í-sponsored project known as AKISA (Adults and Kids in Santa Ana) was established to serve the needs of the Laotian and Cambodian populations by helping the newly arrived refugees adjust to their surroundings, including helping the children learn English.[165] In response to the unprecedented waves of Asian immigrants during the 1980s, the American Bahá'í community published guidelines to facilitate the integration of Indo–Chinese refugees into the Bahá'í community. "We have the good fortune of being able to share this land as a refuge, as well as to facilitate the contribution of each of the diverse cultures not only into the U. S. but into the American Bahá'í community as well."[166]

The Bahá'ís also made considerable efforts to locate Bahá'í refugees who had been in the United States for "up to 10 years with little or no contact with their local Bahá'í communities." In 1989, coordinators of the U.S. Bahá'í Refugee Office visited ten cities throughout central California to help reintegrate the refugees into the larger Bahá'í community.[167]

The American Bahá'í Community's concern for building a truly multi-ethnic community extended naturally to those Southeast Asian refugees who were not Bahá'ís. For example, the Bahá'ís in Des Moines, Iowa,

---

162. *Bahá'í News* (January, 1973): 5.
163. *The American Bahá'í* (December, 1985): 12.
164. *The American Bahá'í* (March, 1985): 8.
165. *The American Bahá'í* (April, 1986): 7.
166. *The American Bahá'í* (July, 1986): 11.
167. *The American Bahá'í* (April, 1989): 2.

resolved to adopt all Cambodian refugees in that state as a service goal for 1989–90. Between 1983 and 1989, a Bahá'í in Tacoma, Washington, who had worked with Southeast Asian Bahá'ís in Thai–Cambodian border camps, conducted literacy classes for Southeast Asian Bahá'í refugees in the area and served on two non-Bahá'í committees in Tacoma. In August, 1991, the U.S. Bahá'í Refugee Office published a notice in *The American Bahá'í* under the caption, "Welcome S. E. Asians," stating that they would "like to remind the friends of the National Spiritual Assembly's standing policy that local Bahá'í communities welcome Southeast Asian Bahá'í newcomers to the U.S. whether or not they have credentials from overseas."[168] Such encouragement by the NSA on behalf of its fellow believers from another country seeking refuge in a strange land demonstrated once again the American Bahá'í commitment to the building of a multi-ethnic spiritual community.

The persecution of Iranian Bahá'ís by the revolutionary regime in Iran during the late 1970s and throughout the 1980s forced many Iranian Bahá'ís to seek refuge in the United States, further increasing the diversity in the American Bahá'í community. In 1979, the National Persian–American Committee was established to "help in the resettlement of the Persian Bahá'ís in the U. S. and their integration into the American Bahá'í community."[169]

Well over a half-century ago, Shoghi Effendi placed high praise on any effort by Bahá'ís to enhance the diversity of the American Bahá'í community: "No more laudable and meritorious service can be rendered the Cause of God, at the present hour, than a successful effort to enhance the diversity of the members of the American Bahá'í community by swelling the ranks of the Faith through the enrollment of the members of these races."[170] Few, if any, among his contemporaries, understood the synergistic influence inherent in the enhancement of diversity within society. "A blending of these highly differentiated elements of the human race, harmoniously interwoven into the fabric of an all-embracing Bahá'í fraternity," Shoghi Effendi wrote in 1938, "and assimilated through the dynamic processes of a divinely appointed Administrative Order, and contributing each its share to the enrichment and glory of Bahá'í community life, is surely an achievement the contemplation of which must warm and thrill every Bahá'í heart."[171]

The Race Unity Committee played a pivotal role during the 1980s in keeping the American Bahá'í Community focused on the key racial issues that contributed to the building and consideration of the emerging multi-

---

168. *The American Bahá'í* (August, 1991): 12.
169. *The American Bahá'í* (June, 1985): 2; Geoffrey Nash, *Iran's Secret Pogrom.*
170. Shoghi Effendi, *Advent of Divine Justice* 54.
171. Shoghi Effendi, *Advent of Divine Justice* 54.

ethnic American Bahá'í Community. *The American Bahá'í* published special sections on racial unity and devoted special sections to particular populations such as Persians, Native–Americans, and Hispanics. The "Race Unity" section in *The American Bahá'í* kept the American Bahá'í community abreast of a wide variety of race unity programs, events, and activities of local Bahá'í communities.[172] The 1985 publication of *The Power of Unity: Beyond Prejudice and Racism,* a selection of writings from the sacred teachings of the Bahá'í Faith as well as from Shoghi Effendi and the Universal House of Justice, compiled by Bonnie J. Taylor of the National Race Unity Committee, provided the American Bahá'í Community with the best available Bahá'í teachings on the relationship of race to the unification of the human family.

Present and Future Challenges Facing the United States Bahá'í Community: Relationship to the Present and Future State of Race Relations in the United States

The advice from 'Abdu'l-Bahá to the Bahá'í community that "it is impossible to unite unless united . . ." constitutes both a promise and a warning to the Bahá'í community in the United States. It is a promise that if the American Bahá'í community continues to work on its own racial problems, guided by the sacred teachings of Bahá'u'lláh and 'Abdu'l-Bahá and the writings of its late Guardian, Shoghi Effendi, and the guidance of its institutions, then it will become the means to transform race relations throughout the United States. The warning is that if the American Bahá'í community does not succeed in uniting itself, it will lose its spiritual opportunity to effect such a transformation.

The present racial challenges facing the Bahá'í community are the same ones facing the nation as a whole: racial, cultural, and class tensions, conflicts, and alienation. Degrees of racial and cultural tensions and polarization can be observed throughout the community life of the American Bahá'í community. The problem of alienation among many African–American Bahá'ís, reflected in cases of "dropping out" or becoming "inactive," has been a problem in Bahá'í community life in the United States as far back as 1927, when Sadie Oglesby, an African–American Bahá'í from Boston, complained at the 1927 Bahá'í National Convention that the Bahá'ís "were neither attracting new black believers nor holding onto those who had once been interested" in the Bahá'í Faith.[173] That this problem of receptiveness and cultural sensitivity still exists is evident in the various black-on-black dialogues throughout the American Bahá'í community.

---

172. For examples of these developments, see copies of *The American Bahá'í* during the mid-1980s.

173. Morrison, *To Move* 161.

Several attempts have been made to address aspects of this alienation of some black Bahá'ís from local Bahá'í community life. During the late 1970s, black Bahá'ís and white Bahá'ís in Michigan organized a "Most Challenging Issue" conference to attract some of these alienated, "inactive" black Bahá'ís back to the Bahá'í community. Beginning in the late 1980s, a Black Men's Conference has been held each summer at the Louis Gregory Institute in Hemingway, South Carolina. What started out as a gathering of a few black Bahá'í men sharing their concerns and hopes as black men in a religious community, still greatly influenced by European–American social mores, has evolved into a fairly large and still growing number of participants. Viewed through the eyes of an outsider or even some Bahá'ís unable to understand the function of such racial gatherings as a necessary remedial step in the spiritual development of both black Bahá'ís and Bahá'í community life, such gatherings might well be seen as a separatist tendency within the American Bahá'í community. However, once seen within the context of a multicultural religious community exploring a variety of methods to heal and unite a wide range of different peoples and individuals at various levels and stages of spiritual and emotional growth, then a gathering such as the Black Men's Conference makes sense. Other racial and ethnic groups within the American Bahá'í community also have had their special gatherings to focus on particular concerns.[174]

Another challenge facing the American Bahá'í community is overcoming the influence of racial patterns, attitudes, and beliefs created by the increase of racial polarization in the larger society. African–American, Native, Asian, European–American, and Iranian–American Bahá'ís are probably as segregated in their daily lives outside the Bahá'í community as are their counterparts in other religious communities. Some Bahá'ís residing in isolated white suburbs have been influenced by the anti-black racism so common in such suburbs. The crucial difference is that, for example, the Iranian–American and European–American Bahá'ís who live in either all-white or predominantly white suburbs have a greater opportunity and obligation through a range of Bahá'í activities and events such as regional proclamations, holy day celebrations, and summer and winter schools, to interact actively with African–American Bahá'ís who reside in either all-black or predominantly black innercity communities. The same situation exists for the African–American Bahá'í who lives in an all-black or predominantly black community. Unlike the vast majority of blacks and whites in the larger society who have little or no opportunity—and, in many cases, no inclination—to create and maintain spiritual bonds that

---

174. Bahá'ís have also supported meetings involving other groups such as women, Native–Americans, and Hispanics. See *The American Bahá'í*, May, 1984; February, 1985; and October, 1990.

reach across the white-suburban–black-ghetto chasm, Bahá'ís from all classes, races, and cultures are obligated by their sacred writings and principles to work for the oneness of the human race and, in the United States, to address "The Most Challenging Issue" of racial polarization.

However, there are still some Bahá'ís, particularly those whose daily lives confine them to largely white interaction, who are uncomfortable with any more than token (and preferably professional) African–American representation within certain Bahá'í communities. African–American Bahá'ís will have to help meet this challenge so crucial to the future development of the American Bahá'í community by not falling into the unintentional trap of being comfortable in token roles dictated in large part by the racial comfort levels of some white Bahá'ís. Instead, they must lovingly assist their Bahá'í brothers and sisters in expanding their racial comfort level to the point where they are not only comfortable in all racial settings but come to have great appreciation for African–Americans, the one race in the United States that they have been most conditioned to fear and hold in contempt.

Such a challenge can be frightening to those Bahá'ís who have grown accustomed to the racial status quo in the Bahá'í community, as "entry by troops" in the Bahá'í Faith will undoubtedly include vast numbers of racial minorities, many of whom will admittedly be from the worst sections of town. Some will be drug-addicts, ex-convicts, people on welfare, angry black, Hispanic, Asian, and Native–American youth from every segment of the underclass, driven by racism to the margins of society. These are the people whom the American Bahá'ís must and will welcome with open arms because the Bahá'í Faith teaches that the application of the principle of the oneness of the human race to the problems of the world will ensure peace, love, and fellowship. To accomplish this great task, the American Bahá'í community must make itself the model by constantly struggling to live up to the teachings of Bahá'u'lláh.

The American Bahá'í community entered the 1990s with increased commitment to its long-cherished goal of proclaiming and practicing racial unity. Local race unity programs and activities gathered momentum during the last decade just as the community was experiencing a significant growth in cultural diversity brought on in part by the recent influx of Indo–Chinese and Iranian Bahá'ís.

In contrast to the understandable concerns—at times bordering on a sensationalistic obsession with racial conflicts—of the media and those working in the field of race relations, the Association for Bahá'í Studies held an unprecedented conference entitled "Models of Racial Unity," in November of 1990, in Atlanta, Georgia. The purpose of this conference was an exploration of "models of racial unity" rather than the traditional focus on racial crises and conflicts. The American Bahá'í Community had first modeled this "new" approach to race relations before they sought to introduce it to the public and the race relations industry. Skeptics had to concede that the American Bahá'í community had spent considerable time applying this approach to their own internal racial problems and were still in the process of doing so.

One of the first fruits of the Models of Racial Unity Conference was a joint project, "Models of Unity: Racial, Ethnic, and Religious," conducted in the Spring of 1991 by the Human Relations Foundation of Chicago and the American NSA. The purpose of the joint-project was "to find examples of efforts that have successfully brought different groups of people together in the greater Chicago area. Both organizations were concerned about the prominence of publicity about interracial violence, confrontation, and conflict, and were convinced that examples of interracial harmony, peaceful coexistence, and unity were common, yet less well known."[175] A key factor in establishing the joint project and one which had motivated the organizers of the Models of Racial Unity Conference in Atlanta earlier was the lack of research on what one researcher has called "the other tradition" in American race relations, namely: the history of racial unity, cooperation, and fellowship.[176] The sponsors of the joint project took a bold first step in this fairly new direction by explicitly stating that "scholarship on interracial interaction has explored the conflicts in detail, but has done little to examine the roots of interracial unity."[177]

In 1991, the NSA also published a statement entitled, *The Vision of Race Unity: America's Most Challenging Issue,* which was regarded as the cornerstone of a national race unity campaign. The NSA insisted that "racism is the most challenging issue confronting America. . . . To ignore the problem is to expose the country to physical, moral, and spiritual danger." The statement that "the application of the spiritual principle of the oneness of humanity to the life of the nation would necessitate and make possible vast changes in the economic status of the non-white segments of the population"[178] would soon apply to the 1992 Los Angeles "riot" in which many poor and marginalized people of color were involved. Since its publication, *The Vision of Race Unity* has been distributed to a wide range of people including teachers, students, organizations, groups, and public officials.

---

175. "Models of Unity: Racial, Ethnic, and Religious" 1.

176. See "The Other Tradition in American Race Relations," Chapter 7 of this book.

177. "Models of Unity: Racial, Ethnic, and Religious," A project of the Human Relations Foundation of Chicago and the National Spiritual Assembly of the Bahá'ís of the United States, February, 1992.

178. *The Vision of Race Unity: America's Most Challenging Issue* 1 and 5.

In April, 1992, several months after the publication of the joint project report, the National Spiritual Assembly of the Bahá'ís of the United States sponsored a Race Unity Conference at the Carter Presidential Center, Atlanta, Georgia. The purpose of the conference was stated thus:

> During the next few years the City of Atlanta will be the focus of efforts to transform its society and to alleviate social illnesses that affect the city and the entire nation. We believe that these efforts can only succeed if the races are united in common purpose and vision. The purpose of this conference is to explore specific actions which may be taken by different groups and institutions to establish racial unity as the foundation for the transformation of our society.[179]

Soon after the NSA held this conference, Los Angeles exploded in violence in the wake of the Rodney King verdict. Responding to the news of the disturbance there and in other cities, the Universal House of Justice sent a letter to the American NSA, which in part stated:

> . . . we reiterate more strongly than before the encouragement we expressed for your campaign to combat racism in the United States. It is highly fitting that during this Holy Year, which marks the centenary of the ascension of the Manifestation of God Who made the oneness of humankind the pivotal principle and goal of His Faith, you should sally forth in a mighty effort to rally the forces which will in His Name and in obedience to His command assist in eradicating this evil from the fair name of your country. . . .[180]

The NSA responded to the racial violence in Los Angeles in several critical ways designed to heal the wounds and contribute to the long-term solution of the basic causes of the violence. In a letter to Los Angeles Mayor Tom Bradley on behalf of the U. S. Bahá'í Community, the NSA wrote: ". . . we join you in your appeal to all our fellow-citizens not to be blinded by anger and hate. . . . the American Bahá'í community, faithful to the teachings of its Founder, has worked for the establishment of race unity in a country blighted by race prejudice that confounds its cherished values, threatens its peace, and poisons the souls of its citizens." The NSA then referred to the principles in its recently published statement, *The Vision of Race Unity* and informed the mayor of its readiness to share the message "with city authorities, private organizations, and individuals who seek such a solution." In addition, the NSA presented to the mayor and the city its jointly sponsored study *Models of Unity*. Concluding their letter to the

---

179. See conference program, "Visions of Race Unity: Race Unity Conference," the Carter Presidential Center, Atlanta, Georgia, Saturday, April 4, 1992. Sponsored by the National Spiritual Assembly of the Bahá'ís of the United States.

180. Quoted in *The American Bahá'í* (July 13, 1992): 1.

mayor, the NSA left him with this message of hope: "We offer you, Mr. Mayor, our cooperation, and pray that Los Angeles will emerge from its trials more enlightened and dedicated to the realization of the great truth that we are all 'the leaves of one tree and the drops of one ocean'."[181]

The NSA then published an open letter to U.S. President George Bush that appeared in several national newspapers:

TO THE PRESIDENT OF THE UNITED STATES:

A CALL TO ELIMINATE RACISM

DEAR MR. PRESIDENT:

No American can look with indifference upon the tragedy relentlessly unfolding in our cities. Its causes lie beyond a particular verdict or a particular act of oppression. **The fires and deaths in Los Angeles are only symptoms of an old congenital disease eating at the vitals of American society,** a disease that has plagued our country ever since slaves were brought from Africa to these shores by their early settlers.

The Abolitionist movement, the Civil War, the Reconstruction, the various legislative acts dealing with civil rights, are so many milestones on the path of progress, but they have fallen far short of society's needs and have not eliminated the ingrained racism that blights our existence as a nation. America's history is a history of advance and retreat, efforts toward improvement and the abandonment of such efforts before they had borne fruit.

The solution to the problem of racism is not simple. Its material requirements are well known. They include the provision of economic security and elimination of poverty, the education of the young and care of the old. But the spiritual requirements have been persistently neglected. **America has not done enough to demonstrate her commitment to the equality and the unity of races,** to the dignity of all human beings whatever their color, and to the moral imperative of extending love and respect to the entire human family.

Ever since its inception a century ago the **American Bahá'í community, inspired by the teachings of Bahá'u'lláh has made the elimination of racism one of its principal goals.** Bahá'ís have ceaselessly warned that discrimination and oppression would lead to strife, that "enmity will increase day by day, and the final result will be hardship and . . . bloodshed." They have worked, and pledge to continue to strive, for the eradication of all forms of prejudice, hatred, and injustice and for the fulfillment of the noble dream of peace and unity of all peoples, races, and creeds.

We appeal to you, Mr. President, and to all our fellow citizens, not to turn away from this "most vital and challenging issue." **We plead for a supreme effort on**

---

181. *The American Bahá'í* (June 5, 1992): 3.

the part of public and private institutions, schools and the media, business and the arts, and most of all to individual Americans to join hands, accept the sacrifices this issue must impose, show forth the "care and vigilance it demands, the moral courage and fortitude it requires, the tact and sympathy it necessitates" so that true and irreversible progress may be made and the promise of this great country may not be buried under the rubble of our cities.[182]

The Spiritual Assembly of Los Angeles began the process of applying the Bahá'í Faith's unique spiritually based balm to the gaping wounds of racial conflict by "mobilizing task forces to provide emergency relief for those most affected by the riots." One group of local Bahá'ís had already been working with the office of the mayor "to design networking forums for community-based race unity groups such as the African–Korean Alliance and the Anti-Defamation League." Another group of Bahá'ís provided emergency transportation to riot-area residents who needed to locate food stores that had survived the flames and violence. They also provided transportation for people who had medical appointments. Still another group made itself available for clean-up crews, and others assisted in conducting discussions at the Center on Racial Unity. The LSA also "designed and implemented a number of outreach programs to help community members such as counseling services for children and adults, Bahá'í and non-Bahá'í, to cope with the emotional and spiritual after-effects of the violence."[183]

One of the National Spiritual Assembly's responses to the Los Angeles disturbance occurred in mid-May in Atlanta where it met with representatives of twenty-nine local Bahá'í assemblies from the surrounding area, members of local spiritual assemblies in fourteen cities in which rioting had taken place to review the Bahá'í communities' responses to the riots and their aftermath, and to consult with the international board of advisors on courses of action.[184] The consultation resulted in a "decision to channel all national efforts in the coming year into one mission—the promotion of race unity." Several weeks later, the NSA announced it was setting up "a two-fold agenda for all Bahá'í communities and individuals in this country: (1) promoting race unity 'in His Name and in obedience to His command'; and (2) supporting the Bahá'í World Congress, which is in itself a marvelous demonstration of the power of Bahá'u'lláh's Covenant to establish the oneness of humanity."[185]

The National Race Unity Committee published in *The American Bahá'í* the following message to the Bahá'í community:

---

182. *The Washington Post,* June 15, 1992, A15. Reprinted *The American Bahá'í* (June 24, 1992): 1.

183. *The American Bahá'í* (June 5, 1992): 3.

184. *The American Bahá'í* (July 13, 1992): 1.

185. *The American Bahá'í* (July 13, 1992): 2.

Bahá'ís should arise to help solve the country's racial problems

Since the principle of the oneness of humanity is the cornerstone around which all the Bahá'í teachings revolve, it becomes incumbent upon Bahá'í communities to arise to address racial incidents that take place in their localities.

As the number of these incidents is increasing around the country, the necessity for Bahá'ís to develop thoughtful and innovative ways to apply healing solutions to racially tense situations has become more urgent.

These incidents create opportunities for us to proclaim Bahá'u'lláh's universal love for the human race, and His teachings regarding our common bonds.

They provide occasions to call forth demonstrations of such noble human values as brotherly love, justice, and compassion, values which have been incorporated in the teachings of the world's major religions, as well as in American culture.

They offer openings to warn about the consequences of prejudice and disunity, and to teach the process of unity and peace given us by Bahá'u'lláh.[186]

Soon after the riots, the National Spiritual Assembly began "its own plan of action including a number of specific measures to increase public awareness of the Bahá'í teachings on race . . . to bring about racial unity in America."[187]

Dr. Robert C. Henderson, secretary-general of the National Spiritual Assembly of the Bahá'ís of the United States, pointed out that American Bahá'ís are "now beginning to emerge as leaders in the arena of race unity. . . ." He pointed to some very impressive examples:

• The acceptance by the Carter Presidential Center in Atlanta of the National Spiritual Assembly's proposal for a joint study of race unity in conjunction with Center's Atlanta Project, . . .
    • the acceptance of a similar proposal by Mayor Tom Bradley of Los Angeles;
    • offers of funding to help publicize the statement on race unity from several major humanitarian foundations;
    • the many and diverse race unity projects being carried out either wholly or in part by Bahá'ís in cities from coast to coast; and
    • work in progress toward establishing not-for-profit consulting groups on race unity under the auspices of the National Spiritual Assembly.[188]

Henderson was confident that the American Bahá'í Community will play a leading role in the solution of the racial crisis in America. "We can already see . . .that if the pace of Bahá'í involvement continues to accelerate, we can soon envision great demands being placed on our resources." According to Dr. Henderson, "No other voice in this country . . . whether

---

186. *The American Bahá'í* (June 5, 1992): 3.
187. *The American Bahá'í* (July 13, 1992): 2.
188. *The American Bahá'í* (July 13, 1992): 2.

black or white, has the credibility or the plan to lead this nation in achieving unity."[189]

The renewed commitment of the American Bahá'í community to exert even more effort toward the solution of the nation's racial problems was not limited to open letters to public officials and proclamations from Bahá'í national spokespersons and representatives. Rather, the commitment radiated throughout the Bahá'í community, expressing itself in hundreds of local grassroots annual Race Unity Day observances. An article in *The American Bahá'í* stated that "there has been a nationwide upsurge in recent weeks in Bahá'í efforts to promote the oneness of humanity. The new level of activity is in part a response to the national attention on the issue since the April riots; it also builds on the momentum generated by the release of the National Assembly's statement on racial unity a year ago." In the same article, William Davis, member of the National Spiritual Assembly, pointed out that "although it is too soon to provide an exact number of race unity activities, all indications point to a degree of effort far surpassing anything we have yet seen." According to Mr. Davis, "What is particularly encouraging is that they [Bahá'í race unity activities] are not limited to any one milieu: from the smallest towns to the largest cities; among Hispanics, African–Americans, Asians and others; and in every social class from the lowest to the highest, the teachings of Bahá'u'lláh are being promulgated."[190]

Conclusion

It has always been a basic Bahá'í belief that the most effective method of solving the racial crisis in the United States is the establishment of genuine love and unity among the races, particularly between black and white; and that such love and unity can only be created through spiritual means. That is why Bahá'ís have always based their approach to racism and racial conflict on Bahá'u'lláh's spiritual principles, which they believe have the power to spiritually transform relationships among races. Others are also beginning to discover and acknowledge the fact that the Bahá'í message of love and unity has a power to unify, heal, and transform a racially fragmented society. Their firm belief in this "spiritual power" enabled Bahá'í local communities all over the United States to hold over 600 separate activities to celebrate Race Unity Day during the same year as one of the worst urban disturbances in American history.[191]

The American Bahá'í community has been a model of racial unity for decades, even as it works on its own shortcomings. Anyone studying the history of this community's long involvement in the struggle for racial justice,

---

189. *The American Bahá'í* (July 13, 1992): 2.
190. *The American Bahá'í* (July 13, 1992): 1.
191. *The American Bahá'í* (July 13, 1992): 5.

unity, love, and fellowship cannot deny that American race relations would be far worse had the American Bahá'í community not existed. Even more important, the contributions made by this community of diverse peoples could not have existed for long without the unifying influence of their belief in their prophet-founder Bahá'u'lláh's teachings on the absolute necessity of recognizing the oneness of humanity. It is this common belief in the principle of oneness that motivates American Bahá'ís to strive so tirelessly for racial unity, and in this striving they have become by far one of the best models of a "working" multicultural spiritual community in the world.

This does not mean that the American Bahá'í community "has arrived" or is anyway "perfect." Rather, it means that this community is very clear about its spiritual role in transforming race relations in America and yet aware of how far it still has to develop as a truly spiritual, unified community. Bahá'ís in the United States have had to overcome many barriers to get to where they currently stand. They have struggled over the years to put into practice the Bahá'í teachings on racial unity within their community life. They have not always been able to avoid all the "pitfalls" along the "long and thorny road," but they have continued to try, keeping faith in the vision of unity expressed in their sacred writings. In 1986, the National Race Unity Committee took the Bahá'ís of the United States another step along the road with the following insightful and challenging words:

> Our American Bahá'í community may soon possess a majority of members who are from minority populations in the United States. Inevitably, our culture as a Bahá'í community must also change. Such a change will manifest itself initially through an increasing appreciation for the cultural offerings—music, food, festivities, manners of speech and dress—of blacks, Hispanics, Native–Americans, Persians, Southeast Asians, and others in the Bahá'í community. But ultimately we must become multicultural so that our community life acquires a character that is flexible, versatile, creative, and blessed with a wide repertoire of cultural responses to daily Bahá'í life. These patterns of our collective life also deserve our attention because they serve to become magnets for the spiritual energy that quickens our community life. As 'Abdu'l-Bahá guides us: "It is impossible to unite unless united."[192]

This is the model that the American Bahá'í community can offer to a country still struggling to solve its racial problems.

---

192. Quoted in *Power of Unity* x–xi.

EPILOGUE

9

A Transformational Agenda for Racial Unity and Social Progress

As I stand here and look upon thousands of Negro faces, and the thousands of white faces, intermingled like the waters of a river, I see only one face—the face of the future.

—Martin Luther King, Jr.

Developing an Agenda that Truly Transforms People and Communities

This book has examined aspects of the history of race relations in the United States. We now have some understanding of how the tradition of white racism evolved and poisoned the very core of American society. We also have some understanding of another tradition in American history: the tradition of interracial struggle for racial justice, unity, love, and fellowship. This latter great tradition has expanded the vision of America, from one that saw this country as a land given by God to whites as their racial manifest destiny to one in which all of humankind could develop a model multiracial community that would be "the city on the hill" for all humankind to emulate. The historic tension between these two opposing traditions has been at the heart of racial problems in the United States. These tensions are still playing themselves out in a million different settings in peoples' hearts, minds, and souls in families and communities throughout the United States and every other multiracial society in the world. The struggle for racial justice, unity, fellowship, and love is at heart a struggle that transcends black–white relations. Rather, it is a struggle driven by the oldest vision and tradition of human history: the struggle to recognize our common humanity, our organic oneness. No matter what form this struggle has assumed—political, economic, cultural—its deepest roots are spiritual in nature. When individuals and communities are connected to the spiritual roots of these struggles, they are transformed.

They become new people. When they are disconnected from the spiritual roots of their struggle, they might gain power, but they are not transformed. They are merely new faces in the same human drama. They are not elevated as human beings and communities. The process of human betterment either stagnates or regresses. Therefore, all struggles for any form of justice—if their objective is to transform people and communities in a way that will elevate them and the larger world—must be grounded in spiritual principles. The present struggle for racial justice, unity, fellowship, and love is in need of an agenda that can guide it along the path to its fullest potential—that of a spiritual leaven for multiracial–multicultural communities around the world.

A transformative agenda is one that—in the process of seeking racial justice, unity, fellowship, and love—transforms and elevates peoples and communities. A transformative agenda explains the interconnection among all the above elements and social progress. A transformative agenda for racial unity and social progress seeks a basic change in perceptions and values about human beings. It seeks to inculcate in all people an appreciation of the organic oneness of the human family. It unabashedly embraces and advocates love for one's fellow human beings as a prerequisite for building and healing communities.

Changing Our Perceptions and Values About People and Communities

New perceptions and values about relationships among peoples and communities are essential to any transformative agenda for racial unity and social progress. Unity must be understood as the key precondition for all forms of social progress. What we need is a new paradigm to help us see old problems in new ways. Psychiatrist H. B. Danesh discusses one such "new way" in his ground-breaking book *Unity: The Creative Foundation of Peace*: "The unity paradigm is an all-encompassing concept, at the same time simple and complex, individual and universal, concrete and abstract, emotional and intellectual, material and spiritual." This unity paradigm, Danesh explains, "challenges us to look at ourselves in new ways and to reappraise our previously-held conceptions in the light of this new perspective on human reality."[1] In the light of centuries of disunity among all kinds of peoples, such a paradigm strains credulity. One has only to survey the present world to see compelling evidence to the contrary. Yet Danesh's argument is persuasive:

> The story of mankind's disunity is also that of its unity. In its march toward maturity, humanity has achieved many remarkable acts of unity, such as the

---

1. H. B. Danesh, *Unity: The Creative Foundation of Peace* 85.

successive creation of family, clan, tribe, state, and nation. Humanity has also achieved a greater degree of understanding and empathy among various races and ethnic groups, and we have seen the powerful contemporary movement for achieving equality between men and women, the remarkable increase in world consciousness concerning the need for a new world order, and, finally, the creation of multinational organizations and world agencies as first steps towards the achievement of unity.[2]

Although Danesh recognizes that these "accomplishments have contributed to the collective growth of humanity, helping mankind to arrive at its present stage of development. However," he cautions, "these are limited unities, no longer appropriate for the needs of humanity today. The emergence of a global society and a united world demand wider unity, the absence of which has made all other types of unity inoperative and even dangerous."[3]

To make his point concerning the limited power of lesser unities, Danesh quotes 'Abdu'l-Bahá, who said:

> From these limited unities mentioned only limited outcomes proceed whereas unlimited unity produces unlimited result. For instance, from the limited unity of race or nationality the results at most are limited. It is like a family living alone and solitary; there are no unlimited or universal outcomes from it.
>
> The unity which is productive of unlimited results is first a unity of mankind. . . .[4]

This focus on unity is a vital aspect of the transformational agenda for racial unity and social progress. Anyone surveying the contemporary racial scene in the United States knows that whites and blacks are still the most racially segregated and polarized races in American society. Most suburban whites and central city blacks not only live in vastly different physical worlds but also hold drastically different views of each other, developed over the decades and transmitted through racial folklore. Since the end of the Civil Rights Movement, major segments of these two communities have fought pitched ideological, political, and even physical battles on a hundred scattered battlefields, from innercity schools to university campuses, from factories to boardrooms.

Ironically, while blacks and whites are divided on many issues, they are at the same time united on many others. While many blacks and Jews fight over affirmative action, they both celebrate the birthday of the Reverend Dr. Martin Luther King, Jr. Many young and old, black Americans and white Americans love the same music and even copy each other's cultural styles. Black street kids' "rappin'" has penetrated to the heart of most, if not

---

2. Danesh, *Unity* 86–87.
3. Danesh, *Unity* 87.
4. Quoted in Danesh, *Unity* 87; *Bahá'í World Faith* 257.

all, white suburbs. Moviegoers of both races crowd in line to see black comics such as Richard Pryor and Eddie Murphy. Many blacks and whites work side-by-side everyday, year in, year out. They lunch together, jog together, share stories of their families, some even visit each other's homes, and a few intermarry and rear families. This list could go on, but the point is clear: notwithstanding the many problems and conflicts that still exist between blacks and whites, there are many points of unity and cooperation which can collectively contribute to a transformational agenda for racial unity and social progress.

Here is where the unity paradigm is most appropriate to contemporary race relations, not only in the United States but also in other multiracial societies. All racial groups have to be educated to understand that at this stage of human evolution on this planet, where interdependence is a structural and intergroup reality, *everyone*, no matter who they are or where they are on the social scale, has a vital role to play in solving the problems associated with racism. This calls for nothing less than a unity of vision and purpose. A transformational agenda based upon the unity paradigm proceeds from the assumption that we are all members of one organic family and community. Whatever hurts one of us, hurts us all and retards the full development of our common good. Conversely, whatever profits the least of us, profits us all. Such an agenda would help those white males who see affirmative action policies and programs solely in terms of how they benefit racial minorities and women to see them instead as enabling minorities and women to contribute more to the common good from which they as white males would also obviously benefit. Applying the unity paradigm to the problems of the cities would enable black central cities and white suburbs to transform their antagonisms into creative strategies to develop the human resources of the *entire* region. All it takes is the realization that in increasingly interdependent metropolitan areas, states, nations, and even the world, unity is the only path to individual and collective growth and development. Only one barrier stands in the way of achieving the unity that could make the above possible: the lack of vision to see that social progress in every multiracial society in the world is inextricably linked to racial unity. The first building block of the transformation agenda is to impart this vision to those who are committed to racial justice, unity, and social progress.

The Building Blocks of a Transformational Agenda for Racial and Social Progress
The Vision: The Organic Unity of the Human Race
To create a truly racially unified society in which all member races are bound together by genuine ties of love, respect, and fellowship, there must be a powerful and inspiring vision of what we want to become as a

community. We must see ourselves as the rose garden 'Abdu'l-Bahá spoke of, blending together in beauty and harmony. We must be able to visualize loving and caring for each other as members of one family. We must come to feel and sense the power we will have as the result of combining our respective racial talents, skills, perspectives, and insights. This vision must be so all-compelling as to enable all member races to relate to each other as one race—the human race. Once this vision is firmly implanted in the hearts and minds of a critical mass of sincere people from various racial backgrounds, we will become the leaven for the spiritual and social transformation of the entire society.

We must impart this vision to our children and youth. Our children should be taught to look for signs of our common humanity. Teachers should inculcate not only recognition of the great heritages of various cultural and racial groups but also the more important recognition and celebration of the organic unity of our species.[5] Then discussions of the history and culture of various groups will not disintegrate into excessive pride, ethnocentrism, envy, competition, or feelings of inferiority. Once children understand that they are linked to every other human being, they will began to feel a kinship with all peoples.

Building on the Tradition of People Working Together

After fixing upon the vision to guide us along the path toward racial unity, we must then begin building upon the existing tradition of people working together. In short, we do not have to re-invent the proverbial wheel. There are many interracial organizations and groups working for the realization of a racially just, cooperative, and caring society. From Focus Hope in Detroit to the Council on Interracial Books for Children in New York to the Interracial Family Alliance in Houston, a growing number of interracial organizations and groups are working to build a racially just and caring society.[6]

Interracial Friendships

A transformational agenda for racial unity and social progress must include the vast reservoir of interracial friendships that often goes untapped. Many of these friendships have already evolved into highly developed forms of human bonding, capable of generating the healing influences so urgently needed in fragmented and wounded sectors of our multiracial community. The most highly evolved of these interracial friendships can offer us models of how best

---

5. For a good description of the form such education to eliminate prejudice might take, see Susan Clay Stoddart, "Education and Moral Development in Children."

6. See the annual interracial march by Focus Hope in the *Detroit Free Press*, October 15, 1990; "The Council on Interracial Books for Children," leaflet. For information on interracial families, see *Communique*, the official newsletter of the Interracial Family Alliance.

to heal interracial conflicts such as the present conflicts between some Jews and blacks as well as between some blacks and Koreans in certain urban communities. Interracial friendships are the oldest forms of the positive tradition of race relations in the history of American race relations. In the 1970s, a white woman and a black woman discussed their interracial friendship in a book entitled *Interracial Bonds*. The white friend commented:

> There are many divisive forces in our society that mitigate against the chances of interracial friendships developing beyond the superficial level. It even amazes me today as I write this and meditate upon the forces in my background which were set in motion in order to prevent such a friendship from ever forming, that I feel compelled to acknowledge the fact that Adah Askew is one of my closest and most intimate friends, one whom I love very dearly.[7]

Her black friend wrote these words about her:

> I've lived next door to Gloria for the past nine years and as time has passed our friendship has grown. The intensity of our relationship amazes many people. Perhaps it's because I'm black and Gloria is white that our closeness surprises folks. . . . The ties which bind Gloria and me are deep. They have withstood the "causes célèbres" of us both—the emergence of my black awareness and Gloria's feminism.[8]

There are thousands of such genuine interracial friendships that we ignore or see as too marginal to make a difference. Too many of us view these relationships as just isolated interpersonal interracial adventures that rarely last beyond the special circumstances that produce them. While some interracial friendships are of such a nature, many are genuine and strong enough to tap for a transformational agenda. We must remember that much of the transformation from racism and racial conflicts has occurred within the bonds of interracial friendships. This is the best-kept secret in contemporary American race relations.

Healing Old Wounds and Creating Unity in Fragmented Communities: Blacks and Jews, and Koreans and Blacks

Any transformational agenda for racial unity and social progress must work on healing the wounds of those blacks and Jews who in the heat of their separate struggles to address their needs have strained their traditional relationship. In some cases, they have both afflicted each other so severely with their accusations and counteraccusations that the possibility of

---

7. Gloria Feman Orenstein, "A Friendship: Part One" in Rhonda Goldstein Blumberg and Wendell James Royce, *Interracial Bonds* 175.

8. Adah Askew, "A Friendship: Part Two" in Blumberg and Royce, *Interracial* 186–89.

reconciliation now seems remote if not highly improbable. Yet, many blacks and Jews are still working together in areas where they do not have to compromise their particular agendas. This unity in diversity is a reality of pragmatic racial–ethnic politics in any pluralistic society. However, a transformational agenda demands much more from both of these long-time allies. Since blacks and Jews have had one of the longest and most effective working relationships of any racial–ethnic groups in recent American history, their combined cultural and spiritual influence is urgently needed to achieve racial unity and social progress. However much some African–Americans and Jews might want to put all their joint history in struggling for social and economic justice behind them and concentrate on their own agendas, the fact is that those very agendas are inextricably linked to developments within the larger society which the transformational agenda must address. Racial justice, unity, love, and fellowship cannot be achieved without the synergistic force of black–Jewish unity and cooperation. Notwithstanding the conflicts between these two traditional allies, they have developed the highest form of interracial friendship and intergroup cooperation, love, and fellowship in the history of black–white relations in this country. This fact alone demands that we work to heal the rifts between these two long-time friends so that they can contribute their great spiritual powers to the transformation of American race relations.

The recent conflicts between Korean–American merchants and African–American customers in New York and other cities reflect another form of fragmentation within the increasingly diverse American society. It is an old problem with some new faces. It also involves conflicts of racial–ethnic group agendas and can only be partially solved through traditional means. Both Korean–Americans and African–Americans need to see their problems from the perspective of the unity paradigm that can more effectively address both groups' problems. Here again, as with blacks and Jews, Koreans and blacks will need the assistance of those who have the vision of a truly unified multiracial society as well as the skills and determination to carry out the transformational agenda for racial unity and social progress.

The Need for a Racial Unity and Harmony Movement

On several occasions there has been mention of the need for a movement dedicated to racial unity and harmony. The National Spiritual Assembly of the Bahá'ís of the United States has been a major voice calling for such a movement in the wilderness of racial conflicts and tensions. In a 1993 statement to the Bahá'ís of the United States, they encouraged Bahá'ís to: "Strive to become leaders in the movement for racial unity and to make Bahá'í communities models of unity which inspire emulation and lead to growth." Much like the civil rights and women's movements, a movement for racial unity and harmony could tap great reservoirs of goodwill and hope within the American collective psyche. More important, as we approach the year 2000 with the gathering momentum of increased racial and ethnic diversity, either we will be more unified or more divided. Nothing short of a mass movement for the achievement of genuine racial unity, love, fellowship, and harmony will be able to deflect an increasingly racially and ethnically diverse United States from a course leading towards more racial and ethnic violence and conflicts. Perhaps the popular 1960s saying[9] sums it up best: "You're either part of the solution or part of the problem." Either we will stand by and be spectators of a social order being destroyed by racial hatred, conflict, and disunity, or we will be participants in a glorious movement to heal racial wounds, bridge racial and ethnic chasms, and build loving and caring interracial relationships within our institutions, organizations, and communities. If we choose the former, history will blame us, but if we choose the latter, we will be known as the healers and builders who prepared the way for all races and peoples to unite in true love and fellowship, and by doing so we will have contributed to the social and spiritual progress of the world.

---

9. Attributed to Eldridge Cleaver in 1968.

Bibliography

'Abdu'l-Bahá. *The Promulgation of Universal Peace: Talks Delivered by 'Abdu'l-Bahá during His Visit to the United States and Canada in 1912.* Comp. Howard MacNutt. 2d ed. Wilmette, Illinois: Bahá'í Publishing Trust, 1982.

———. *The Secret of Divine Civilization.* Trans. Marzieh Gail. 3d ed. Wilmette, Illinois: Bahá'í Publishing Trust, 1975.

———. *Selections from the Writings of 'Abdu'l-Bahá.* Trans. Marzieh Gail et al. Haifa: Bahá'í World Centre, 1978.

———. *Will and Testament of 'Abdu'l-Bahá.* Wilmette, Illinois: Bahá'í Publishing Trust, 1944.

Allen, Robert L. *Reluctant Reformers: Racism and Social Reform Movements in the United States.* Garden City, New York: Doubleday and Co., Anchor Edition, 1975.

Allport, Gordon W. *The Nature of Prejudice.* Reading, Massachusetts: Addison-Wesley Publishing Company, 1954.

Amaker, Norman C. *Civil Rights and the Reagan Administration.* Washington, D.C.: The Urban Institute Press, 1988.

Askew, Adah. "A Friendship: Part Two." In *Interracial Bonds,* edited by Rhonda Goldstein Blumberg and Wendell James Royce. New York: General Hall, 1979.

Bahá'í World, The. Volumes 1–12. Reprinted Wilmette, Illinois: Bahá'í Publishing Trust, 1980–81. Also, *A Compendium of Volumes of the Bahá'í World, an International Record, I–XII, 82–110 of the Bahá'í Era (1925–1954).* Comp. Roger White. Oxford: George Ronald, 1981.

Bahá'u'lláh. *Gleanings from the Writings of Bahá'u'lláh.* Trans. Shoghi Effendi. 2d ed. Wilmette, Illinois: Bahá'í Publishing Trust, 1976.

———. *Tablets of Bahá'u'lláh Revealed after the Kitáb-i-Aqdas.* Comp. Research Department. Trans. H. Taherzadeh et al. Rev. ed. Haifa: Bahá'í World Centre, 1988.

———. *The Hidden Words of Bahá'u'lláh.* Trans. Shoghi Effendi. Rev. ed. Wilmette, Illinois: Bahá'í Publishing Trust, 1975.

Balyuzi, H. M. *'Abdu'l-Bahá: The Center of the Covenant of Bahá'u'lláh.* London: George Ronald, 1971.

Baron, Harold M., and Bennett Hymer. "The Negro Worker in the Chicago Labor Market." In *The Negro and the American Labor Movement,* edited by Julius Jacobson. Garden City, New York: Anchor Books, 1968.

Baron, Harold M. "The Demand for Black Labor: Historical Notes on the Political Economy of Racism." *Radical America* 5.2 (March–April, 1971): 1–46.

Bastide, Roger. "Color, Racism, and Christianity." *Dædalus* 96.2 (Spring, 1967): 312–27.

Bayley, David H., and Harold Mendelsohn. *Minorities and the Police: Confrontation in America.* New York: The Free Press, 1969.

Bell, Derrick A., Jr. *Race, Racism and American Law.* Rev. ed. Boston: Little, Brown and Company, 1980.

Benokraitis, Nijole V., and Joe R. Feagin. *Affirmative Action and Equal Opportunity: Action, Inaction, Reaction.* Boulder, Colorado: Westview Press, 1978.

Benyon, John, and John Solomos, eds. *The Roots of Urban Unrest.* Oxford: Pergamon Press, 1987.

Berkhofer, Robert F., Jr. *The White Man's Indian: Images of the American Indian from Columbus to the Present.* New York: Vintage Books, 1979.

Bernal, Martin. *Black Athena: The Afroasiatic Roots of Classical Civilization.* Vol. 1. *The Fabrication of Ancient Greece 1785–1985.* New Brunswick, N.J.: Rutgers University Press, 1987.

———. "Roots." *New Republic* 206.10 (March 9, 1992): 4–7.

Berry, Mary Frances. *Black Resistance/White Law: A History of Constitutional Racism in America.* New York: Appleton-Century-Crofts, 1971.

Blauner, Bob. *Black Lives, White Lives: Three Decades of Race Relations in America.* Berkeley: University of California Press, 1989.

Boskin, Joseph. *Urban Racial Violence in the Twentieth Century.* Beverly Hills: Glencoe, 1969.

Botwinick, Michael, ed. *Africa in Antiquity.* Vol. 1. *The Arts of Ancient Nubia and the Sudan: The Essays.* New York: The Brooklyn Museum, 1978.

Branch, Taylor. *Parting the Waters: America in the King Years 1954–63.* New York: Simon and Schuster, 1988.

Buswell, J. Oliver, III. *Slavery, Segregation and Scripture.* Grand Rapids, Michigan: William B. Eerdmans Company, 1964.

Cahn, Edgar S., ed. *Our Brother's Keeper: The Indian in White America.* New York: New Community Press, 1969.

Capeci, Dominic J., Jr. *Race Relations in Wartime Detroit: The Sojourner Truth Housing Controversy of 1942.* Philadelphia: Temple University Press, 1984.

Cashmore, Ellis, and Eugene McLaughlin, eds. *Out of Order?: Policing Black People.* London: Routledge, 1991.

Clark, Kenneth B. *Dark Ghetto: Dilemmas of Social Power.* New York: Harper & Row, 1965.

Confronting Racial Isolation in Miami: A Report of the U.S. Commission on Civil Rights. Washington, DC: U.S. Government Printing Office, June 1982, v. 26.

Danesh, H. B. *Unity: The Creative Foundation of Peace.* Ottawa, Canada: Bahá'í Studies Publications, 1986.

Darden, Joe T., Richard Child Hill, June Thomas, and Richard Thomas. *Detroit: Race and Uneven Development.* Philadelphia: Temple University Press, 1987.

Deloria, Vine, Jr. *God is Red.* New York: Dell Publishing Company, 1975.

Dillingham, Harry C., and David F. Sly. "The Mechanical Cotton-Picker, Negro Migration, and the Integration Movement." *Human Organization* 25.4 (Winter, 1966): 344–51.

Du Bois, W. E. B. *The Autobiography of W. E. B. Du Bois: A Soliloquy on Viewing My Life from the Last Decade of its First Century.* New York: International Publishers, 1968.

———. "The Races Congress." *The Crisis* (September, 1911): 200–209. Vols. 1–2, Nov. 1910–Oct. 1911. Authorized Reprint Edition. New York: Arno Press, 1969.

———. *The Souls of Black Folk: Essays and Sketches.* Greenwich, Connecticut: Fawcett, 1961.

Etter-Lewis, Gwen. Unpublished paper on black Bahá'í women.

Foner, Philip S. *Organized Labor and the Black Worker 1619–1973.* New York: International Publishers, 1976.

Fontaine, Pierre-Michel, ed. *Race, Class and Power in Brazil.* Los Angeles: Center for Afro-American Studies, University of California, 1985.

Franklin, John Hope. "History of Racial Segregation in the United States." *The Annals of the American Academy of Political and Social Science* 304 (March, 1956).

———. *The Emancipation Proclamation.* Garden City, New York: Doubleday & Company, Anchor Books, 1965.

Franklin, John Hope, and Alfred A. Moss, Jr. *From Slavery to Freedom: A History of Negro Americans.* 6th ed. New York: McGraw-Hill, 1988.

Frazier, E. Franklin. *Race and Culture Contacts in the Modern World.* Boston: Beacon Press, 1965.

Gara, Larry. *The Liberty Line: The Legend of the Underground Railroad.* Lexington: University of Kentucky Press, 1967.

Gelfand, Mark I. *A Nation of Cities: The Federal Government and Urban America, 1933–1965.* New York: Oxford University Press, 1975.

Ginzburg, Ralph. *100 Years of Lynchings: A Shocking Documentary of Race Violence in America.* New York: Lancer Books, 1962.

Glatthaar, Joseph T. *Forged in Battle: The Civil War Alliance of Black Soldiers and White Officers.* New York: The Free Press, 1990.

Glazer, Nathan. *Affirmative Discrimination: Ethnic Inequality and Public Policy.* New York: Basic Books, 1975.

Gordon, David M. *Theories of Poverty and Underemployment: Orthodox, Radical, and Dual Labor Market Perspectives.* Lexington, Mass.: D.C. Heath & Company, 1972.

Gossett, Thomas F. *Race: The History of an Idea in America.* New York: Schocken Books, 1965.

Gregory, Louis G. *A Heavenly Vista: The Pilgrimage of Louis G. Gregory.* Washington, D.C.: R. L. Pendleton, 1911.

———. "Light on Basic Unity." *The Star of the West* 22.7 (October, 1931): 220–23.

———. "Racial Amity in America." *The Bahá'í World, 1936–38.* Vol. 7. New York: Bahá'í Publishing Committee, 1939: 652–66. Vols. 1–12 reprinted Wilmette, Illinois: Bahá'í Publishing Trust, 1980–81.

Gross, Bella. "The First National Negro Convention." *The Journal of Negro History* 31.4 (October, 1946): 435–43.

Guttentag, Jack M., and Susan M. Wachter. *Redlining and Public Policy.* New York: New York Graduate School of Business Administration, 1980.

Hanke, Louis. *Aristotle and the American Indian: A Study in Race Prejudice in the Modern World.* Bloomington: Indiana University Press, 1959.

Harding, Vincent. *There is a River: The Black Struggle for Freedom in America.* New York: Harcourt Brace Jovanovich, 1981.

Hatcher, William S., and J. Douglas Martin. *The Bahá'í Faith: The Emerging Global Religion.* San Francisco: Harper and Row, 1984.

Hawkins, Homer, and Richard Thomas. "White Policing of Black Populations: A History of Race and Social Control in America." In *Out of Order?: Policing Black People,* edited by E. Cashmore and E. McLaughlin. London: Routledge, 1991: 65–86.

Henri, Florette. *Black Migration: Movement North, 1900–1920.* Garden City, NY: Anchor, 1976.

Herodotus. Trans. A. D.Godley. 4 volumes. Cambridge: Harvard University Press, 1921.

Higginbotham, A. Leon, Jr. *In the Matter of Color: Race and the American Legal Process, The Colonial Period.* New York: Oxford University Press, 1980.

Hintz, Fritz. "The Kingdom of Kush: The Meroitic Period." In *Africa in Antiquity.* Vol.1. *The Arts of Ancient Nubia and the Sudan: The Essays,* edited by Michael Botwinick. New York: The Brooklyn Museum, 1978.

Hiro, Dilip. *Black British, White British.* London: Eyre and Spottiswoode, 1971.

Hirsh, Arnold R. *Making the Second Ghetto: Race and Housing in Chicago, 1940–1960.* Cambridge: Cambridge University Press, 1983.

Hoffman, Edward. *The Right To Be Human: A Biography of Abraham Maslow.* Los Angeles: Jeremy P. Tarcher, 1988.

Homer. *The Iliad.* Trans. Robert Fagles. New York: Viking, 1990.

———. *The Odyssey.* Trans. Robert Fitzgerald. Garden City, New York: Doubleday, 1961.

Hornsby, Alton, Jr. *The Black Almanac.* 4th ed. Woodbury, NY: Barron's Educational Series, 1977.

Hornsby, Helen, comp. *Lights of Guidance.* 2d ed. New Delhi, India: Bahá'í Publishing Trust, 1988.

Horsman, Reginald. *Race and Manifest Destiny: The Origins of American Racial Anglo-Saxonism.* Cambridge: Harvard University Press, 1981.

Hosokawa, Bill. *Nisei: The Quiet Americans.* New York: William Morrow & Company, 1969.

Hughes, Langston. *Fight for Freedom: The Story of the NAACP.* New York: W. W. Norton & Company, 1962.

Ives, Howard Colby. *Portals to Freedom.* Rev. ed. London: George Ronald, 1976.

Jacobson, Julius, ed. *The Negro and the American Labor Movement.* Garden City, NY: Anchor Books, 1968.

James, C. L. R. *The Black Jacobins: Toussaint L'Ouverture and the San Domingo Revolution.* 2d ed. New York: First Vintage Press Edition, 1963.

Jaynes, Gerald David, and Robin M. Williams, Jr., eds. *A Common Destiny: Blacks in American Society.* Washington, D.C.: National Academy Press, 1989.

Johnson, Charles. "Substitution of Negro for European Immigrant Labor." In *National Conference of Social Work Proceedings.* May–June, 1926.

Johnson, Lemuel A. *The Devil, the Gargoyle, and the Buffoon: The Negro as Metaphor in Western Literature.* 2d ed. Port Washington, New York: Kennikat Press, 1971.

Jordan, Winthrop D. *The White Man's Burden: Historical Origins of Racism in the United States.* New York: Oxford University Press, 1974.

Joshua, Harris, and Tina Wallace. *To Ride the Storm: The 1980 Bristol "Riot" and the State.* London: Heinemann, 1983.

Kaufman, Jonathan. *Broken Alliance: The Turbulent Times Between Blacks and Jews in America.* New York: Mentor, 1988.

Kellogg, Charles Flint. *NAACP: A History of the NAACP.* Vol. 1, 1909–1920. Baltimore: Johns Hopkins Press, 1967.

Koch, Adrienne, and William Peden, eds. *The Life and Selected Writings of Thomas Jefferson.* New York: Modern Library, 1944.

Kuper, Leo, ed. *Race, Science and Society.* Paris: The UNESCO Press, 1975.

Leclant, Jean. "Egypt in Nubia during the Old, Middle, and New Kingdoms." In *Africa in Antiquity.*Vol.1. *The Arts of Ancient Nubia and the Sudan: The Essays,* edited by Michael Botwinick. New York: The Brooklyn Museum, 1978.

Lefkowitz, Mary. "Not Out of Africa." *New Republic.* 206.6 (February 10, 1992): 29–36.

Litwack, Leon F. *Been in the Storm So Long: The Aftermath of Slavery.* New York: Vintage Press, 1980.

Locke, Alain. *The New Negro.* New York: Albert and Charles Boni, 1925.

Logan, Rayford W. *The Betrayal of the Negro: From Rutherford B. Hayes to Woodrow Wilson.* Rev. ed. London: Collier Books, 1965.

Mehlinger, Louis R. "The Attitude of the Free Negro toward African Colonization." *The Journal of Negro History* 1.3 (July, 1916): 276–301.

Miller, John Chester. *The Wolf by the Ears: Thomas Jefferson and Slavery.* New York: Free Press, 1977.

"Models of Unity: Racial, Ethnic, and Religious." Wilmette, Illinois: Human Relations Foundation of Chicago and National Spiritual Assembly of the Bahá'ís of the United States, February, 1992.

Mokhtar, G., ed. *Ancient Civilizations of Africa.* Vol. 2. *General History of Africa.* Paris: The UNESCO Press, 1990.

Morrison, Gayle. *To Move the World: Louis G. Gregory and the Advancement of Racial Unity in America.* Wilmette, Illinois: Bahá'í Publishing Trust, 1982.

Mosse, George L. *Toward the Final Solution: A History of European Racism.* New York: Harper Colophon Books, 1980.

Moynihan, Daniel P. *The Negro Family: The Case for National Action.* Washington, D.C.: Office of Policy Planning and Research, U.S. Dept. of Labor, March, 1965.

Murray, Florence, ed. "National Defense Chronology for the Year, 1941." In *The Negro Handbook.* New York: Wendell Mailliet and Company, 1942.

Muse, Benjamin. *The American Negro Revolution: From Nonviolence to Black Power.* New York: Citadel Press, 1970.

Nash, Gary B. *Red, White, and Black: The Peoples of Early America.* 2d ed. Englewood Cliffs, New Jersey: Prentice-Hall, 1982.

Nash, Gary B., and Richard Weiss, eds. *The Great Fear: Race in the Mind of America.* New York: Holt Reinhart and Winston, 1970.

Nash, Geoffrey. *Iran's Secret Pogrom.* Sudbury, Suffolk: Neville Spearman, 1982.

Newby, I.A. *Jim Crow's Defense: Anti-Negro Thought in America, 1900–1930.* Baton Rouge: Louisiana State University Press, 1965.

Orenstein, Gloria Feman. "A Friendship: Part One." In *Interracial Bonds,* edited by Rhonda Goldstein Blumberg and Wendell James Royce. New York: General Hall, 1979.

Orfield, Gary. *Must We Bus? Segregated Schools and National Policy.* Washington, D.C.: The Brookings Institution, 1978.

Perry, Mark Lloyd. "The Chicago Bahá'í Community, 1921–1939." Unpublished dissertation, University of Chicago, 1986. Excerpted as "Pioneering Race Unity: The Chicago Bahá'ís, 1919–39." *World Order* 20.2 (Winter, 1985–86): 41–60.

Pollack, Norman, ed. *The Populist Mind.* Indianapolis and New York: Bobbs-Merrill Company, 1967.

Power of Unity: Beyond Prejudice and Racism, The. Bonnie Taylor, comp. Wilmette, Illinois: Bahá'í Publishing Trust, 1986.

Priese, Karl-Heinz. "The Kingdom of Kush: The Napatan Period." In *Africa in Antiquity.* Vol.1. *The Arts of Ancient Nubia and the Sudan: The Essays,* edited by Michael Botwinick. New York: The Brooklyn Museum, 1978.

Quarles, Benjamin. *Black Abolitionists.* New York: Oxford University Press, 1969.

Report of the National Advisory Commission on Civil Disorders. New York: Bantam Books, 1968.

Rosen, Sumner M., "The CIO Era, 1935–55." In *The Negro and the American Labor Movement,* edited by Julius Jacobson. Garden City, NY: Anchor Books, 1968: 188–208.

Ross, B. Joyce. *J. E. Spingarn and the Rise of the NAACP, 1911–1939.* New York: Atheneum, 1972.

Rotberg, Robert I. *The Rise of Nationalism in Central Africa: The Making of Malawi and Zambia, 1873–1964.* 3d ed. Cambridge: Harvard University Press, 1971.

Ruchames, Louis. *Race, Jobs, & Politics: The Story of the FEPC.* New York: Columbia University Press, 1953.

Ryan, William. *Blaming the Victim.* New York: Pantheon, 1971.

Santa Cruz, Hernán. *Racial Discrimination.* New York: United Nations, 1971.

Scott, Emmett J. *Negro Migration during the War.* New York: Arno Press, 1969.

Segal, Ronald. *The Race War.* New York: Viking Press, 1967.

Seminar on International Assistance and Support to Peoples and Movements Struggling against Colonialism, Racism, Racial Discrimination and Apartheid. New York: United Nations, 1986

Shinnie, P.L. *Meroë: A Civilization of the Sudan.* London: Thames & Hudson, 1967.

Shogan, Robert, and Tom Craig. *The Detroit Race Riot: A Study in Violence.* Philadelphia: Chilton Books, 1964.

Shoghi Effendi. *The Advent of Divine Justice.* Rev. ed. Wilmette, Illinois: Bahá'í Publishing Trust, 1984.

———. *Citadel of Faith: Messages to America/1947–1957.* Wilmette, Illinois: Bahá'í Publishing Trust, 1965.

———. *Dawn of a New Day: Messages to India 1923–1957.* New Delhi: Bahá'í Publishing Trust, 1970.

———. *The Unfolding Destiny of the British Bahá'í Community: The Messages from the Guardian of the Bahá'í Faith to the Bahá'ís of the British Isles.* London: Bahá'í Publishing Trust, 1981.

———. *The World Order of Bahá'u'lláh.* 2d ed. Wilmette, Illinois: Bahá'í Publishing Trust, 1974.

Sinkler, George. *The Racial Attitudes of American Presidents: From Abraham Lincoln to Theodore Roosevelt.* Garden City, New York: Doubleday and Company, 1971.

Sitkoff, Harvard. *The Struggle for Black Equality, 1954–1980.* New York: Hill and Wang, 1981.

Skidmore, Thomas E. "Race and Class in Brazil: Historical Perspectives." In *Race, Class and Power in Brazil,* edited by Pierre-Michel Fontaine. Los Angeles: Center for Afro-American Studies, University of California, 1985.

Snowden, Frank M., Jr. *Before Color Prejudice: The Ancient View of Blacks.* Cambridge: Harvard University Press, 1983.

————. *Blacks in Antiquity: Ethiopians in the Greco–Roman Experience.* Cambridge, Mass.: Belknap Press, 1970.

Special Measure of Love, A: The Importance and Nature of the Teaching Work among the Masses, Messages from Shoghi Effendi and the Universal House of Justice. Wilmette, Illinois: Bahá'í Publishing Trust, 1974.

Spero, Sterling D., and Abram L. Harris. *The Black Worker.* New York: Columbia University Press, 1931.

Spiller, G., ed. *Inter-Racial Problems: Papers from the First Universal Races Congress Held in London in 1911.* Rev. ed. with Introduction by H. Aptheker. New York: Citadel Press, 1970. Originally published as *Papers on Inter-Racial Problems, Communicated to the First Universal Races Congress Held at the University of London, July 26–29, 1911.* London: P. S. King and Son, 1911.

Stanton, William. *The Leopard's Spots: Scientific Attitudes toward Race in America 1815–59.* Chicago: University of Chicago Press, 1960.

Star of the West, The. Chicago: Bahá'í News Service. Vol. 1.1 (March 21, 1910)–14.12 (March, 1924). Reprinted in 8 bound volumes. Oxford: George Ronald, 1978.

Stoddart, Susan Clay. "Education and Moral Development in Children." *The Journal of Bahá'í Studies* 1.1 (1988): 59–75.

Taeuber, Karl E., and Alma F. Taeuber. *Negroes in Cities: Residential Segregation and Neighborhood Change.* New York: Atheneum, 1969.

Taherzadeh, Adib. *The Covenant of Bahá'u'lláh.* Oxford: George Ronald, 1992.

Takaki, Ronald T. *Iron Cages: Race and Culture in Nineteenth-Century America.* Seattle: University of Washington Press, 1982

————. *Strangers from a Different Shore: A History of Asian Americans.* New York: Penguin, 1989.

Thomas, Richard W. "Looking Forward: The Detroit Experience after the Riots of 1943 and 1967." In *The Roots of Urban Unrest,* edited by John Benyon and John Solomos. Oxford: Pergamon Press, 1987.

Tilson, Everett. *Segregation and the Bible.* Nashville: Abbingdon Press, n.d.

Trigger, Bruce G. "Nubian, Negro, Black, Nilotic?" In *Africa in Antiquity.* Vol.1. *The Arts of Ancient Nubia and the Sudan: The Essays,* edited by Michael Botwinick. New York: The Brooklyn Museum, 1978.

Tuttle, William M., Jr. *Race Riot: Chicago in the Red Summer of 1919.* New York: Atheneum, 1972.

Tygiel, Jules. *Baseball's Great Experiment: Jackie Robinson and His Legacy.* New York: Vintage, 1984.

Universal House of Justice. *The Promise of World Peace.* Wilmette, Illinois: Bahá'í Publishing Trust, 1985. Also published in an annotated edition as "To the Peoples of the World." *Bahá'í Studies* 14. Ottawa, Canada: Association for Bahá'í Studies, 1986.

Vercoutter, Jean, et al., eds. *The Image of the Black in Western Art: From the Pharaohs to the Fall of the Roman Empire.* Cambridge: Harvard University Press, 1976.

Vision of Race Unity, The: America's Most Challenging Issue. A Statement by the National Spiritual Assembly of the Bahá'ís of the United States. Wilmette, Illinois: Bahá'í Publishing Trust, 1991.

Vose, Clement E. *Caucasians Only: The Supreme Court, the NAACP, and the Restrictive Covenant Cases.* Berkeley: University of California Press, 1959.

Wallerstein, Immanuel. *The Modern World-System: Capitalist Agriculture and the Origins of the European World-Economy in the Sixteenth Century.* New York: Academic Press, 1976.

Walvin, James. *The Black Presence: A documentary history of the Negro in England, 1555–1860.* London: Orbach and Chambers, 1971.

Ward, Allan L. *239 Days: 'Abdu'l-Bahá's Journey in America.* Wilmette, Illinois: Bahá'í Publishing Trust, 1979.

Washburn, Wilcom E., ed. *The Indian and the White Man.* Garden City, NY: Anchor Books, 1964.

Weiss, Nancy J. *The National Urban League: 1910–1940.* New York: Oxford University Press, 1974.

Wesley, Charles H. "Lincoln's Plan for Colonizing the Emancipated Negroes." *The Journal of Negro History* 4.1 (January, 1919): 7–21.

Weston, Rubin Francis. *Racism in U.S. Imperialism: The Influence of Racial Assumptions on American Foreign Policy, 1893–1946.* Columbia, South Carolina: University of South Carolina Press, 1972.

Wilkins, Roy, with Tom Mathews. *Standing Fast: The Autobiography of Roy Wilkins.* New York: Viking, 1982.

Wilkinson, J. Harvie, III. *From* Brown *to* Bakke*: The Supreme Court and School Integration, 1954–1978.* New York: Oxford University Press, 1979.

Williamson, Joel. *A Rage for Order: Black/White Relations in the American South Since Emancipation.* New York: Oxford University Press, 1986.

Wilson, William Julius. *The Truly Disadvantaged: The Inner City, the Underclass, and Public Policy.* Chicago: University of Chicago Press, 1987.

Wood, Forrest G. *Black Scare: The Racist Response to Emancipation and Reconstruction.* Berkeley: University of California Press, 1970.

———. *The Arrogance of Faith: Christianity and Race in America from the Colonial Era to the Twentieth Century.* New York: Alfred A. Knopf, 1990.

Wood, L. Hollingsworth. "The Urban League Movement." *The Journal of Negro History* 9.1 (January, 1924): 117–26.

Woodward, C. Vann. *The Strange Career of Jim Crow.* Rev. ed. New York: Oxford University Press, 1974.

Index

L. Robertson